An Introduction to Business Law

Bridget Walker and Terry Payn

Stanley Thornes (Publishers) Ltd

First published in 1995 by:
Stanley Thornes (Publishers) Ltd
Ellenborough House
Wellington Street
CHELTENHAM
Glos. GL50 1YW
UK

ISBN 0 7487 1882 6

Typeset by Tech-Set, Gateshead, Tyne and Wear
Printed and bound in Great Britain by Redwood Books, Trowbridge, Wiltshire

Contents

Preface

We have both been responsible for teaching students who are studying law as part of their studies on a business course. We have both taught law to business students at the University of Bradford and Terry has also taught students at Leeds Metropolitan University and elsewhere. What our breadth of teaching experience has proved to us is that there is a widespread need for a straightforward approach to law for business students.

This book was inspired by our own experiences of teaching (and learning how to teach) business students. One of the main problems which students experience is often that the subject appears ludicrously complex. The knee jerk reaction to it is often 'Well why do I need to know this, I don't want to be a lawyer anyway.' This book does not aim to create lawyers. It aims instead to guide the reader gently along the path to an understanding of basic principles such that he or she can
i)   Handle straightforward business affairs effectively
ii) Recognise when they may need the help of a lawyer
iii) Be equipped to deal effectively with a lawyer in the business context.

Moving on from the text itself we need to say one particular thank you and that is to Francis Dodds of Stanley Thornes Publishers. His kindly chivvying and his own considerable input have played no small part in ensuring that this text was completed.

Bridget Walker and Terry Payn
August 1995

A note on using the text. Most of the chapters in this book conclude with case-study exercises for you to complete. Notes on these exercises are contained in a separate lecturer's pack available to lecturers adopting the text for their students. The pack also contains notes on a range of case-study exercises situated within relevant chapters, together with additional exercises for students.

Table of cases

Table of legislation

Table of treaties/conventions

1 What is the law and how does it affect business people?

Objectives

By the end of this chapter, you should:

- be able to understand the nature and purpose of law
- understand that there are divisions of different types of law
- understand the distinction between criminal and civil, public and private law
- understand how the law affects business people
- understand the nature of legal reasoning
- be able to answer the questions in the case study exercise at the end of the chapter.

✎   **CASE STUDY 1**

You are the managing director of a small business, Smith Limited, producing components for computers. You agreed to supply Jones Limited with an urgent order on condition that it arrives not later than 08.00 hours tomorrow. Overnight there is an attempted burglary in which one of your security guards is shot, and the burglar is caught leaving the premises. The resulting delay means that you have to rush the order without the usual quality check. In an attempt to get the order to the customer on time, the driver fails to notice a pedestrian who steps out into the road suddenly and is injured in the ensuing impact. When the order finally arrives it is too late. Subsequently Jones Limited say that they want compensation for their own lost order and tell you that the component which you supplied failed to meet government safety standards.

Preferably in groups, discuss and then write down the possible ways the law might be involved in this scenario and what purpose the law is attempting to serve.

1   What is the law?

This may sound like a silly question! We all know from our everyday dealings how some parts of the law work. We know, for example, that it is 'illegal' to park on double yellow lines and that if we do we will face a fine. We also know that shoplifting is 'illegal'. We know, too, that if you fail to pay your credit card debt the credit card company is likely to 'sue' you for repayment of the money that you owe them.

We can see from these examples that the law comprises a set of rules which indicate what is acceptable behaviour. It is a means of ensuring that there is some institutional social control over how society as a whole functions and also a way to regulate dealings and settle disputes between individual members within that society. The whole system is designed to ensure that society as a whole and individuals respect certain values and behave in a socially, politically and economically acceptable way.

2 What types of law are there?

Think about the examples that we have just looked at. The purpose behind the legal rule which says that you cannot park on a double yellow line is probably to prevent traffic congestion. It is there to define, prevent and, if need be, punish a form of socially unacceptable behaviour: parking your car where it will cause congestion. The purpose of the rule which says that you cannot run up a credit card bill and then not pay it is probably to ensure that the economy can work effectively. It is there to regulate dealings between individuals and to provide some protection if someone fails to honour his or her side of the bargain. If banks and other institutions could not lend money, safe in the knowledge that they are entitled to it back, our whole economy would grind to a halt.

These two roles of the law in (a) defining acceptable behaviour and (b) regulating dealings between individuals have given rise to two different branches of the law: criminal law and civil law.

2.1 Criminal law

Criminal law generally aims to ensure that everyone conforms to certain standards of behaviour. Some of it may be designed to ensure that the economic system can function effectively (e.g. shops would not be able to maintain a profit if they had no recourse against shoplifters). Other aspects of the criminal law simply indicate what is, and what is not, acceptable behaviour. In most areas this is quite clear and the social reasoning behind it is understandable. The law relating to assault, for example, stops people using violence as a means of getting their own way and encourages respect for the individual.

In other areas the reason for the rules is less clear, for example, on the issue of drugs. Our particular legal system says that alcohol is a socially acceptable drug (although behaviour which is induced by it may not be). Even the Chancellor of the Exchequer had a glass of whisky next to him during one budget speech! Cannabis on the other hand is not a drug which is accepted in our society. There are those who would argue that if alcohol is acceptable why not cannabis? There are those who would go even further and say that cannabis should be more acceptable, since they would argue that it causes fewer social problems. The fact remains that the values of our society are reflected in the law. Even if, as some would argue, there is no real justification for the distinction, those are this society's accepted values which are being upheld.

Now look at the case study and the first answers you gave.

1 What matters do you think may be covered by the criminal law?

2 In each case what objective do you think society is trying to achieve?

You have probably already decided that the shooting of the security guard was illegal and that the burglar will be prosecuted and is likely to be imprisoned.

Most people agree that stealing goods is wrong and that using violence to do it is particularly unacceptable. You may also have agreed that the law may be used to prosecute the driver if he or she is guilty of a driving offence (you may not have spotted that, as a company, you might face prosecution if the driver was breaking the speed limit on your instructions). In this case, the law is being used to enforce reasonable standards of driving to protect road-users and pedestrians.

Finally, you may well have seen that your company might be prosecuted for infringing official safety standards governing the components you have manufactured. Here the law is used to protect consumers from potentially dangerous goods.

2.2 The civil law

The purpose of civil law is somewhat different. It has less to do with maintaining the standards of society generally and more to do with creating a system of rules which enable relationships between individuals to function with as little dispute as possible. The civil law helps these relationships in two ways. Firstly, the established law acts as a set of guidelines within which individuals can structure their dealings. It has basically a practical focus for allowing people to get on with ordinary business activity as easily as possible. Knowing the law means that a business person knows where he or she stands and can deal with others with some confidence and security. Secondly, if things do go wrong, the civil law provides a mechanism for resolving disputes.

Look again at the first answers you gave when looking at the case study.

1 What matters do you think may be covered by the civil law?

2 What reasons do you think society has for creating laws in these cases?

You may have decided that, if you are not prepared to give them compensation, Jones Limited might want to take you to court for breaking your agreement with them so that they can recoup some of their losses. As we saw earlier, the law sets up rules on what constitutes a valid agreement so that both parties know their respective rights and responsibilities and can deal with each other confidently. When something goes wrong and someone loses out, the law provides a forum for sorting out the rights and wrongs of the case. If you cannot sort it out between yourselves, you and Jones Limited can use the law to define what obligations you have towards each other and, if you can't agree on a satisfactory solution, it can provide procedures for deciding who is right and how they ought to be compensated.

You may not have spotted that the pedestrian injured by the lorry may also use the law to sue you for negligence so as to get compensation for her injuries. As we shall see in Parts 4 and 5, the law also provides a framework for deciding degrees of responsibility in those situations where unrelated individuals come into contact, one party's actions cause harm to the other, and the injured party seeks compensation.

2.3   Public law and private law

A different way of seeing what types of law there are is to consider the distinction between public and private law. This distinction is based on who or what the law is trying to regulate. If the law is trying to regulate individuals and their behaviour towards other individuals then it is often called private law. If, however, the law is trying to regulate the government and its various institutions and bodies and how they behave then it is often called public law. Public law also includes those aspects of law where the state itself regulates the behaviour of individuals. It is concerned with the relationship between the state and its citizens, whether it is the law which governs how the state should be run, or the laws which the state itself enforces to control the behaviour of its citizens. This distinction is shown in the diagram opposite.

It helps to put criminal and civil law in the context of the law as a whole. Criminal law is a distinct branch of public law concerned, as we have seen, with ensuring individuals conform to certain standards of behaviour and with the way the state enforces those standards on those individuals who fail to conform. It covers a wide range of socially unacceptable acts from, as we have seen, parking on double yellow lines and shoplifting through to robbery, assault or murder.

Civil or private law takes in, as the diagram shows, a range of different branches of the law from family and property law through to the law of contract and tort. All these branches of the law provide a set of rules which define the obligations of individuals to one another and a forum for settling disputes if the parties cannot agree any other way.

3   How does the law affect business people?

Look at the case study again.

1 Which branches of the law shown in the diagram might cover the various legal problems you have identified?

Let us begin with Smith and Jones. In breaking an agreement by, in this case, failing to meet an agreed deadline, Smith Limited would appear to be in *breach of contract*, dealt with under contract law. The pedestrian may decide to sue

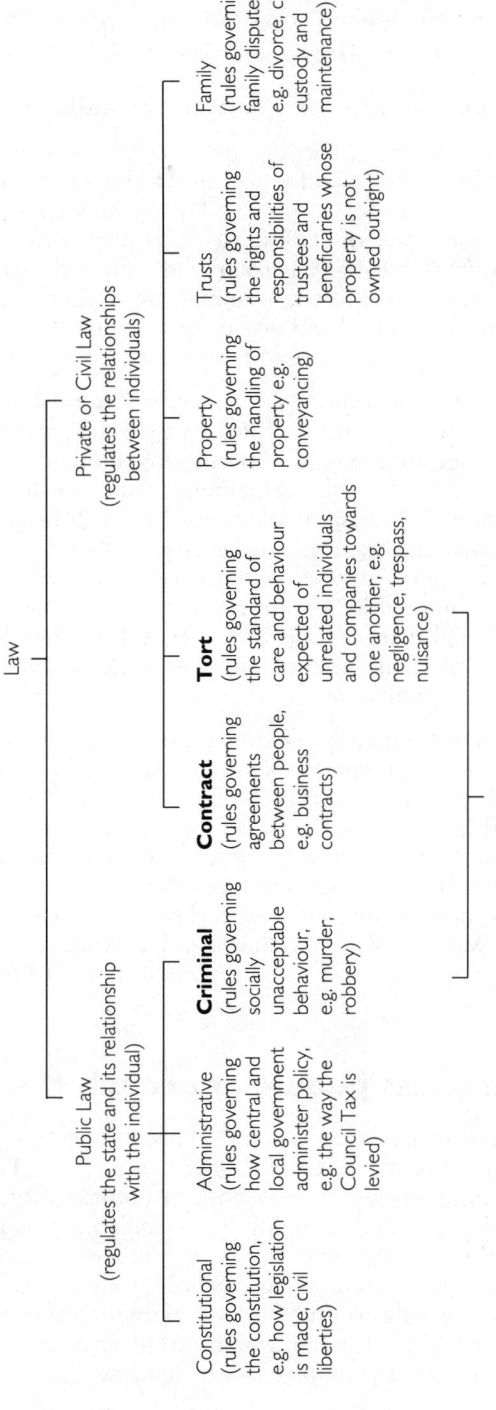

Law

Public Law
(regulates the state and its relationship
with the individual)

Private or Civil Law
(regulates the relationships
between individuals)

Constitutional
(rules governing
the constitution,
e.g. how legislation
is made, civil
liberties)

Administrative
(rules governing
how central and
local government
administer policy,
e.g. the way the
Council Tax is
levied)

Criminal
(rules governing
socially
unacceptable
behaviour,
e.g. murder,
robbery)

Contract
(rules governing
agreements
between people,
e.g. business
contracts)

Tort
(rules governing
the standard of
care and behaviour
expected of
unrelated individuals
and companies towards
one another, e.g.
negligence, trespass,
nuisance)

Property
(rules governing
the handling of
property e.g.
conveyancing)

Trusts
(rules governing
the rights and
responsibilities of
trustees and
beneficiaries whose
property is not
owned outright)

Family
(rules governing
family disputes
e.g. divorce, child
custody and
maintenance)

The main scope of business law

Figure I

you for negligence in causing her injuries, in which case you will be dealt with under the law of *tort*. The state itself may want to prosecute you and your driver for producing unsafe goods and bad driving and for having, therefore, committed a *criminal offence*. Though a business may from time to time be affected by, for example, property law, it is in these three areas, contract, tort and crime, that it is most likely to come into contact with the law.

Criminal law is often of relevance to business people in terms of the criminal liability which they may face for failing to ensure the safety of their workforce and the public, for failing to comply with provisions designed to limit environmental pollution, or for failing to comply with relevant taxation provisions, for example. This liability is usually set out with reasonable clarity in the appropriate legislation. Where the criminal law is concerned, it is really a matter of ensuring that you take legal advice as to what things you must avoid doing and then follow that advice. There is very little room for argument.

What criminal law affects your business will vary enormously depending on the type of business that you run. For example, a waste disposal firm must comply with the criminal law requirements for monitoring methane gas production at waste disposal sites. A road haulage business must ensure that its vehicles comply with Department of Transport standards or it will be guilty of a criminal offence. A firm of financial advisers must ensure that it complies with the Financial Services Act 1986 or those giving advice will be guilty of a criminal offence. It would be impossible in one book to deal with all the aspects of criminal law which might arise. This book therefore largely limits itself to looking at the business person's relationship with other firms or individuals and not at liability under the criminal law.

Civil law is clearly of relevance to business people in the way it sets down guidelines for the kinds of agreement they make and defines the responsibilities they may have to others with whom they come into contact whether, as in the case of Jones Limited, as part of normal business activity or, in the case of the pedestrian, through a more unexpected route. Most firms make a conscious effort to avoid liability under the criminal law, but all make regular use of the civil law in the agreements they make on a day-to-day basis, for example. An understanding of how the law of contract and of tort affects their business dealings is especially important and is the principal theme of this book.

4   How do business people approach the law?

In most cases businesses will avoid going to the extreme of taking someone to court. We like to call this the *least risk of litigation line*. Litigation involves dispute which often ends up being dealt with in court. Going to court is often expensive, time consuming and stressful. Most sensible people try to arrange their affairs so that they do not end up having to argue the matter in court. Business people, then, may look at law in a slightly different way to some lawyers. They will be looking to enter into deals which are unlikely to be the subject of a dispute. They are usually looking to arrange their affairs in such a way that they follow the most certain points of the law.

For business people it must always be remembered that the law is there as a guide and as a last resort. Very often business people have to consider not only whether they would be likely to succeed if they sued the other party, but also what effect suing them would have on their future business.

In his book *An Introduction to Law*, Phil Harris observes that:

> '... In the sphere of commercial agreements and business contracts, research ... has suggested that people in business rarely invoke the law as a means of resolving business disputes over their contractual agreements, mainly because this is seen as having the effect of perpetuating the conflict and polarising the disputants, instead of resolving the particular problem without damaging the continuing business relationships of the parties.'

Looking back at the case study, if you have engaged in a good business relationship with Jones Ltd up until the delayed order, you both might want to compromise rather than damage that relationship at each other's expense. Recognising that it was not all your fault, Jones Ltd might see it as more sensible to discuss, for example, partial compensation or a discount on subsequent orders. You might also try to agree ways of avoiding the problem in future.

Having said that, business people cannot entirely avoid legal reasoning and possible disputes. However well we try to order our affairs things will not always go to plan. When the unexpected happens you must be able to apply legal reasoning to decide what you think the likely outcome of the situation is, and plan your tactics accordingly.

5   Civil and criminal procedure

The distinction between civil and criminal law is also reflected in the differing procedures that a business person might encounter in each. We will look in detail at how one might use the courts, for example, later in the book. Here we introduce some of the fundamental questions relating particularly to proof. It is important to grasp these principles early, particularly as they help the non-lawyer to understand the nature of legal reasoning.

5.1   Civil procedure

What type of law affects me?
Civil actions concern disputes between private individuals, in which one party is trying to acquire a remedy for the wrong which they have suffered.

When proceedings based on civil law are brought the *plaintiff* (the person who has been wronged and is bringing the proceedings) *sues* the *defendant* (the alleged wrongdoer) in the civil courts. It is up to the plaintiff to start proceedings by approaching the court and initiating a writ or summons for the defendant to come to court to answer the case against him or her. In order to 'win', the plaintiff must bring evidence to the court (in terms of either physical evidence or witnesses) to prove his/her case. If the plaintiff is successful then the defendant is found *liable* and an appropriate order will be made by the court. This order will give effect to the plaintiff's *remedy*. This is very often *damages* (financial compensation).

5.1.1   The burden of proof

Who must prove their story?
If you do decide to sue, who is going to have to prove their story? The answer is that the *burden of proof* is on the plaintiff. If you imagine a pair of scales, the burden of proof means that they start off tipped very slightly against the plaintiff. It is the plaintiff's job to bring evidence to tip them in his or her favour. Until the plaintiff does that, the defendant does not need to defend him/herself at all.

5.1.2   The standard of proof

How much proof must be provided?
How much evidence must the plaintiff bring in order to tip the scales into his or her favour? The answer is that the plaintiff must show that, *on a balance of probabilities,* what he or she is saying is more likely to be true than what the defendant says. If you imagine the pair of scales again, this 'standard of proof' means that the scales need only tip very slightly in the plaintiff's favour.

5.2   Criminal offences

Criminal offences are, as one might expect, governed by criminal law. Murder, grievous bodily harm (GBH) and theft are all well-known crimes. So too are speeding and tax evasion.

Crimes represent conduct considered by society to be undesirable to the extent that the law prohibits such behaviour and makes it a criminal offence. The wrongdoer ('*the defendant*') is *prosecuted* and if found guilty is punished. This is really the objective of criminal law – to punish the guilty party. Crime is viewed not only as a wrong against an individual or individuals but also as against the state itself. Hence it is usually the state itself in the name of *the Crown*, represented by the Crown Prosecution Service ('CPS'), which initiates and carries out a prosecution against a defendant. The police will often be the first to detect that a crime has been committed, to arrest and charge an individual in some cases, and to accumulate evidence. However, they will hand over the actual prosecution to the CPS. Because it is the state that prosecutes, that is why criminal cases in English law are referred to as 'The Crown against So and So'. In American films you will hear the same type of thing referred to as 'The State against so and so' or 'The People against so and so'.

5.2.1   The burden of proof

In criminal cases a defendant is 'innocent until proven guilty'. This means that it is the prosecutor's job to show that a crime has, on the face of it, been committed. If the prosecutor does not show this, the defence lawyers will not call any evidence but will instead ask the court to rule that there is 'no case to answer'. If the court agrees, that is the end of the matter. If the court thinks that the prosecution has shown some evidence that the crime was committed then the defendant must bring his or her evidence and convince the court otherwise.

5.2.2 The standard of proof

The prosecution must prove its case *beyond all reasonable doubt.* This is a higher standard than is required in the civil courts and is designed to ensure that, as far as humanly possible, if someone is going to be branded as a criminal, we can be sure that the guilty party is really guilty. The idea is that it is better for a guilty person to go free than for an innocent one to be convicted. Needless to say, that is the Utopian view. Television programmes like 'Rough Justice' have shown that even this high standard is not foolproof. It does however mean that you do not, as in civil cases, ask yourself which story is most likely to be true. Instead you ask yourself whether you are sure that the defendant's story could not be true.

Table 1.1 Differences between criminal and civil law

Characteristics	Criminal Law	Civil Law
Purpose	to ensure individuals conform to certain standards of behaviour	to provide rules to enable individuals to bargain and to settle disputes between them
Who brings an action against whom?	the state *prosecutes* a *defendant*	a *plaintiff* sues a *defendant*
What standard of proof is required?	the prosecution must prove its case *beyond all reasonable doubt*	the plaintiff must prove his/her case on a *balance of probabilities*
What happens to the defendant?	he/she is *convicted* if proven *guilty* and *acquitted* if proven *innocent*	a defendant may be proved to be *liable* or *not liable*
What kind of punishment may be given?	fine, community service, probation, imprisonment	compensation or *remedy* in the form of, e.g., *damages*

6 How do you study law?

Probably this seems a very stupid question. You probably already know how to study a number of subjects. Law though is different. Students who have been used to other disciplines often find it very difficult and frustrating to find that there is often no 'right' answer in law. Law is a system of rules which will often apply slightly differently depending on the facts of the case.

The academic or practising lawyer will look at the matter and will look at the possible outcomes. Say there is a dispute between X and Y. Lawyers will then try and construct an argument that favours X. Then they will construct an argument which favours Y. From the two arguments they will decide which is the stronger and therefore which, if the matter were to go to court, would be *the most likely* to win. Occasionally the argument in favour of one party will be so much stronger than that in favour of the other that the lawyer will say that one party has *no case*. Very seldom do they actually mean this. What they usually mean is that the other party is most unlikely to win!

As we have seen, whether one party will have a strong case or not also depends on the burden of proof required by a criminal or civil court. In a civil case, the plaintiff must prove his or her case on the balance of probabilities. The skill of the lawyer lies in interpreting the evidence to his or her client's advantage in light of the rules laid down by the law and tipping the scales enough to prove or disprove the case for the client. As we shall see in Chapter 3, things are complicated even further by the way lawyers interpret the rules using previous cases!

7   How can business people cope with legal jargon?

Any good lawyer should be able to explain legal principles and concepts in plain English so that their client is not confused. Business people, however, need to have some independent understanding of how the law works. It is important, for two reasons, for business people to understand some of the terms which lawyers use. Firstly, they need to be able to deal with basic concepts of law themselves without recourse at every turn to a lawyer for an explanation. Secondly, even if the matter is complex and a lawyer is needed, a great deal of valuable time will be wasted if every term and concept has to be explained by the lawyer.

In order to help you with some of the legal jargon this book does two things:

- it attempts to explain each term as you come across it and to repeat the explanation from time to time
- in case you come across a term which you don't fully understand, a glossary of terms is included at the end of the book. This glossary is fairly simple but should enable you to follow the development of the principles of law without feeling as if you were dealing with a brand new foreign language. (Sometimes when listening to a group of lawyers talking, that is what it can sound like!)

Remember, if you do come across a term which you don't understand either look it up or ask someone. Often people don't like to ask for fear of looking silly. Our experience is that you will very seldom be the only one who doesn't understand something and often students and staff will be grateful to have an opportunity to clear up the problem! Even when you get into business itself, if your lawyer uses terms which you do not understand tell them and ask them to explain it. Lawyers spend a long time training to be experts in their field. If everyone could be expected to understand the law and its terminology straight away none of us lawyers would have jobs at all! A lawyer who is incapable of explaining the law or legal terminology should not be in practice.

Summary

Law has two fundamental roles, reflected in two differing branches of the law:

- *criminal* law provides a set of rules which ensures individuals conform to certain standards of behaviour
- *civil* law provides a set of rules which allows individuals to bargain confidently and to resolve their differences when something goes wrong.

Business people will often use the law only as a last resort, but need to know enough to understand their responsibilities and what the options are if something goes wrong.

Legal reasoning is concerned with constructing the strongest case from the evidence: civil and criminal law have differing rules concerning the strength of the case needed to win.

 CASE STUDY 2

This is rather less a case study and more a practical exercise. You should, preferably, do this exercise in a group. If possible there should be four of you. You each now take one of the following roles (if you cannot get together in a group you can do it on your own by considering each role in turn):

1 The owner of a wine merchant retail outlet
2 The owner of a building firm which is carrying out repairs to the wine merchant's shop
3 A customer of the shop
4 A shoplifter in the shop

Having decided which role you will take now, on your own, write down in respect of each of the other people two types of factual scenario between you and each of them which might involve the law.

Once you have done this, get back together again and go through each scenario. Try to work out whether criminal or civil law is involved and, simply from your own knowledge of the law so far, indicate what names you might be able to give to the problem, what steps those involved might take and the questions of proof involved.

You may find that, when you have worked through this book, you need to change your ideas from these initial ones. But at least you are beginning to think of everyday business situations in terms of *the law*.

2 Where does EC law fit in?

Objectives

By the end of this chapter you should:

- appreciate the significance of European Community Law as it relates to and is part of English law
- be able to identify the name and role of the main institutions of the European Community
- be able to explain how the different types of European Community law interact with and influence English law.

1 The significance of European Community law – the historical background

As early as 1951 the Treaty of Paris established the European Coal and Steel Community ('ECSC') when six countries agreed to place the production of coal and steel under their joint international control.

In 1955 the Foreign Ministers of the six members of the ECSC agreed to: 'pursue the establishment of a United Europe through the development of common institutions, a progressive fusion of national economies, the creation of a common market and harmonisation of social policies ...'

These original aspirations culminated in the six member states of the ECSC signing the Treaty of Rome. Article 2 of the Treaty of Rome says:

'The Community shall have as its task, by establishing a common market and progressively approximating the economic policies of member states, to promote throughout the Community a harmonious development of economic activities, a continuous and balanced expansion, an increase in stability, an accelerated raising of the standard of living and closer relations between the states belonging to it.'

In January 1972 the UK signed the Treaty of Accession in Brussels and became a full member of the EEC as from 1 January 1973.

In February 1986 the member states (now 12) signed the Single European Act amending the EEC treaty. As a result the Treaty of Rome had added to it a new Article 8A which in part said:

'The community shall adopt measures with the aim of progressively establishing the internal market over a period expiring on December 1992 ... The internal market shall comprise an area without internal frontiers in which the free movement of goods, persons, services and capital is ensured within the provisions of the Treaty ...'

The preamble to the Single European Act talked in terms of the member states transforming '... relations as a whole among their states into a European *Union* ...' (emphasis added). A treaty adopted in the Dutch city of Maastricht in December 1991 was signed in February 1992. This is the Treaty on European Union (TEU) usually referred to as 'the Maastricht Treaty'. The TEU created the European Union consisting of the three 'pillars'. These three pillars consist of the central pillar, viz. the existing communities and their law, hence EC law. The two other pillars are Cooperation on Common Foreign and Security Policy (European Political Cooperation under the Single European Act) and Cooperation in Justice and Home Affairs. These latter two 'pillars' are not incorporated into the EEC treaty as amended by the TEU and are therefore non-Community competences not subject to the control of the European Court of Justice. Hence we do not talk in terms of EU law, there being no such thing. Article A of Title 1 of the treaty provides that the member states shall '... establish amongst themselves a European Union ...' and goes on to state that the treaty marks '... a new stage in the process of creating an ever closer union among the peoples of Europe'.

A number of member states have expressed reservations as to the steps envisaged in order to achieve an 'ever closer union', in particular monetary union.

2   Community institutions

There is a single institutional framework comprising the Council of Ministers, the Commission, the European Parliament and the Court of Justice. These institutions implement the objectives of the European Union. (A fifth institution, the Court of Auditors, is to be added as a result of the Maastricht Treaty.)

2.1   The Council of Ministers

The Council of Ministers of the European Communities consists of one minister from each of the member states. Which particular minister sits on the Council depends on the particular topic under discussion. For example, it is likely to be the Minister for Agriculture when European agricultural policy is being discussed.

In essence the Council is the decision-making body of the European Communities. Its power as a law maker, however, is restricted to the extent that it only has the power to decide whether or not to adopt proposals put forward by the Commission. It cannot create its own proposals.

The methods of voting used by the Council are obviously of great importance. There are three:

- Unanimity – where all the member states must agree
- Simple Majority – where at least seven member states must support the proposal
- Qualified Majority – which is a system of weighted voting where the 'big four', France, Germany, Italy and the UK, have ten votes each, Spain has eight and other states have fewer still. The total votes available are 87 and a qualified majority requires 62 votes.

As a result of the Luxembourg Accords of 1966 it is possible, where vital national interests are at stake, for a state to insist on unanimous voting, though the Accords have increasingly fallen into disuse. The Single European Act of 1986 has not affected these provisions but has increased the areas where qualified voting applies. For example, the bulk of the legislation required to achieve the internal market is now to be agreed by the method of qualified majority voting.

2.2   The Commission

The Commission is the executive body of the Communities. The Commission presently consists of 20 members who act independently of the member states who appoint them. The five largest member states (i.e. France, Germany, Italy, the UK and Spain) can appoint two Commissioners each while the ten smaller countries can appoint one commissioner each. The length of appointment of each Commissioner is five years (since January 1995) and each Commissioner takes responsibility for EU policy such as competition policy, economic and financial affairs, regional policy, etc.

The Commission is responsible for formulating Community policy. There are two main ways in which the Commission plays a part in influencing European Community law.

Firstly, it initiates and drafts most Community legislation; such proposals are then put to the Council for the Council to consider and, if it is in agreement, enact.

Secondly, by virtue of Article 155 of the Treaty of Rome, '… in order to ensure the proper functioning and development of the Common Market the Commission shall ensure that the provisions of this Treaty and measures taken pursuant to it are applied.'

This second function confers on the Commission the task of ensuring that the treaty and legislative measures arising out of it are observed. In order to carry out this task the Commission has power to initiate proceedings against member states, the Council of Ministers, the Parliament, individuals and businesses. For example, one of the forms of Community legislation is *directives*, which we look at later in this chapter. Article 169 of the Treaty of Rome states that:

'if the Commission considers that a member state has failed to fulfil an obligation under this treaty, it shall deliver a reasoned opinion on the matter … if the state concerned does not comply with the opinion of the Commission the latter may bring the matter before the European Court of Justice.'

The Commission is the institution that enforces the Community's competition rules (Articles 85 and 86). These rules aim to achieve a perfectly competitive market for business in the member states. The Commission has extensive powers (set out in Regulation 17/62/EEC) to investigate complaints or to conduct general enquiries in business sectors where it suspects that competition may be restricted. The Regulation specifies the sanctions that the Commission may use and also empowers it to grant individual exemptions where, for example, conduct which would otherwise be anti-competitive is shown to be of benefit to the consumer.

2.3   The Parliament

The European Parliament was created by the Treaty of Rome in 1957 and was then known as 'the Assembly'. It is now called the Parliament. It was not, at the outset, intended to be a democratic body and even when members of the Parliament became directly elected, in 1979, it cannot be compared to our own Parliament. The functions and powers of the two are very different indeed.

Since June 1979 MEPs (Members of the European Parliament) are directly elected by voters within the member states. Currently there are 626 MEPs (since the accession of Austria, Finland and Sweden in June 1994). The MEPs group together in terms of their political position rather than their nationality. Members are elected for five years.

Unlike our own Parliament it has limited legislative powers. The Treaty of Rome gave the Parliament a purely advisory and consultative role. The Council and the Commission consult with the Parliament before taking decisions. This minor role gave rise to criticisms of a 'democratic deficit' in the legislative process. The Single European Act began the process of increasing the Parliament's powers by introducing a cooperation procedure whereby the Parliament may propose amendments to legislation. The co-decision procedure which was introduced by Maastricht gives the Parliament a power of veto.

The Parliament can also put questions to the Council and the Commission. Article 144 of the Treaty of Rome confers on the Parliament the power to dismiss the full Commission. Needless to say this is a very extreme measure and has, to date, never been used. The Parliament also has considerable powers over the Community's budget. The Parliament, if you like, 'holds the purse strings'. It receives the preliminary draft budget from the Council. It can then take one of three courses:

- it can approve the budget
- it can suggest modifications to it
- it can reject it.

2.4   The European Court of Justice

The European Court of Justice sits in Luxembourg and is the supreme authority on all aspects of European law. Article 164 of the Treaty of Rome states that '… the Court of Justice shall ensure that in the interpretation and application of this treaty the Law is observed.'

The decisions of the European Court of Justice are binding on member states and there is no right of appeal.

There are 15 judges, one from each of the member states. Judges are appointed for terms of six years which may be renewed.

Article 167 says that the judges '... shall be chosen from persons whose independence is beyond doubt and who possess the qualifications for appointment to the highest judicial offices in their respective countries'.

Unlike English court procedure, there is an absence of emphasis placed on oral argument and much greater reliance on written submission or pleadings. The judges themselves play an active role in the hearing rather than simply listening to the evidence and speeches which are presented to them. The judges are assisted by nine *advocates general* whose task it is to give an independent opinion of the case to the court. The court, following continental practice, gives a single judgment and no dissenting judgments are given. The judgments are also short, terse and to the point with little or no indication of the reasoning upon which it is based. (English law students invariably wish English judgments were similar!)

The jurisdiction of the Court includes the following:

- One of the most important functions of the Court is to give preliminary rulings on the interpretation of the Treaties or of any Acts of Community institutions. Article 177 of the Treaty of Rome says that any court or tribunal in a member state may request such a ruling.
- If a member state fails to comply with its treaty obligations then an action may be brought against it by another member state or by the Commission. The Court will decide the dispute and will issue a judgment which is in the form of a declaration outlining in what way the obligation is not being complied with and what the member state must do to make amends.
- Actions may be brought against Community institutions by other institutions, member states, private individuals or companies. The action might allege, for example, that the particular institution has infringed the treaty or misused its powers.

In an attempt to relieve the burden upon the Court and reduce delays, a Court of First Instance was established in 1989 under the provisions of the Single European Act. This court has 12 judges appointed by member states, and three to five of these will sit together to hear some cases. Jurisdiction is limited to disputes between the Community and its servants and to applications for judicial review of certain actions of the Council or Commission. There is a right of appeal to the full Court on a point of law.

2.5   What role does the European Court of Human Rights have?

It often seems very confusing when you listen to the news and they talk about the different institutions of the European Union. The European Court of Human

Rights stands alone. It is not part of European Community law. European Community law deals mainly with the economic interests of the member states. The European Court of Human Rights is a separate institution whose role is to protect individuals' human rights against potential abuse by the member states and has jurisdiction only over states which are signatories to the European Convention on Human Rights.

3   Community law-making acts

Article 189 of the Treaty of Rome lays down the legislative powers of the Community institutions. It says that 'in order to carry out their task the Council and the Commission shall ... make *regulations*, issue *directives*, take *decisions*, make *recommendations* or deliver *opinions*.'

We need therefore to understand what each of these things is:

- a regulation has general application and is binding, in its entirety, and is *directly* applicable in all member states
- a directive is also binding on all member states. The difference here is that it is the general result to be achieved which is binding. *How* it is achieved is left to the individual states
- a decision is binding on those to whom it is addressed as are recommendations and opinions.

3.1   Regulations

The idea then is that *regulations* are directly applicable in all member states without any need for future legislation. However not all regulations are as simple as that.

In **case 128/78 Commission v UK (Re Tachographs)** the UK had failed to implement part of a regulation relating to the introduction of tachometers in commercial vehicles. It was held that national legislation was necessary in order to create a new criminal offence.

3.2   Directives

Directives do not become applicable immediately. They are binding on states as to the result to be achieved but each member state has discretion about how it is actually done. It may be that a member state is reluctant to implement a directive for a number of reasons. For example, it might be the case that implementing the directive would give individuals rights to receive compensation where none existed before.

This was the situation when the Commission issued the **Acquired Rights Directive (EC/77/187)** which offers a greater measure of protection to employees who find themselves caught up in the situation where a business changes hands. The UK government with considerable reluctance implemented the directive through the **Transfer of Undertakings (Protection of Employment) Regulations 1981**. It refused however to allow these regulations to apply to undertakings which were not in the nature of a commercial venture. In this way they ensured that their policy of compulsory competitive tendering could flourish without the danger of individuals 'rocking the boat' by claiming compensation. Nowhere in the original directive was there any reference to the non-applicability to non-commercial ventures such as local councils. A decision of the European Court of Justice resolved the issue by holding that the directive did cover non-commercial undertakings.

> In **Dr Sophie Redmond Stitchting v Bartol [1992]** the plaintiff was a foundation in Holland giving assistance to drug addicts. It was originally aided by grants from a local authority; from the beginning of 1991, however, the grants were transferred to a similar organisation. Some of the plaintiff's employees were offered new contracts of employment; those who were not offered employment pleaded that a transfer had occurred within the meaning of the Acquired Rights Directive. The Dutch courts referred the matter to the ECJ who held that a transfer of an undertaking had taken place.

No mention was made of the undertaking being in the nature of a commercial venture and it must be assumed that a directive applying to local-authority-related non-commercial organisations in Holland also applies to local authorities in the UK. As a result of this decision, amending legislation had to be passed in the UK to bring the domestic rules into line with the directive as interpreted by the European Court.

If, as a result of a member state's failure to implement a directive, an individual has suffered loss, then that individual may be able to claim compensation from the government. Compensation can be claimed if the following provisions are satisfied:

- the directive concerned must have conferred rights on individuals
- those rights can actually be identified from the directive
- there is a causal link between the state's failure to implement the directive and the damage suffered by the individual in question.

3.3   Decisions, recommendations and opinions

Decisions of the Council or the Commission are binding in their entirety on the person or body to whom they are addressed. They do not have general legislative effect.

Recommendations and opinions are only a reflection of the views held by the Council and Commission on European Community policies. They are not in any way binding but are merely of persuasive value.

4 Case law

In your study of English law you will quickly become accustomed to the idea of the decisions in earlier cases becoming binding on courts when making later decisions (the doctrine of binding precedent). As far as the Court of Justice is concerned it has no law-making powers. Its decisions relate only to the case that it is hearing at the time; they are binding on the domestic courts within the member states but in relation to its own decisions there is no doctrine of binding precedent. The situation is slightly different when looking at interpretation of the Treaties. A trend is beginning to emerge where there appears to be an increasing reliance on previous decisions. Although previous decisions as to how a treaty should be interpreted are not precedents, they do appear to have considerable persuasive authority.

5 Acceptance of European Community law by the UK

In 1972 the UK passed the European Communities Act which ensured the acceptance of the law of the European Communities into English law. Section 2(1) of the European Communities Act provides that European Community law is to be applied in the UK. It states that any 'rights powers ... and restrictions from time to time created or arising under the Treaties ... are, without further enactment, to be given legal effect or used in the United Kingdom, shall be recognised ... and be enforced allowed and followed accordingly.'

This section ensures that, in general terms, when Parliament legislates, its legislative power is *subject* to legislation of the European Union which is directly applicable (i.e. regulations). The practical effect of this is that if, for example, a regulation is applied and it conflicts with existing UK law, then the UK law is automatically repealed. The European Community law provision applies and not UK law.

The sovereignty, or overriding power, of the UK Parliament has, as it were, been 'put on hold' as far as matters of the European Union are concerned. In **Macarthy's Ltd v Smith [1979]** Lord Denning said 'if ... our legislation is deficient – or is inconsistent with Community law ... then it is our bounden duty to give priority to Community law.'

Here Lord Denning is expressing a clear commitment to the supremacy of Community law. However, there is a sting in the tail because in the same case Lord Denning recognises that, like any other statute, the **European Communities Act 1972** could technically be repealed by the UK Parliament. He goes on to say: '... if the time should come when our Parliament deliberately passes an Act with the intention of repudiating the Treaty or any provisions in it ... and says so in express terms then ... it would be the duty of our Courts to follow the statute of our Parliament.'

What in effect Lord Denning is saying is that we have agreed to accept everything in European Community law. The UK is bound by all EC law and cannot simply pick and choose which bits it likes and which it doesn't. If there is something with which the UK disagrees it has two choices:

- either to accept it
- or to withdraw from the Union entirely.

While withdrawal from the European Union and repeal of the European Communities Act are highly unlikely, they are in theory possible and so, to that extent, the UK Parliament retains control.

Summary

You should now be able to:

- explain the roles of the Community institutions:
  the Council of Ministers
  the Commission
  the European Parliament
  the European Court of Justice
- explain Community law-making acts
  Regulations
  Directives
  Decisions
  Recommendations and Opinions
- distinguish between their different effects and applicability
- identify the statute whereby English law is governed by European Community law and explain to what extent, if at all, it would be possible for the UK to reject the provisions of the European Union.

3 How does the law evolve?

Objectives

By the end of this chapter, you should:

- understand the distinction between statute and common law
- be able to explain the legislative process, delegated legislation and statutory interpretation
- understand the role of precedent in the evolution of the law
- be able to understand the key features of a case.

Introduction: statute and common law

In English law we tend to think of Parliament as being responsible for making the law. The law which is made by Parliament is called *statute*. There are however many matters which are not covered by an Act of Parliament and on which the judges have had to make up their own set of rules. Law which has been devised by the judges in this way is called *common law*.

In this chapter, we will look first at the way statute law develops, before going on to look at the evolution of the common law. We will also look at the hierarchy of particular courts as it impacts on the way law develops.

I Legislation

We have already seen that, to a certain extent, the UK has by joining the European Union accepted that there are matters on which EC law will take precedence over UK law and certain situations where the law which the UK makes will be prescribed by EC directives and regulations.

Where a matter is not one which affects the European Union the UK is however free to make its own laws or *legislation*. Legislation is quite simply law enacted by Parliament in the form of *Acts of Parliament* otherwise known as *statutes*. We do not intend, in a book of this kind, to go into great detail on how an Act of Parliament is created but there are certain stages and terminology with which you need to be familiar in order to understand how the law may affect you as a business person.

Most legislation starts its life being introduced by the current government. (Private Members Bills, started by an individual Member of Parliament, often with the backing of a special interest group, are a comparatively small part of the proposed legislation dealt with by Parliament.) An Act of Parliament may start off life in the form of a *green paper*. This is a device which seeks the response of interested parties to the government's preliminary proposals. The green paper is then followed by a *white paper*. The white paper is advance notice of the more definite proposals upon which the final legislation will be based. There will then follow a draft *Bill* which will have been prepared by Parliamentary draftsmen. The Bill will then pass through various stages in both the House of Commons and the House of Lords and if it is successful in overcoming any obstacles during these stages it will then acquire the *Royal Assent* and become an *Act of Parliament*. The obstacles which the Bill may face before becoming an Act may be in the form of lengthy debate followed by voting on all or particular parts of it. Two things are worthy of note in respect of this procedure. First, the House of Lords can debate and vote on any Bill but its powers to prevent legislation coming into force are limited. (The idea is that, as the elected house, the wishes of the House of Commons should not be frustrated by the House of Lords which is not elected.) The House of Lords therefore only has the power to block what is known as a *money bill* (in other words one containing only financial and taxation provisions). Its only real power in relation to other Bills is that if the House of Lords is opposed to a Bill it can be delayed by the House of Lords for up to one year.

The second matter which deserves some mention is the Royal Assent. The Royal Assent is, by convention, necessary before any Act can become law. The sovereign does not however have any realistic say in the matter. It is simply unthinkable that a monarch would refuse the Royal Assent. To do so would certainly cause uproar and a complete reconsideration of the role of the monarchy. The Royal Assent is realistically a final rubber stamp.

1.1   Delegated legislation

Not all legislation goes through the fairly lengthy procedure which we have just looked at in section 1. Parliament frequently resorts to the use of *delegated legislation* as a method of creating the enormous volume of rules which are necessary to:

- implement government policies, and
- cope with the increasing complexities of modern society.

In order for delegated legislation to be possible there must be an enabling or parent statute which contains within it a clear indication of authority to delegate to a particular person or post holder (e.g. the Secretary of State) or a body (e.g. a local authority) the power to make new law. Law created in this fashion is every bit as authentic and effective as law made by an Act of Parliament.

The use of delegated legislation is justified by the following reasoning:

- Parliament has not got time to create all the law required by the time-consuming route which is taken by primary legislation (Acts of Parliament)
- much of the law in the form of rules and regulations contains complex technical details which require special expertise to implement and

understand (many MPs and peers would not have the expertise to assess the merits of a particular provision)

- legislation which has been delegated can easily and quickly be adapted to changing circumstances and can allow for a swift response to emergencies.

The main criticisms of delegated legislation are:

- powers conferred can sometimes prove to be far in excess of what might originally have been anticipated
- once delegated, the control over the legislation is often limited and the only really effective way of dealing with say a Secretary of State who stretched his or her powers to the limit might be to attempt to *repeal* the parent Act. Something which itself would not be particularly easy with a strong party in a majority in the House of Commons!
- publicity is often inadequate. Delegated legislation may become part of English law with very little notice and finding out what has been brought into force in this way can require a headache-inducing session in the law library!

A less convincing argument against delegated legislation is that it diminishes the sovereignty of Parliament. No doubt it does to a certain extent. Compare this, though, in the light of our increasing integration into the European Union with the resulting loss of sovereignty.

2   Statutory interpretation

Judges also have a role to play when it comes to 'shaping' statutory provisions. When the Parliamentary draftsmen draft a Bill they will do their best to think of every possible situation and to make provision for it. They will almost certainly not succeed. There will inevitably be some situation in which the application of the Act or its wording appears ambiguous. When a case comes before the court based on a provision in an Act, the judge will be required to *interpret* and apply the statute. It is *not* the judge's role to disagree with the statute and come to a different decision. (That would be to usurp the supremacy of Parliament. The judges must apply the law which Parliament has created.) Within the bounds of arguable options, however, it is open to the judges to shape the law by the way in which they interpret and apply any piece of legislation that is ambiguous. In the past, judges have applied certain guidelines in interpreting statutes and these guidelines have become known as the rules of statutory interpretation.

The literal rule
This is, by tradition, the first resort of the judges. What it means is quite simply that words, if they are clear and unambiguous, must be given their common and ordinary meaning. If a literal interpretation produces manifest absurdity then that is just too bad. The reasoning is that Parliament will have to come along later and amend the provision. An example of this is:

Fisher v Bell (1961) in which statute made it an offence to 'offer for sale' flick knives. A shop keeper displaying flick knives in his shop window was prosecuted. His defence was that he was not offering for sale the flick knives but displaying them. His defence succeeded when the judge applied a literal interpretation of the statute. It required amending legislation to correct the error of the Parliamentary draftsmen.

The golden rule

This rule suggests that where wording in a statute is capable of two or more literal meanings then the interpretation should be adopted which produces the most acceptable and least absurd result.

In **Re Sigsworth (1935)**, on a literal interpretation of the Administration of Estates Act 1925, an only son who had murdered his mother would inherit her estate since she had died without leaving a will. The golden rule was applied to prevent this from happening.

The mischief rule

This rule says that the court should examine the statute to see what 'mischief', or problem, inherent in the judge-made or common law the statute had been passed to remedy. The words of the statute should then be interpreted in such a way as to achieve this objective.

These are the three main rules although further lesser rules do exist, for example, '*noscitur a sociis*' which means that a word should be interpreted by the company it keeps. In other words the context of the word and the wording is important. Another rule says that you should assume that if something has been left out of a statute it was an intentional omission and the words should be interpreted restrictively so as not to include it. Also the '*ejusdem generis*' rule which means that where specific words are followed by general words then the general words should be interpreted in the light of the specific words. A classic example of this is the expression, 'cats, dogs, or other animals'. The term 'other animals' should, on the basis of this rule, be interpreted so as to coincide with the meaning of the particular words 'cats, dogs ...'. In other words, domestic animals.

3 Common law

It is very tempting to think of the evolution of the law as complete once you have looked at the process by which legislation 'gets onto the statute books'. It must be remembered, however, that there are some matters which have never been the subject of Acts of Parliament. What has happened is that in the past disputes have arisen and the courts have been asked to adjudicate on the matter. In the absence of any statute covering the point the judges had to do what they thought best. In this way judge-made legal rules developed and as they developed so did the system of *precedent*. By this means, then, a whole system of rules and principles developed. These rules and principles are often still applied today. Only if the particular point has been dealt with by legislation will the *judge-made law* become obsolete. Until then, statutory rules and what you may see referred to as *common law rules* continue to exist side by side.

It must be said that when a judge is called upon to resolve a dispute between two parties (called *litigants*), he or she is not autonomous to the extent that he/she can reach whatever conclusion he/she feels to be appropriate. A judge *must* decide the issue in question by referring to previous cases decided in court either at the same level as the one in which that judge is sitting or at a higher level.

The status of the court is significant in determining whether its decisions are binding or merely persuasive. Where the facts of the case that the judge is hearing are the same or similar to the one under review, the judge must usually apply the same reasoning as the judge(s) in the earlier case used. In other words once a line of argument has been used to settle a dispute, the judge should use the same line of reasoning unless there are exceptional reasons for not doing so. The previous or earlier cases which have this constraining effect are referred to as *precedents*.

English law is governed by the doctrine of binding judicial precedent in that if the reasoning in a relevant precedent is not applied (e.g. if it was overlooked or rejected because it was mistakenly believed to be inapplicable), then the case under review will be wrongly decided and will have to be heard again on appeal.

3.1 The hierarchy of the courts

The basic rule of thumb is that the reasoning applied in higher courts is binding on lower courts. We will look at the basic structure of the courts system in Chapter 5, showing the hierarchy of individual courts. On the following page we include a detailed diagram which illustrates possible lines of appeal from lower to higher courts.

3.2 The European Court of Justice

We have already looked in Chapter 2 at the role of European Community law in English law. As one would expect, the decisions of the European Court of Justice are binding on courts in the UK. The European Court itself, however, does not consider itself bound by its own earlier decisions. In other words it feels free to change its mind and decide a case differently if it thinks it appropriate.

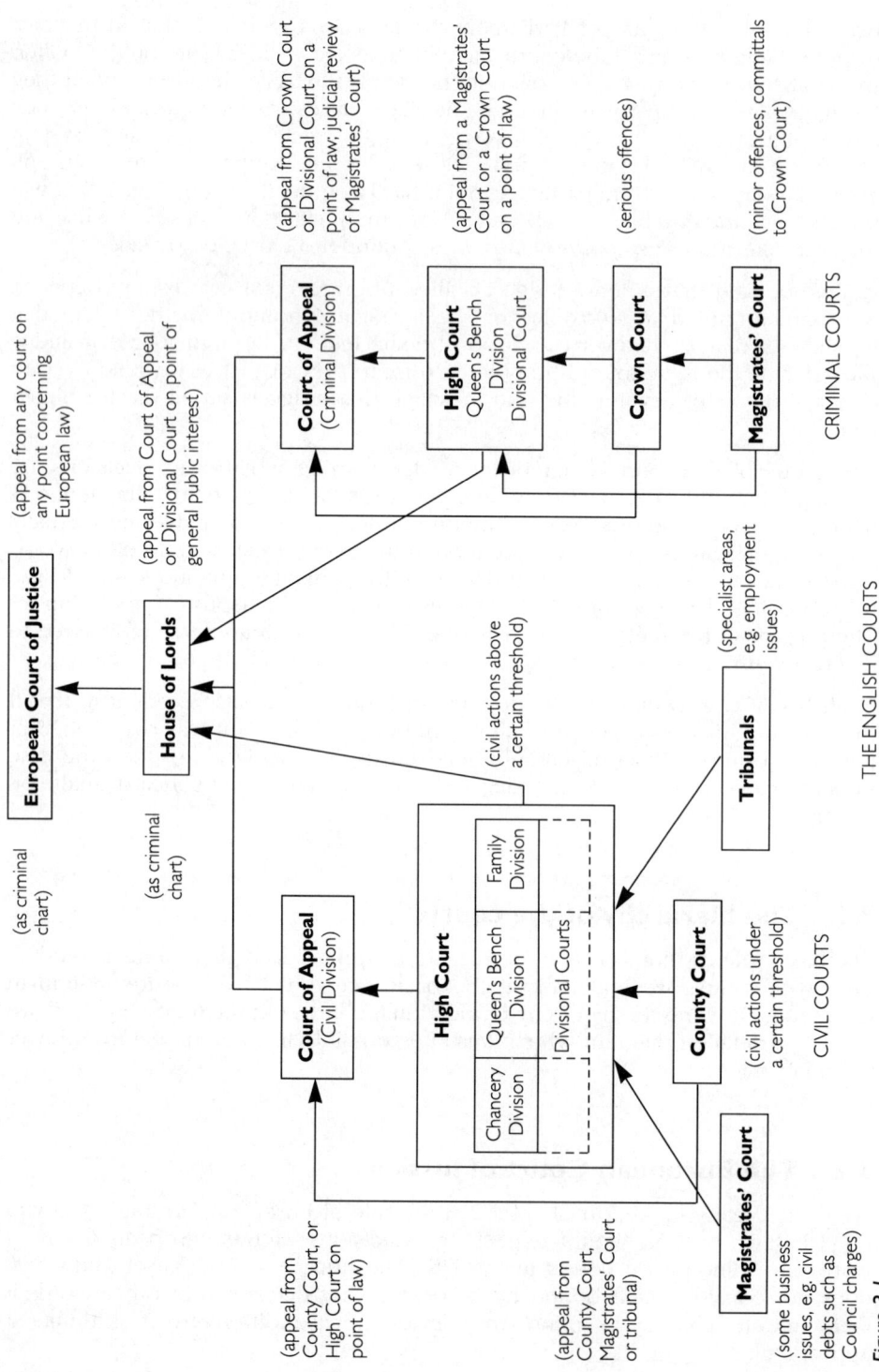

Figure 3.1

3.3 The House of Lords

First of all we should be clear that when we talk about the House of Lords as a court, we are not talking about the same thing as the House of Lords in its role as the upper house of Parliament. In this context the House of Lords simply means the court of last resort (or the 'highest' court) in the UK. Those who take part in the decisions are all senior judges and not simply there by virtue of being peers in the House of Lords.

Decisions of the House of Lords are binding on all other English courts. The House of Lords originally felt that it should follow its own previous decisions. This rule meant that no allowance could be made for changing times, nor could the court ignore a decision, even if it felt that it had been wrongly decided. Whilst this situation might be acceptable in a lower court from which an appeal could be made, it was a very rigid system indeed to apply to what was then the 'highest court in the land'! In 1966 this changed; in the Practice Direction of 1966, Lord Gardiner, then the Lord Chancellor, stated that:

> '... their Lordships nevertheless realise that too rigid adherence to precedent may lead to injustice in a particular case and also unduly restrict proper development of the law. They propose therefore to modify their present practice and, while treating former decisions of this House as normally binding, to depart from a previous decision when it appears right to do so ...'

A recent example of such departure is **Murphy v Brentwood District Council (1990)** in which the House of Lords declared that the case of **Anns v Merton London Borough Council (1977)** was wrongly decided and they duly departed from their earlier decision.

3.4 The Court of Appeal (Civil Division)

This court is inevitably bound by decisions of both the European Court and the House of Lords. Its decisions bind lower courts and it is bound to follow its own previous decisions with three exceptions:

- where the previous decision was decided *per incuriam* – or through lack of care. This usually means that in deciding the previous case the court overlooked a key earlier decision which was binding on it
- where the House of Lords has, in the meantime, reached a different conclusion to that of the previous Court of Appeal decision. In that case the Court of Appeal will be obliged to follow the new House of Lords decision and ignore its previous decision
- where there are previous decisions of the Court of Appeal which conflict. (Despite what has been said this can happen – take it from us!) Then obviously both or all decisions cannot be followed. The court can follow the decision which it thinks appropriate.

These principles are collectively known as the rule in Young's case (**Young v Bristol Aeroplane Co (1944)**).

3.5 Court of Appeal (Criminal Division)

This court is bound by the decisions of both the European Court and the House of Lords. Its decisions bind lower courts. The rule in Young's case applies except that the Criminal Division has much greater ability to depart from one of its own previous decisions where the freedom of an alleged criminal is at stake.

In **R v Spencer (1985)** is was said that '... if a man be in prison and in the judgment of the court wrongly in prison, it should not allow such matters as [precedent] to stand in the way ...'

3.6 The High Court

The High Court has two roles. It deals with civil cases that are considered too important for lower courts. Sitting as a *divisional* court, it hears appeals from lower courts.

A single High Court judge does not bind another High Court judge sitting alone, although such a decision would be regarded as persuasive. However when two or more High Court judges sit together as a *divisional court* their decision will be binding on any other divisional court as well as on a High Court judge sitting alone.

The High Court is bound by decisions of the Court of Appeal (both divisions) and the House of Lords. If there are two decisions, one of the Court of Appeal and one of the House of Lords, which conflict (and it can happen!), then the High Court is strangely bound to follow the decision of the 'next one up', i.e. the Court of Appeal.

3.7 Inferior courts (Crown, County, Magistrates, etc.)

The lower courts, since they rarely, if ever, have their cases reported, do not create precedent but of course they are bound to follow decisions reached in the higher courts.

4 Reading cases

Once you have grasped the role of precedent in the way the law evolves, you can begin to understand why lawyers place such importance on knowing the relevant *case* law in any particular legal area. They will use the precedents suggested by previous cases to help substantiate the argument they are making on your behalf. For the non-lawyer, some familiarity with past cases which have helped to establish, challenge or reinforce a precedent is important in understanding the nature of a particular aspect of the law.

Civil cases are normally referred to by the names of the people engaged in the law suit. For example, in **Donoghue v Stevenson** the plaintiff (Donoghue) was suing the defendant (Stevenson). Whenever we refer to a case we also give a date after the case. That date is the date on which the case was reported in the law reports. Sometimes cases are named after the property in dispute, e.g. Re No. 139 Deptford High Street. (Re simply means 'in the matter of'.)

Not all cases are reported. Most cases which are decided in the more important courts find their way into the law reports. A law library contains not just legal text books but also Law Reports where all reported cases can be found should you need to refer to them or to look at a point which is dealt with in the case a little more closely. In using this book you will not, unless your course tutor asks you to, need to refer to the cases in the law library because when we mention a case we usually give a (very brief) explanation about the rationale or significance of the case.

If you do venture as far as the law library you will discover, if you look at the reports, that a case report contains several parts. It contains an account of the facts and evidence which were considered. Then it contains the judgment itself. The judgment is the judge's speech in which he or she explains, usually at some length, the reason he or she has decided the case in favour of the winning side.

When judgment is given in a case the judges usually say quite a lot! Indeed most law students who have to read and dissect judgments probably think they say too much! For your purposes, however, not all of the judgment is relevant. Much of it will in any event be a re-explanation of the facts. Other parts may simply be observations that the judge has made which have no real bearing on the case itself – they are, if you like, asides. The part of the judgment which future judges will have to apply in resolving future disputes is the statement of the law which forms the basis of the decision. It is the principle of law on which the decision itself is based. This is known as the *ratio decidendi* of the case (which is thankfully usually abbreviated to the *ratio*). It is the *ratio* (the reason for the decision) which is the crucial aspect of a judgment and which is binding on future judges. Let's look at a few examples.

 CASE STUDY 1

If you turn to Chapter 8, page 73, you will see the case of **Hyde v Wrench (1840)**. There you will find a brief résumé of the facts and the *ratio* of the case, i.e. the legal reasoning on which the decision was based.

Have a look at that case and see if you can write down a short principle of law which forms the basis of that decision.

The type of statement which could represent the *ratio* in this case is *a counter offer immediately terminates the original offer*. In this context the facts and indeed the decision are to a certain extent superfluous for our purposes. They are obviously of importance to the parties themselves. (They are likely to be much more interested in the result of the case than any principle of law which it might establish for future cases.)

Again, preceding this case on page 72 is the case of **Byrne v Van Tienhoven (1880)**. The case includes a brief résumé of the facts. Again the *ratio* can in fact be worked out quite independently of the facts and the decision itself. Have a go ...

The *ratio* is the principle of law on which the decision is based. The principle of law which can be applied from this case to future cases is that *withdrawal of an offer only becomes effective when the fact of withdrawal is communicated to the person to whom the offer was made*.

Don't worry too much; the significance of these points of contract law will make more sense later on: for the moment they have simply served as examples of what the *ratio* of a case is.

Much of what a judge will say in reaching a decision will not actually form the basis of that decision. He or she will digress; certain statements will be said which appear to be principles of law. However, in order for a principle of law to be the *ratio decidendi* it must be the principle of law on which that decision is based. The judge may make other statements of what he or she believes to be the law. If, however, those statements are not the principles on which the decision is based they are said to be *obiter dicta* statements. (This is often abbreviated to '*obiter*'.) These digressions are not binding on future judges in the sense that the *ratios* are. They are said to be merely of persuasive authority in the sense that they may be followed if it is felt that the court in which the *obiter* statement was originally made is of major importance. The important difference though is that if a *ratio* is ignored then the case will most likely be wrongly decided. If an *obiter* statement from an earlier case is ignored, then the case will not be wrongly decided as a result. The *obiter* statements are merely there for guidance not to bind judges in later cases.

   CASE STUDY 2

Let's turn to an example of *obiter dicta*. If you turn to Chapter 14, page 224, you will find the case of **Hedley Byrne v Heller & Partners (1964)**. Here it was held by the House of Lords that the defendants would have been liable in the tort of negligence for a misstatement had it not been for the fact that they were able to rely on a clause which specifically excluded liability.

Have a look at that case and try to identify:

- who won
- the legal principle why they won (the *ratio*)
- another statement of legal principle of some importance but not directly relevant to the result in that case (the *obiter dicta*).

Briefly the answers are (and don't cheat by looking at this first!)

- the defendants won
- the reason they won was because the exclusion clause was effective in avoiding liability
- they would have been liable if there had been no exclusion clause.

This last statement is *obiter* since it is hypothetical. An exclusion clause did exist and it prevented the imposition of liability in this particular case. Interestingly, however, what started its life as *obiter dicta* went on to become part of English law in later cases.

Summary

You should now be able to:

- explain what is meant by legislation
- understand the significance of delegated legislation
- explain the role of the judges in relation to legislation

- explain the methods of interpreting statutes
- explain what is meant by common law
- understand what is meant by the doctrine of binding judicial precedent
- understand what is meant by the hierarchy of the courts and its significance in relation to the doctrine of precedent
- explain the meaning of *ratio decidendi* and be able to locate examples from case excerpts
- explain the meaning of *obiter dicta*.

 Case Study 3

Simon is employed by Megabuck Enterprises as a sales representative. During the course of his employment, as a result of his alleged careless driving, he is involved in a road accident. After being questioned by the police, he is accused of conduct contrary to section 1 of a statute in that he was 'in charge of a vehicle while not in full control of his faculties through impairment due to the consumption of whisky, brandy, gin, vodka or other such substances'.

Simon claims that he had taken a tranquilliser and in order to 'wash it down' had drunk half a can of lager.

Apply the three main rules of statutory interpretation (that is, *the literal rule, golden rule and mischief rule*) to the wording of the statute and in each case try to think what conclusion the court might arrive at. Do they differ?

4 What kind of wrong has been done?

Objectives

By the end of this chapter you should:

- understand what is meant by the term 'cause of action'
- understand why it is so important to identify the area of law which is involved and the precise wrong which has been done
- understand some of the major categories into which law is divided
- understand how different acts may have different consequences depending on which law is applied
- recognise when a business person may find themselves liable for criminal acts of their company
- understand what is meant by 'vicarious liability'
- understand what is meant by 'limitation of actions' and how it relates to different categories of law.

1   What type of wrong counts?

There may be all sorts of things which we consider to be 'wrong'. You may consider that it is wrong to tell lies. You may consider that it is wrong to be unkind. You may consider that it is wrong not to pay your bills promptly.

Many things may be considered 'wrong' but not all of them have the potential for landing the person who committed the wrong in court. First of all we need to look again at the distinction between crimes and other types of law. The criminal law is society's means of controlling its members so that it can function efficiently. In this context something as straightforward as telling lies may give rise to criminal liability. Imagine that a vehicle is involved in a collision. At the time, it is being driven by Mr Jones. Mr Jones already has several penalty points on his licence and fears that another, even minor, conviction might mean he would lose his licence. Mr Jones persuades Mrs Jones to say that she was driving. If this is subsequently found to be untrue, then both Mr and Mrs Jones could be prosecuted for having told this lie in this context. No damage has been caused but this type of behaviour is seen as threatening the effective functioning of the judicial system and of society.

In the area of civil law, you need to prove not only that the person about whom you are complaining has done something 'wrong' but also that that particular wrong has caused you some damage. Imagine that someone is selling you a car. He may tell a number of lies about how long he has owned the car and how many miles it does to the gallon. It might be, however, that you would have bought the car even if he had only owned it for a short while and, because it was a special edition, you didn't care how good its petrol consumption was. In which case, his lies have caused you no damage. They may be irritating but they are not *actionable* – that is, you cannot sue him because of the lies he told.

2   Establishing a formal legal link

We have just seen that if the case that you are bringing is based on civil law, you will need to show that you suffered some damage because of what the defendant did or did not do. That alone though is not enough.

Imagine that I come up to you and tell you that you smell and that no one likes you! You will probably be extremely upset and may feel that I have damaged you. (Certainly the courts have been able in some cases to put a price on injured feelings in the form of injured reputation in cases of libel and slander.) The question is: can you sue me? The answer is no. I may have committed a moral 'wrong' and you may have suffered damage as a result, but there is no existing formal legal link by which you can sue me. Had I made that same remark to your colleagues you might have been able to sue me for slander. (Slander requires the statement to have lowered you in the estimation of right-thinking people generally.) Slander is a well-established formal legal link by which one person can sue another. This formal legal link is known as a *cause of action*. Simply saying or doing something which causes damage is not enough for liability under the law. You must also identify an existing cause of action, into which definition the particular conduct falls.

3   Criminal law or civil law

We have already looked at the reason for having legal rules. We have also looked at the division between *civil law* and *criminal law*. We saw that the role of the civil law is to regulate the behaviour of individuals and companies towards one another. The role of the criminal law is to regulate the behaviour of individuals and companies in relation to the needs of society as a whole.

In the last section we looked at the idea of a *cause of action*, that is, the formal legal link which is required for one party to bring court proceedings against another.

The law as a whole needs to be broken down further into different areas of law. We need to know which area of law to apply and why.

CASE STUDY 1

Last night you were driving home when a car pulled out from a side road in front of you without any warning. You were unable to stop and so the two vehicles collided and your car has been written off.

Make a list of all the areas of law which might be relevant to this scenario.

Your list should include:

- criminal law; was the other driver driving carelessly to an extent that they should be punished by society using the *criminal law*
- negligence; (we shall see later that this comes within an area of law known as *tort*). Should the other driver have to pay you compensation for the damage to your car – after all the accident was his fault!
- contract law; this may come into the situation in terms of your rights in relation to your insurance company. You will have a *contract* with the insurance company and the terms of that contract will determine, for example, whether they must provide you with a hire car while yours is replaced.

This case study should help to show that there may be many areas of law which arise in respect of even a single incident. We need to look now at what these areas of law are. We will look at them each in more detail in later chapters but for now we simply need to be able to distinguish them.

4   What is the source of the law?

Whatever the category of law that you are dealing with, there are likely to be two main sources of law. The first is statutes. Statutes are introduced by and through Parliament. The second source of law is sometimes referred to as *common law*. This includes law which has come about historically through decided cases in the courts. It is, in effect, judge-made law and in so far as it does not conflict with any statute it exists side by side with them.

5   Criminal acts

The basis of liability for criminal acts is that they are acts which society regards as undesirable. They may be offences which relate to the state (such as treason or public order offences). They may be offences which reflect society's respect for private property (such as theft and burglary). Or they may be offences against individual citizens which the state prohibits (such as assault or murder).

There are other crimes which relate to the protection and functioning of society as a whole and these are the ones which most business people will need to be aware of. Examples of these types of crimes are pollution or the infringement of provisions which protect consumers.

The basis of liability in tort is that society regulates the behaviour of individuals towards each other. Business people are likely to come across liability in tort on a fairly frequent basis. Often the acts may give rise both to a liability in criminal law to the state and a liability in civil law to an individual. If this is the case the usual type of civil law involved will be the law of tort.

5.1 Purely criminal acts

There are some acts which are only ever likely to be criminal; for example, failing to produce your driving licence when required to by a police officer. No one has suffered any harm because you have failed to do it and so no individual is going to be able to sue you.

5.2 Acts which involve both crime and tort

An example is bad driving which also causes damage to you or your property. This is both a crime because society requires a certain standard of care when driving a vehicle and a tort because you have suffered damage as a result of the driver's negligent behaviour.

5.3 Acts which are only torts

A common example of this is the tort of trespass. If an individual strays onto land which belongs to another individual this is not usually a criminal offence. (Many of those signs which say 'Trespassers will be prosecuted' are in fact deterrents. There is usually no power to prosecute the trespasser under the criminal law.) The property owner's rights to enjoy the property are, however, something which society sees fit to protect and so the land owner could not only remove you from the land (using *reasonable* force) but also bring proceedings to prevent you repeating the trespass. If any damage was sustained to the land they could also sue for compensation.

5.4 Acts which are neither crimes nor torts

Remember what we said in section 2 about establishing a formal legal link. In the case of criminal law you must show that it is an established form of crime. In the case of tort you must show that it is an established form of tort. Simply because there is a consensus that an act is likely to damage society does not make it a crime. Simply because you suffer damage through someone else's actions does not make it a tort.

Consider, for example, the situation of invasion of privacy. When a certain person's privacy is invaded there is always the argument to be made that it is in the public interest to know that such person 'swings naked from the chandeliers in wild sex orgies'. Those who make this argument will say that we need to know what 'type' of people are running the country. But imagine that it is someone in your town who has been behaving in this way. An ambitious young reporter might decide to 'reveal all'. There is unlikely to be any crime committed, although many people may think it socially unacceptable behaviour. The revelations made by the reporter may be extremely damaging to the individual concerned (for example, if he is a shopkeeper a number of people may stop coming to his shop). There is however no established tort which has been committed. Damage resulting from the behaviour of another is not always a tort.

6   Torts

To start with, this is a strange word. It is a category which includes such things as trespass and negligence, two concepts with which you are probably more familiar. You may have noticed with the majority of crimes that there is a suggestion of 'fault' on the part of the criminal. A prime example of this is the crime of theft. If you 'innocently' take something, say a coat from a cloakroom, believing it to be your own, that is not theft. Theft requires a guilty mind as well as a guilty act.

Many torts require a similar, although perhaps less morally culpable, state of mind. The act done by the person who caused the damage must generally be done either deliberately or without care or consideration as to the consequences of the action.

7   Contract

Contract is a special category of civil liability. Contract law is a set of legal rules which regulate not standards of behaviour generally but the behaviour of two parties with regard to a formal relationship which they have already entered into. We are not here talking about how an individual's or a company's behaviour might affect society generally or other members of society individually. We are looking instead at three main issues:

- firstly, resolving disputes on interpretation of the contract. If the parties cannot agree on what exactly is required of them by a term of the contract then the courts can adjudicate and decide for them
- secondly, the law will step in to make a commercial relationship workable where something is missing from the agreement but is procedural rather than the substance of the agreement. Imagine the situation where you order a text book for your studies from a book shop. The book shop takes a deposit and says it will order the book. Despite your repeated enquiries, five months later they say that it is still not in stock. Nothing was said when you ordered the book about how long it would take. Is it fair to imply into the agreement that the book must be available within a reasonable time and you can have your deposit back? Or must you wait another five months and then buy the book – by which time you may well have finished that course! The answer is that, if

you had asked both parties at the beginning whether the book should be provided within a reasonable time, it would surely be yes. In this type of situation the law may imply terms, which have not actually been discussed, into the contract between the parties

- thirdly, the law will step in to prevent certain abuses of power in contracts. Generally these provisions are designed to protect non business people against business people who, knowing the law better, may try to include unfair conditions in the contract and so take advantage of the consumer's lack of knowledge. An example of this type of provision is the **Unfair Contract Terms Act 1977** which is looked at in Chapter 9.

8 Criminal liability

Most people can be liable for crimes. In some situations a company can be liable for crimes as well. Business people should take particular note of this. To some people it may seem a somewhat strange idea since a company is actually inanimate! Not only is it actually possible to prosecute a company (for it can be effectively punished by imposing a fine on it) but also the directors of companies may find themselves *personally* liable for the crimes which the company has committed and directors can be imprisoned!

Exceptionally some individuals or organisations can routinely escape liability for crimes, for example foreign diplomatic staff.

Minors under a certain age are not usually prosecuted for certain crimes as they are regarded as being incapable of having the necessary 'guilty mind' (known as *mens rea*). Those who are insane are seldom prosecuted for crimes since they will be regarded as 'unfit to plead'. In other words they cannot really defend themselves. Instead they are often 'detained at Her Majesty's pleasure' in a mental institution!

9 Liability in tort

9.1 Who can be liable?

Liability for tort can be imposed on any individual or company. In the case of a firm which is a partnership rather than a company, all the partners may be liable. Minors and the mentally ill cannot escape liability for tort either. The only concession to their status is where the particular tort requires some sort of mental culpability and the individual is shown not to have the necessary mental capacity to be responsible for his or her actions. So for example in the case of negligence, an adult who pokes someone's eye out with a stick is likely to be liable for negligence – after all you might expect someone to get hurt if you play around with sharp sticks. On the other hand a toddler who causes the same injury cannot really be held morally, or legally, responsible.

9.2   What if more than one person was involved?

If more than one person is responsible for the tort then both will be liable for the consequences. The liability will be what is called *joint and several* liability. This means that either one or both can be sued for the whole amount of the damage.

9.3   Can you be liable for someone else's acts?

In criminal law an individual is usually only responsible for his/her own behaviour. In the law of tort the situation is different. The main difference, which is of vital importance to the business person, is the concept of *vicarious liability*. This is looked at in more detail in Chapter 14. Essentially, an employer may be sued for the negligent acts of his/her employee if those acts were done by the employee while working. The injured person can sue the worker or the employer or both. The only restriction is that they cannot recover the amount of money that the injury is 'worth' twice.

The lesson for employers is that they should make sure that they are fully insured against potential liability not only for their own mistakes but also for those of all their employees.

10   Liability in contract

This question is a question of *capacity* which is looked at further in Chapter 8. Suffice it to say that most people who are aware enough to enter into a contract can be sued if they fail to perform it. A company can, since the **Companies Act 1985**, be required to perform any contract to which it commits itself, notwithstanding that it may be strictly outside its powers, which are contained in the formal documents by which it was created.

Whether or not a minor can be sued on the basis of a contract which he/she enters into depends largely on the nature of the contract. This is looked at in more detail in Chapter 8.

11   Are there any time limits?

With regard to crimes there is no time limit. Once a crime has been committed you can be prosecuted for it however long afterwards it is discovered. Some minor offences, for instance minor road traffic offences, require the Crown Prosecution Service to decide whether or not to prosecute within six months.

In the case of complaints relating to contracts, proceedings must be brought within six years of the date when the cause of action accrued or 12 years if the contract is in the form of a *deed*. Proceedings for the recovery of possession of land must be brought within 12 years.

In the case of torts most proceedings must be commenced within six years. There are special rules limiting claims to being brought within three years for actions involving personal injury. There are also special rules where the damage that has been suffered cannot be discovered until some time after the actual wrong was done. For example, it may take some time for you to realise that your extension has been built with inadequate foundations – it may only start to show cracks after four years anyway!

Where the person who has suffered damage is under a *disability* (for example, he or she is a minor or is mentally ill) the time limits will not apply until after the disability has ceased. So for example a 12-year-old boy who is injured in a car accident actually has nine years in which to start proceedings. The three year time limit does not start until he reaches 18, the age of majority.

Summary

You should now be able to distinguish between the role of:

- the criminal law, the law of tort and the law of contract
- statute and common law.

You should also be able to look at the following case study and decide what types of wrong may have been committed.

 CASE STUDY 1

Recently you employed a roofer to do some work on the roof of your house. You came home yesterday to find that the builder had been and had:

- taken a large number of antiques which you had stored in the roof void
- apparently put his foot through your bedroom ceiling
- done a completely inadequate job of mending the roof – the rain still pours in.

Consider what areas of law might apply in respect of this situation.

5 In what ways can I settle disputes?

Objectives

By the end of this chapter you should:

- understand the role of the court system in dispute resolution
- know how different methods of negotiation may be employed to settle disputes
- understand which type of court a particular case would be likely to start in
- understand what is meant by alternative dispute resolution.

1   Do I have to go to court?

We tend to think that once a dispute of a legal nature starts, the inevitable conclusion is that the matter will 'go to court'. (This is perhaps partly the influence of television drama where the cases which don't make it to court are very seldom featured!) This is, however, far from the usual course that a dispute will take. Most civil cases are settled out of court. Many are settled (a compromise is reached) before court proceedings are issued at all. With other cases court proceedings are started, often with the intention simply of showing the other party that the complainant 'means business'. Of the disputes where court proceedings are actually started fewer than 10 per cent actually reach a court hearing.

It should become clear from this that any discussion of dispute settling has to include not only a consideration of the different types of court and formal dispute settling mechanisms but also a consideration of how negotiation might be used to help to settle the dispute.

2   Negotiations

Before a matter ever becomes a serious dispute there is likely to have been a period of negotiation between the parties. Whatever the matter, for example whether someone has not paid their account on time or whether goods supplied

41

under a contract are faulty, there is likely to be a period of negotiation when the initial problem is discovered. If the 'negotiation' takes the form of bad-tempered correspondence threatening legal proceedings you may not feel that this counts as negotiation. It is however all part of an attempt to settle the problem without having to bring court proceedings.

2.1   Negotiation strategies

There are two main forms of negotiation which are recognised. It is useful for you as a business person to recognise these so that:

- you can consider carefully which form of negotiation is most likely to achieve what it is that you want to achieve
- you can recognise what tactics the other party in the dispute seems to be using.

2.1.1   Competitive or adversarial negotiation

This type of negotiation works on a simple assumption. The assumption is that a point gained by one party is a point lost by the other. This method works by attaching a price to everything that the parties are aggrieved about and trying to get monetary compensation in accordance with that estimate. It is characterised by a formal approach involving the making of statements and arguments, and of offer and counter-offer, rather than asking questions in order to see how the dispute might most easily be resolved. The aim is to 'win' and to this end some information may be kept secret.

2.1.2   Cooperative or problem solving negotiation

The idea of this approach is that a dispute can usually be solved by trying to engage in a joint decision-making process. Instead of entrenching positions, the idea of the negotiation is to explore what the matters are which concern the parties and what they really want to achieve out of the situation. Out of that it is seen as possible to find a solution in which both parties feel that they have gained from the process. Rather than a 'tug-of-war' type situation where one party feels they have won and the other lost, instead, each party can feel that they have gained *something* from a situation which could have ended up a lot worse. The approach of the negotiators in this method should not be secretive. The parties should 'lay all their cards on the table'; there should be a recognition by each side of the need to reach a *fair* compromise.

2.1.3   Which method is best?

Which method is best depends on what it is that you are trying to achieve. Consider the following case study.

 CASE STUDY 1

You are the manager of a retail electrical shop. Sam Jones bought a fridge-freezer last week. Yesterday he telephoned to say that the freezer had broken down and that he demanded a replacement. When your repairman inspected the fridge-freezer he said that the damage could only have been caused by mistreatment of the unit. It had received a heavy blow to the external electrical unit. In his opinion he thinks that Mr Jones is responsible for the damage and the fact that the unit no longer works.

Mr Jones is coming to see you today 'to find out what you are going to do about it'. Consider your position.

Stage 1

1 Write down the points you would want to make if you were to adopt the adversarial approach.

2 Write down the points which you would need to consider if you chose to adopt the problem-solving approach.

You will probably find that the list for 1 takes the form of a list of *arguments*. You will probably have dwelt on your lack of fault and Mr Jones's own fault. You have probably also thought in terms of the monetary cost of a new fridge-freezer.

With 2 you should have found that you had a list not of arguments but of the *interests* of each party. You should be thinking about not only the monetary cost of a new fridge-freezer but also the wider perspective of whether that customer is likely to tell his friends about the service he received and what the long-term implications of a mutually acceptable compromise might be.

Stage 2

Now consider which of the approaches is most appropriate.

There is no right answer to this. It depends on your objectives. If your major objective is to build up a reputation as a customer-friendly and responsive store it may be worth while bearing the cost of the replacement simply so that Mr Jones is happy and tells his friends as much (or at least doesn't complain about you. Remember criticism usually travels faster than praise!). If on the other hand your major objective is to keep down costs because the business is running to a very tight profit margin, the short-term costs of replacing the fridge-freezer may mean that you 'take a hard line' in your negotiations with Mr Jones.

Stage 3

Get together with a friend and try to produce a list of at least five factors which might influence what style of negotiation you would choose to adopt on any particular occasion.

3 Dispute settling mechanisms

What we have looked at so far in this chapter are *methods* of settling disputes. What we need to look at now are the formal mechanisms to which negotiators can resort if the dispute cannot be resolved in the early stages. This is what we tend to think of as 'going to court'. Often a case which cannot be resolved will end up in one of the courts. We need therefore to look at which court is likely to be used and why, but also at other mechanisms which could be used. The mechanisms for resolving disputes which are not part of the formal court system are often referred to under the heading of *alternative dispute resolution.*

3.1   Which court would I use?

Within our legal system the court structure provides a mechanism where disputes of varying degrees (often degrees of value) can be concluded. The role of the court is:

- to decide what the facts of the dispute are. (Each party's story or perception of the facts is likely to be different – even where neither is being dishonest or deliberately untruthful.)
- to locate the rules of law to be applied
- to apply those rules and in so doing resolve the dispute by achieving a solution.

3.1.1   Does the court deal with civil or criminal law
We have already looked at the basic structure of the courts system. In Chapter 7 we will look at what actually happens in a civil court. What we need to consider now is which type of court deals with which type of case. On the next page, a simplified version of figure 3.1 describing the structure of the English courts is reproduced for quick response – please see page 26 for the full version.

Most courts hear both civil and criminal disputes (e.g. the High Court) but some are confined to either civil or criminal cases. For example, the County Court deals only with civil cases and the Crown Court deals only with criminal cases. We will outline the differences in the next section.

3.1.2   Courts of first instance and appeal courts
Individuals do not have the right to decide which court will hear their case. All cases must start and be heard in a *court of first instance.* Once the decision of that court has been given, only then can the case be taken on appeal to one of the appellate courts. So when a dispute is heard in a court for the first time then the court will be a court of first instance or a court of original jurisdiction (e.g. a County Court). When a dispute is resolved in a court of first instance and both parties are satisfied to leave it at that, then the case will go no further. However, if the losing party is dissatisfied then in certain circumstances he or she may be allowed to appeal to a higher court (e.g. the Court of Appeal). In the following discussion it will be helpful to refer to the diagram, which shows the lines of appeal in certain circumstances. Some courts have a peculiar status in that they may be a court of first instance for some cases and a court of appeal for others. The High Court, for example, may be the court of appeal for a case which started off in a more minor court.

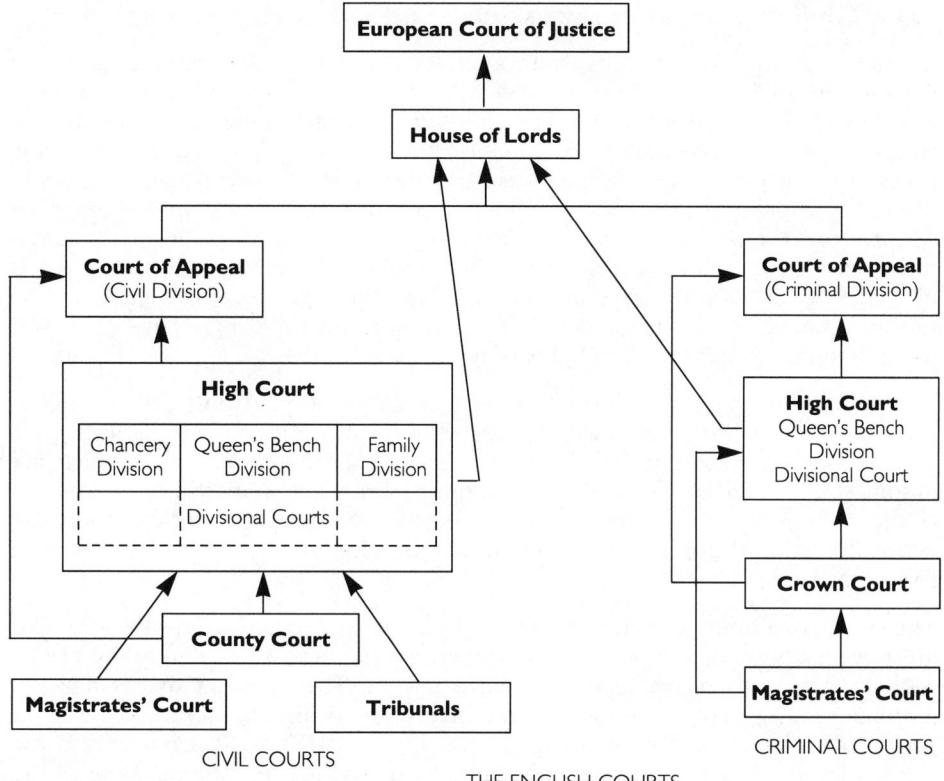

Figure 5.1

CIVIL COURTS

CRIMINAL COURTS

THE ENGLISH COURTS

3.2   Criminal law and the courts

Proceedings for a criminal case usually begin in a Magistrates Court. Magistrates courts have two basic roles in the criminal justice system. The first is to try a range of minor criminal offences, for example most traffic offences, for which they can usually only impose prison sentences of up to six months or fines of up to £5000. Their second role is to take on some of the burden of administering criminal law, for example in the issuing of summonses, arrest and search warrants, and the granting of bail. They are also responsible, via committal proceedings, for deciding whether a case is sufficiently serious to go on to a higher court and for making the appropriate arrangements to do so. Most people facing a criminal charge will appear first in a Magistrates Court.

Serious criminal offences are then tried, in most instances, in a Crown Court before a judge and jury – the setting which you are most likely to be familiar with on television. Depending on the circumstances, appeals may then be heard by the High Court or the Court of Appeal. There are strict rules governing when an appeal can be made. In general terms an appeal needs to be 'by case stated', in which a lower court refers to a higher court the relevant facts and arguments surrounding a disputed point of law for adjudication. Final appeals on a point of law judged to be of particular public interest may be made to the House of Lords, or on any point which may contravene European law to the European Court of Justice.

3.3   Civil law: the County Court and small claims

County courts are of immense importance in practice since most of the civil litigation in England and Wales is dealt with in the County Court. The purpose of the County Court is to provide a forum whereby civil disputes of a local nature can be resolved comparatively quickly and cheaply. The court is usually presided over by a single judge. Amongst the types of matter that the County Court is competent to deal with are most types of proceedings (proceedings for defamation of character being one notable exception). The value of the claim must usually not be expected to exceed £25,000. If the value of the claim is likely to be £25,000 to £50,000 then the case can first be heard either in the County Court or in the High Court. If the amount of the claim exceeds £50,000 the case will be heard in the High Court.

In addition to the usual formal procedure the County Court has a special procedure for dealing with small claims. There is in fact no such thing as a small claims court. It is simply an expression that is used for those cases which are automatically referred to the County Court arbitration system when the amount of the claim is small. Currently, claims need to be under £1000 though there are proposals to raise the limit to £3000 and to provide a similar 'fast-track' service for claims under £10,000.

The principle underlying small claims is to provide a forum where people who are not legally qualified can feel more comfortable making or defending claims without having to resort to employing a lawyer. The value of this is that the amount of any claim will be comparatively small and it would be counter productive if such a dispute involved the high cost of legal services and the inevitable delay and expense associated with the court system. People are therefore encouraged by the system to conduct their own case in an informal, usually private, atmosphere. Generally speaking the system is quick, cheap, and straightforward. As an example, unlike the County Court and other courts generally, there are no rules about what evidence is allowed to be brought before the court and what is not. There is also the added incentive for disputants of not having to run the risk of paying their adversary's legal costs should they lose, as the winner can claim only very limited expenses and not legal fees.

The types of disputes which can be dealt with under the small claims procedure are extremely wide – literally anything from a defective purchase to the provision of a service which falls short of satisfactory, a disastrous holiday, a minor injury, a dispute with a neighbour or a landlord, or a claim for repayment of a debt. A claim will be suitable for arbitration if it is not too complex and can be expressed as a sum of money.

It is important to ensure that a claim does come within the £1000 limit. Even if the claim is originally in excess of £1000 it is permissible to reduce the claim in order to acquire the benefits of the procedure. If a claim is for more than £1000 then it can only be dealt with by arbitration if both parties agree, but the party who loses runs the risk of having to pay the costs of the action. If a claim estimated to be in excess of £1000 turns out in fact to be within the jurisdiction of the small claims procedure, then even if a party wins they may not be entitled to costs.

3.3.1 Magistrates Courts

Magistrates Courts are of course mainly concerned with criminal cases. There is, however, a limited jurisdiction with regard to family proceedings, recovery of certain civil debts (e.g. council tax) and the granting of licences for gaming and the sale of alcohol.

3.3.2 High Court

The High Court consists of three divisions which deal with civil cases. These are the Queens Bench, Chancery and Family. The Queens Bench Division has the widest jurisdiction of the three and is the one where most straightforward cases will be heard. It is the usual court of first instance for those cases which simply cannot be heard in the County Court because of the monetary value of the claim.

3.3.3 Crown Court

As with the Magistrates Court the Crown Court is predominantly concerned with criminal matters. It can, however, hear appeals relating to some of the civil matters which have first been decided in the Magistrates Court.

3.3.4 The Court of Appeal (Civil Division)

The head of the Court of Appeal is known as the Master of the Rolls. Judges in the Court of Appeal are known as Lord Justices of Appeal (often abbreviated to LJ after the surname). There are normally three judges to hear an appeal; sometimes only two may hear a case. Occasionally, where the case is of special importance, there may be five judges hearing the same case. Decisions are reached on a majority basis. Judges who disagree with the majority decision are allowed to give dissenting judgments which are included in reports of the cases in the Law Reports.

Appeals in the Civil Division come from all three divisions of the High Court, from the County Court and from certain tribunals such as the Employment Appeal Tribunal.

3.3.5 The House of Lords

The House of Lords is the final court of appeal in this country for both civil and criminal matters. It is composed of Lords of Appeal (Law Lords). Five Law Lords normally sit to hear an appeal and decisions are reached on a majority basis. As in the Court of Appeal, judges who disagree with the majority can give their own judgments explaining why they disagree and these judgments are also recorded in the Law Reports.

3.3.6 Court of Justice of the European Community

The House of Lords is the final court of appeal in relation to law which is of a purely domestic nature. However if a dispute contains some aspect relating to the European Community, then any English court or tribunal may request and in some instances must request advice from the European Court on any point of European Community law which applies.

3.3.7 The European Court of Human Rights

This court is part of a system separate from the European Community's Court of Justice. This court has authority over a government which is a signatory to the European Convention for the Protection of Human Rights and Fundamental

Freedoms (ECHR). The Court can decide whether or not a signatory state has breached one of the fundamental rights. One might expect this to be of limited importance to the business person. (For example, the right to freedom from torture and inhuman or degrading treatment is not likely to crop up in the course of business.) However, this is not always the case; for example, Article 1 of the ECHR protects the right to peaceful enjoyment of possessions. The protection of the treaty is afforded to persons within the jurisdiction of the member state. At the time of writing the European Court of Human Rights was hearing a case brought by a firm, Air Canada, against the British state for impounding an aircraft at Heathrow airport. The result remains to be seen. It is clear, however, from the cases which are being brought that the provisions of the ECHR are being used with increasing ingenuity by business people in dispute with a government or a government institution.

4   Tribunals

During the twentieth century there has gradually emerged a large number of specialised bodies resembling to a certain extent traditional courts. The function of these tribunals is to dispense justice quickly, informally, cheaply and efficiently. Tribunals are established by statutes. Many of the tribunals resolve disputes which have arisen as a result of social legislation which confers benefits (such as Income Support and Unemployment Benefit) on individuals. The conferring of these many benefits is inevitably bound to give rise to numerous disputes and the argument is that the resolution of such disputes or conflicts is better suited to a mechanism handled by people who are not necessarily legally qualified but who have special expertise in the areas concerned. In fact tribunals usually consist of three members. At least one of them (usually the chairman) is legally qualified but the other members of the panel will be lay people. The informality of the system is reflected in the discouragement of legal representation. Legal Aid is not usually available. The tribunal can be expected to be sympathetic to those who choose to represent themselves or have a non-lawyer friend as their representative. The person who loses in a tribunal can appeal to the ordinary court system – but only if they believe that a point of law was wrongly decided, not the facts.

5   Arbitration

Often in the commercial world the potential parties to a dispute will prefer to avoid taking their problem to a court of law. They may wish to avoid the publicity, likely cost and the possible delay. They may therefore agree, at the outset of their relationship when they enter into their initial contract, that if any disputes do arise then such disputes will be referred to arbitration. What happens is that the parties present their arguments to an arbitrator. The arbitrator is chosen by a mechanism which again is agreed at the outset between the parties. He or she will be an individual with special expertise in the subject matter but will not necessarily have a legal qualification. The arbitration is done in private and once the arbitrator's decision is made, it is, because the parties originally agreed it would be, as binding as a decision of the court.

It should be clear from this that this type of arbitration is based on the *contract* between the parties. The agreement by them in the contract that, in the event of dispute, arbitration is mandatory is enforceable on the basis of the contract. It was feared that arbitration provisions might be included in some contracts with consumers where it was inappropriate to do so. Therefore the **Consumer Arbitration Agreements Act 1988** provides that an arbitration clause in a contract cannot be enforced against a customer where the amount in question is under £1000. In other words where the claim would, in any event, come within the small claims procedure in the County Court. If the amount is more than £1000, the arbitration clause may be enforced between the parties providing it is not detrimental to the customer's interests.

6 The Ombudsman

The function of the Ombudsman is to deal with alleged matters of maladministration. There are different Ombudsmen for different areas of concern, including Local Government and the Health Service. The idea is that they can investigate and make recommendations about matters which are clearly unsatisfactory. Often it is a question of the standard having fallen short of that expected and a matter has been dealt with badly rather than wrongly. If the matter has been dealt with wrongly, according to law, the individual might have some redress through the courts. If it is simply dealt with badly, the individual may be justified in feeling aggrieved but cannot point to anything which is actually wrong in law and therefore cannot sue. It is usually one of the principles of the Ombudsman that matters should not be referred to him or her where they could be pursued through the court system. To that extent the Ombudsman is perhaps not really an 'alternative' dispute resolver but rather an additional one.

Summary

You should now be able to:

- explain what is meant by adversarial negotiation
- explain what is meant by cooperative negotiation
- explain factors which might influence the type of negotiation employed in any particular dispute
- understand the mechanism for small claims in the County Court
- understand in which circumstances you would expect a case to start in the High Court and in which the County Court
- explain the difference between a court of first instance and an appellate court
- explain what is meant by arbitration and when it will be the method of resolving a dispute.

You will be able to consolidate your skills from the case study which is at the end of Chapter 7.

6 How can lawyers help?

Objectives

By the end of this chapter you should:

- understand the role of different types of legal personnel
- understand the ways in which a lawyer may be able to help a business person.

1 What types of lawyers are there?

For the non-lawyer it is often quite difficult trying to understand what different types of lawyer there are and what are their roles.

1.1 The difference between a barrister and a solicitor

The main distinction which causes lay people some difficulty is the distinction between *solicitors* and *barristers*. A common misconception is that barristers are solicitors who have been promoted! This is not the case. The English legal system is one of the few which has a divided profession in that there are two types of lawyer, each with their own particular role, training and regulating body. Law graduates wanting to go on to become lawyers make the decision about what branch of the profession they will join. Once that decision is made the courses that they take in order to qualify are entirely different.

1.2 Solicitors

At one time it might have been fair to say that the solicitor was like a medical GP. He or she was the first person to whom a member of the public would turn. If the problem was of a more specialised nature then the matter would be referred to a specialist in that particular field – usually a barrister. Although this is still the role of some of the smaller high street solicitors' firms, it is probably true to say that all solicitors now have some particular areas of specialism and, in the larger firms, many solicitors specialise in simply one small area of law.

In fact the question of specialism is no longer one which distinguishes the two professions.

At one time the question of *rights of audience* (meaning who had the right to represent clients in which courts) would have been a significant distinction, since the higher courts were limited to barristers. Since the **Courts and Legal Services Act 1990** solicitors can apply for rights of audience at all levels. However it will take time for more solicitors to apply for extended rights of audience, and it remains to be seen how many actually take up the opportunity. For the immediate future the ability of barristers to appear in the higher courts is likely to remain a practical distinction between the two professions.

The remaining outstanding feature is that of access. A barrister may not deal directly with a member of the public but can only deal with clients who are referred to them by a solicitor. Members of the public can simply walk in off the street and make an appointment with a solicitor. They cannot do that with a barrister; the barrister must instead be employed by a solicitor on behalf of the solicitor's client.

1.3 Barristers

Barristers are the consultant specialists of the legal world. Many specialise in advocacy. Others are simply experts in particular areas of the law and spend most of their time writing *opinions* in respect of a particular problem which has been referred to them. They may also be asked to draft documents of a particularly specialised nature and often to draft the documents which will be required if a dispute goes to court.

1.4 Legal executives

The Institute of Legal Executives (ILEX) is the professional body of a significant number of legal employees. Legal executives cannot set up a legal practice on their own account nor can they form partnerships. They are legally trained and, under the supervision of a solicitor, they may carry out much of the routine legal work in a solicitor's practice or in industry.

1.5 Para legals

The recession has seen the increasing use of para legals. These are usually people who are not legally qualified but who do have some legal training. They cannot be called solicitors because they are not qualified as such. Neither are they qualified as legal executives. They are in effect clerks with a significant amount of knowledge and expertise in their area of work. However, unlike solicitors and legal executives, they are a disparate group and do not have any regulating professional body.

1.6 Lawyers in industry and commerce

These are often referred to as *in-house lawyers*. They may be from any of the legal professions or they may be para legals. They are however employed directly by a particular firm or company and they do not provide legal services to anyone other than that company and, if required, to its employees.

2   Other sources of legal advice

Solicitors' firms are not the only organisations which can provide advice on a legal matter. Many other organisations have significant legal expertise and many other professionals offer advice of a legal nature.

2.1   Accountants

Probably of significant importance to the business person will be the accountant. The business may employ its own *in-house accountants* or it may engage the services of a firm of chartered accountants. The legal advice of the accountant is likely to be predominantly in the field of *revenue law*, in other words taxation. It will usually be vital for a firm's success that the lawyers and accountants that it engages have a close working relationship. Their combined advice is likely to be the most effective for the firm.

2.2   Law centres

Law centres are not often used by business people. The original intention of the creation of the law centres was to satisfy unmet legal need. In other words it was recognition of the fact that there are a number of people who would benefit from legal advice but who, because of their financial or cultural backgrounds, may not feel able to make use of a solicitor.

2.3   Citizens' Advice Bureaux

The Citizens' Advice Bureaux ('CABs') were designed to provide advice on a number of matters, not all of them strictly the work of lawyers. The CABs however can provide preliminary advice on legal matters and most have a surgery session which is manned by a local solicitor who will give brief initial advice free of charge and, if necessary, either take the case on or refer the individual to a firm of lawyers who could help. Again, the use which a business person makes of the CAB is likely to be limited. They are really designed to help the individual citizen. They will not be able to provide detailed legal advice but they will refer a client on to appropriate lawyers where necessary.

3   Change in the legal professions

The last decade has seen considerable change in the legal professions. Many of these changes were brought about by the **Courts and Legal Services Act 1990**, others by change within the individual professional bodies.

3.1   Property selling

Until 1985 solicitors enjoyed a monopoly of conveyancing work. Only solicitors were permitted to draw up a contract for the sale of land or a conveyance of land. The **Administration of Justice Act 1985** permitted a new group of individuals, *licensed conveyancers*, to do conveyancing work. The Law Society also changed its rules in 1985 to allow solicitors to get involved in property selling. This meant that firms of solicitors who chose to set up 'property shops' could offer a complete service from advertising to completing the sale.

3.2   Rights of audience

Until the **Courts and Legal Services Act 1990** only barristers had rights of audience (that is, the right to represent a client) in the higher courts. Solicitors could represent clients in the County and Magistrates courts but, with only a very few exceptions, in any other court they were obliged to employ a barrister.

Solicitors who can prove that they have the appropriate experience and hold the appropriate certificate can now represent clients in the higher courts without having to employ a barrister.

It is also possible for other professional bodies to put forward appropriately qualified and experienced members for a certificate entitling them to present a case in the higher courts. For example, the Chartered Institute of Patent Agents applied for certain of their members to have that right.

3.3   Partnerships

Section 66 of the Courts and Legal Services Act enables solicitors to form partnerships with non-solicitors. These partnerships would be referred to as *multidisciplinary partnerships*. The most likely combination is solicitors and accountants. In theory it would be possible for solicitors and barristers to enter into partnership. In practice the Bar's professional rules prohibit it.

Section 89 of the Act also introduces the possibility of *multinational partnerships*, that is, lawyers from different countries entering into partnerships. Such a firm would obviously be of considerable use to a business person who was involved in an export or import business and needed advice about how the laws of the two different countries would affect him or her.

3.4   The practical effect of changes to date

Although these changes have already come about, the take-up of them has been comparatively slow. The great majority of lawyers firms are neither multidisciplinary nor multinational and most solicitors have not taken up the opportunity to apply for rights of audience in the higher courts.

4   Legal aid

The Legal Aid scheme is the main state funded scheme that operates to provide legal advice and assistance for those who cannot afford it. The provision of legal aid takes various forms and the rules as to who qualifies are different for each type. All legal aid, though, is subject to a means test. That is, it should only be available for those who cannot afford to pay for it themselves. This of itself means that legal aid is unlikely to be of great importance to business people. It is even less likely to be of interest to a business person when you realise that, if a case is successful, the money spent on legal representation can be recouped by the Legal Aid Board from the money which the losing side is ordered to pay to the winner of the case.

Business people are most likely to encounter legal aid when the person on the other side who is either suing them, or being sued by them, has legal aid. If the other party in a case has full legal aid then, when negotiating, it must be remembered that the legally aided person has little or nothing to lose personally if the case is unsuccessful.

5   How can lawyers help business people?

It is tempting to think that lawyers are only likely to be used by business people when they are either suing someone or being sued. This is a very narrow view of the help that lawyers can provide. Set out below is a sample of the types of matters which a lawyer may be able to help you with.

5.1   Setting up a business

Many businesses are set up by two or more people together. The lawyer can provide practical help here as to the type of business which would be most suitable for you. For example, should the business be run as a *partnership* or as a *limited company*? This will depend on the type of business and what your priorities are. For example, if you and the person you are thinking of setting up a business with are concerned about the effect failure of the business would have on the finances of your respective families, then a limited company may be preferable. (In all usual circumstances if the business collapses your losses will be limited to the amount of money that you actually put into the business. The family home, for example, cannot be seized by dissatisfied creditors.)

Whichever type of business you decide upon, the lawyer can help you further. If you decide on a limited company the lawyer can arrange for you to buy a readymade 'off the peg' company and can help you with the formalities which are required under the Companies Acts. If you decide on a partnership you could simply go ahead without any further consideration of you and your partner's relationship. If you do though, the provisions of the **Partnership Act 1890** will apply to your relationship. Unless you know what these provisions are (which the lawyer can tell you) you cannot possibly know whether they are what you both had in mind. Most lawyers will advise you to have a *partnership agreement* drawn up. Where the provisions of such an agreement conflict with those of the Partnership Act the provisions of the agreement prevail. What is more, the partnership relationship may be much easier to manage if you both know, at the outset, what you expect of each other.

5.2   Taxation

Following on from the setting up of the business you will have to consider how it is taxed. No one likes to pay more tax than they have to. *Tax evasion* is illegal and may result in imprisonment for all involved. *Tax avoidance* on the other hand is perfectly legal. It is simply arranging one's affairs, within the rules, to take best advantage of the provisions. The combined advice of a good lawyer and a good accountant may be able to save even a small business thousands of pounds in unnecessary tax bills.

5.3   Contracts

Any type of business is going to be involved, from the outset, in making contracts with, for example, suppliers and customers. Many of these contracts could be dealt with without legal advice and may work out quite successfully without advice. Consulting a lawyer before entering into a contract may however save a considerable amount of money and heartache. The lawyer can explain the terms of a proposed contract to you and may, if you wish, negotiate new terms for you. You might decide that the firm should have its own standard terms of contract and the lawyer can help you to decide on your objectives and can draw up an agreement which reflects the needs of your particular business.

5.4   General advice – in particular, avoiding criminal liability

When setting up a business there may be all sorts of provisions which will apply to you about which you know nothing. Trade organisations may be able to help you with some of these. Lawyers too should be able to advise you as to what provisions, such as health and safety, environmental, etc, you may be required to comply with. It may be money well spent in order to avoid the bad publicity and a fine which might follow a prosecution for non-compliance.

5.5   Employment advice

If you envisage employing any workers in the business, it is likely also to be worth your while asking a lawyer to guide you through the employment law provisions. You need to know, among other things:

- what you can and cannot ask a potential employee at interview lest you be accused of race or sex discrimination
- what you can and cannot ask of an employee, for example, in terms of overtime or out of hours work

- what your responsibilities are for controlling the behaviour of your workers in so far as they may be putting other workers or members of the public at risk
- what procedure you should follow if you need to discipline or sack an employee
- what procedure you should follow if you need to make an employee redundant
- in connection with any of these what, if any, financial liability you will face.

5.6   Disputes

This is the area where we traditionally think of lawyers as being of help. They can advise you about the likelihood of success of a case in court and they can deal with all the formalities leading up to a court case. Nevertheless even in this traditional area the view of the lawyer should not be so restricted. You must remember that the lawyer should be helping you, the client, to achieve what you want. You should make sure that you employ a lawyer in whom you have confidence. You will need a lawyer who

- is able to *listen* to what it is that you want
- can help you to *prioritise* your needs and objectives
- can *advise* you about the legal and practical effects of different possible courses of action
- can *negotiate* effectively what you want and in the manner that you want. (Think back to the last chapter and what we discussed about the different styles of negotiation. If what you want from a dispute is not simply to win but to keep a valued customer, then a cooperative style of negotiation is likely to be best.)

Summary

You should now be able to:

- explain the difference between a barrister and a solicitor and in what circumstances and by what route you might employ the services of each
- understand the difference between other types of legal personnel whom you may encounter
- know where to look for other types of legal advice
- identify the matters where you might benefit from the help of a lawyer during the course of your business career
- list the factors which are of importance to you in choosing a lawyer to help you in your business.

You will be able to consolidate your skills from the case study which is at the end of Chapter 7.

7 What happens in court and what are my remedies?

Objectives

By the end of this chapter you should:

- understand the types of matter which you should consider before commencing proceedings in the courts
- be familiar with some of the terminology surrounding proceedings
- understand the stages which a case may go through before it is actually heard in court
- have a basic knowledge of the procedure when a case does come to court
- understand what is meant by the term 'remedies'
- be able to explain how money judgments can be enforced
- be familiar with some common types of non-money judgments.

1 The stage before court proceedings

Only the most pugnacious of people respond to a dispute by heading straight for court proceedings. As a business person you are likely to find that the majority of disputes are best settled by other means than a court hearing. Court hearings are really a form of adjudication which is of use when both parties have effectively stopped talking and cannot even attempt to reach a compromise. The vital stage before court proceedings are considered is the *negotiation* stage. Sometimes court proceedings are used as an attempt to 'show the other side that you mean business'. Starting proceedings can be a useful way of doing this and focusing the parties' minds on the issues. As a 'tactic', however, it must be used carefully – it can have the opposite effect and polarise the parties in their positions.

It is of course possible to start court proceedings without the advice of a lawyer, although this is only really sensible in the case of small claims. Whether you choose to employ a lawyer or not there are a number of factors which you need to take into account in deciding whether to sue the other party.

1.1 Do you want to 'win'?

The first matter which you must consider is what your own objectives are. If you want to settle the dispute to the satisfaction of both parties and to continue with a productive trading relationship, then court proceedings are *extremely* unlikely to achieve that objective. Even threatening proceedings is likely to destroy an effective commercial relationship. Commercial agreements, like personal relationships, can usually survive disagreements if they are handled sensitively by both sides.

If you decide that the importance of success in this particular dispute is more important than any possible relationship then, and only then, should you begin to consider court proceedings.

1.2　Is it worth while suing the other party? Will they be able to pay?

If the person or firm which you are thinking of suing has fallen on hard times then you must remember that 'you cannot get blood out of a stone'. Whatever amount the court might order the other side to pay, it is going to be pointless if the firm goes into liquidation or if the individual goes bankrupt. There are seldom any 'winners' where insolvency is involved. Even if the other side is an individual you must remember that, if they have few possessions and a low income, it may take you years to get your money back.

1.3　Litigation risk

Lawyers often refer to 'the litigation risk' of a case. Really this reflects the fact that you can never be 100 per cent sure that you are going to win. Some cases are more likely to win than others. For example, if you are suing on a cheque which has bounced your chances of success are very good. However, many cases which reach court involve each party telling a slightly different story about what happened, when, and how. Part of the judge's job is to decide which story is the truth. Remember that judges are not superhuman. The only way in which they can make this decision is to listen to all the evidence and decide which version they think is likely to be the true one. If your witnesses are telling the truth but don't sound convincing, and the other party's witnesses are 'lying through their teeth' but doing it convincingly, the other side will win!

Whether or not you should sue should include a consideration of how well your witnesses are likely to come across when they give their evidence.

1.4　The costs of proceedings

A lawyer must always advise a client as to the matter of costs. Even if the proceedings are 100 per cent successful and the court orders the other side to pay your costs, you are unlikely to recover *all* of your own costs of bringing the proceedings. The costs must go through a process known as *taxation* and the practical result is that the amount which the other side has to pay is reduced to what was, in the opinion of the court, *strictly* necessary in order to win the case. The balance of the actual costs incurred remains to be paid by you.

Even if you are successful the court may not make an order for the payment of costs. If you are successful in winning compensation of £1500 but your own lawyers' costs amount to £1600 it is something of an empty victory!

The worst scenario of course is that you may lose the case. If you do lose you must remember that not only will you fail to get the compensation which you wanted but also

- you may be ordered to pay compensation to the other party
- you may be ordered to pay the other party's legal costs
- you will still have to pay your own legal costs.

The cost of unsuccessful litigation may be very high indeed.

1.5 Do you want the dispute resolved quickly?

If what you are looking for is for the dispute to be resolved quickly, either because you need the money, or because of the stress of the dispute, then court proceedings are not likely to be your answer. Even comparatively straightforward cases can take years to be finally resolved.

1.6 Any other considerations?

There is always the matter of publicity. Once court proceedings are brought, the matter will become public knowledge. You may feel that the risk of attracting adverse publicity to you or your firm outweighs what you might gain from proceedings.

2 Commencing proceedings

If, having gone through all the points in section 1 above, you decide that you do want to bring court proceedings then you need to understand what documents need to be prepared, and why, before the case is heard in court.

In a civil case the first step is the *pleadings*. The pleadings require each party (if they have not already done so) to state clearly what their position is. The *plaintiff* (that is, the person bringing the proceedings) will state what the complaint is. In the High Court this is called a *writ*; in the County Court it is called a *summons*. The *defendant* then responds by presenting a *defence*. The defendant may feel not only that the plaintiff's claim is unjustified but also that in fact it was the plaintiff who was at fault and should therefore owe him money. If this were the situation the defence would include a *counterclaim*. If either party wants more details of anything which is said in the pleadings they can formally ask for *further and better particulars*, in other words, more detail. If there are any documents which one party has which the other party thinks they should see they can apply for *discovery* of the documents.

All these procedures must be done within specified time limits. There may be a preliminary hearing which is referred to as a *summons for directions* in the High Court or a *pre-trial review* in the County Court. This preliminary hearing is usually purely procedural. Eventually a date will be fixed for the hearing itself.

3   What happens in court?

If you are going to be involved in a case you need to have some idea of what is likely to happen when you get to court. Both parties are likely to be represented by lawyers (often barristers). Because it is the plaintiff's task to 'prove' his case it is the plaintiff's lawyer who will start off with a short statement of what the case is about and what his client is trying to show. The plaintiff's witnesses (often including the plaintiff himself) are then called to give their evidence. The plaintiff's lawyer will take them through their version of events (known as *evidence in chief*). Then the defendant's lawyer will have a chance to *cross-examine* the witness. After that the plaintiff's lawyer will be given a chance to readdress any matters which were dealt with by the defendant's lawyer.

Very occasionally, after this stage, the defendant's lawyer may claim that the plaintiff has not proved his case. If this is true there is no point wasting everyone's time by making the defendant bring all his evidence. The judge has the power at this stage to say that the case has no real foundation and to put a stop to it. This happens, though only very occasionally. If the plaintiff's case is so weak this will usually be spotted earlier in the proceedings and the matter brought to an end at that stage.

Assuming that the plaintiff does make out a reasonable case then it is the defendant's turn. The defendant's lawyer will call the defendant's witnesses (often including the defendant himself). They will be asked to tell their story. The plaintiff's lawyer will then get a chance to cross-examine these witnesses and the defendant's lawyer can re-examine them on any additional matter which has been raised.

After the evidence come the speeches. First the plaintiff's lawyer will make a speech. Then the defendant's lawyer. The purpose of these *closing speeches* is to sum up, for the judge, the facts in relation to the law. Obviously each lawyer does this from his/her own client's point of view.

The judge will then give his or her *judgment*. This is the judge's decision.

After the decision the judge may hear additional argument from the lawyers as to *costs*. It is not always true to say that costs will be awarded to the winner. Sometimes there can be negotiations before the hearing of the case which are kept secret until after the hearing. Imagine, for example, that during such secret negotiations the defendant had offered the plaintiff £2000 to settle the case, and at the actual hearing the judge awarded £1800 damages. The defendant certainly has a moral argument that he should not have to pay all the costs of the case as his offer had been reasonable and the costs of going to court were unnecessary. In this situation the plaintiff is likely to find himself responsible for a considerable amount of costs.

Occasionally the judge will want to think the matter over further before making a decision. This is called a *reserved judgment*.

CASE STUDY 1

You are one of the directors of a firm producing dairy products such as yoghurt and cheese. Recently a delivery of milk was sampled by your director in charge of quality and found to include a rat hair. You rejected the delivery, for which you had paid in advance, and are considering suing the supplier.

Write a memo to the other directors dealing with the following issues:

- what factors should be considered when deciding whether the matter should be taken to court
- what the procedural stages are before the matter comes to court
- who may be required to give evidence and what will happen in court
- what factors should be considered if the supplier has offered to repay 75 per cent of the money.

4 What do we mean by remedies?

If you do decide to go to court you need to know:

- what solution of the dispute you are looking for
- what order the court is likely to make.

Remedies is the term which is applied to all the types of order that it is possible for the court to make.

Remedies can be divided into two groups. Firstly, there are those orders which require the payment of monetary compensation (known as *damages*). Secondly, there are other orders which the court can make which can either require someone to do something or to refrain from doing something which they should not do.

In addition to these two categories we also need to look at what the court will do if the losing party refuses to comply with the court order.

5 Monetary compensation

The most usual form of court order is that the court makes an order for payment of damages, i.e. monetary compensation. This requires the parties, and the court, to have put a monetary value on all the damage which has been suffered. Where the case is about a breach of contract and the profit that the plaintiff has lost, this is comparatively straightforward. Consider however the situation where the case involves compensation for injury after a car accident. The task of putting a monetary value on the loss of a limb, partial disablement or constant pain is a difficult one. The problem becomes even more pronounced where one is trying to compensate for mental trauma. The question of what value should be put on a particular type of damage is said to be one of *quantum* of damages.

Once the court has decided how much the damage the winning party has suffered is worth, it is then that the judge will order the losing party to pay that amount.

If the losing party refuses to pay after he has been ordered to do so, there are various ways in which the judgment can be enforced and the loser made to make the payments. The most common ways in which these can be enforced are:

5.1 A writ of fi. fa. or a warrant of execution

This additional order of the court enables the sheriff or bailiff of the court to go to the debtor's premises and take goods to the value of the judgment debt. The most common reasons for failure of this type of action is that a large number of personal belongings cannot be taken and in the case of other types of goods, such as electrical goods or cars, many people rent them or buy them on hire purchase. In either event the goods do not actually belong to the debtor and so they cannot be seized.

5.2 A charging order

If a judgment debtor owns land it is possible for the court to make an order that the debt should attach to the land (similar to the way that a mortgage does). This means that eventually, when the property is sold, the judgment debt must be repaid.

5.3 An attachment of earnings order

Where the judgment debtor is in employment, it is possible for the court to make an order requiring the debtor's employer to deduct a certain amount each week or month from the debtor's wages. If the debtor is employed this can be a most effective means of recovering the judgment debt – albeit that you will not get payment in one lump sum.

6 Judgments other than for money

It may be that what you wanted out of the court proceedings as well as, or instead of money, was some other type of order. Not all orders are available in all cases since it will depend on the circumstances, but below are examples of the types of order which may be obtained.

6.1 An order for specific performance

This order is usually only encountered in relation to contracts for the sale of land. It is a discretionary remedy and the court can look at all the circumstances of the case in deciding whether or not to order it. The effect of an order for specific performance is to force the parties to go through with the contract. The basis for the special treatment of contracts for the sale of land is that land is regarded as being unique. What the buyer should get is that piece of land which he agreed to buy and not simply money compensation. If the person who is ordered to perform the contract were to refuse, the court could itself deal with the necessary paperwork.

6.2 An order for rescission

An order for rescission is an order which allows parties to a contract to withdraw from the contract. The type of situation where this might be ordered is where one party was induced to enter into a contract either by fraud or by undue influence. Once the contract is rescinded the losing party cannot claim any rights under the now non-existent contract. (See further in Chapter 11 later.)

6.3 An injunction

An injunction usually orders someone to refrain from doing something (e.g. trespassing on someone else's land). Occasionally though a *mandatory injunction* may be available. This type of injunction requires the person to whom it is directed to actively do something. This type of injunction is quite uncommon as the courts often take the view that an order for money compensation will allow the winner to do whatever is required anyway.

If a person is ordered by injunction to do or not to do something, and they refuse to comply with the injunction, they can be imprisoned. Usually individuals cannot be imprisoned in civil cases. (The days of Dickens's debtors' prisons are long gone!) The reason for imprisonment in the case of failure to comply with an injunction is that the individual is effectively 'thumbing his nose' at the power of the court. The imprisonment will be for contempt of court, not for having lost the original case.

6.4 An order for possession

This type of order relates to land. An owner may obtain an order for possession against a squatter. A landlord may obtain an order for possession against a defaulting tenant. A bank or building society may obtain an order for possession when a property owner fails to keep up the repayments on a mortgage.

Summary

You should now be able to:

- list the factors which should be considered before starting court proceedings
- explain the following terms:
  plaintiff, defendant, pleadings, writ/summons, defence, counterclaim, further and better particulars, discovery

- explain what is likely to happen when a case comes before the court
- understand what is meant by the term remedies
- explain what is meant by the term 'quantum' and its importance in the case of money judgments
- explain how a money judgment might be enforced against a loser of a case who is recalcitrant
- explain the circumstances in which non-money judgments may be made.

✎   **CASE STUDY 2**

Look back at the situation you faced as Smith Limited in Chapter 1. Given the size of the lost order, Jones Limited is seeking compensation of £50,000. The pedestrian, who was only slightly hurt, has indicated to you that she will be happy to settle for under £1000. Jones Limited is one of your longest established customers with whom you have had a previously good working relationship. You are aware that they are under some financial pressure. Now, consider the following.

---

1 What are the main business issues that you should bear in mind in considering who might deal with the claims made by Jones Limited and the pedestrian? What type of options could be open to you in dealing with those claims?

2 What type of negotiation might you adopt in each case? How might you make use of the services of an arbitrator?

3 Where and how might proceedings start in either case and in what form? At what stage and when might you need to use the services of a solicitor or barrister?

8   When does a contract exist?

Objectives

The purpose of this chapter is to explain how the law decides whether a contract exists or not. You should read it before the chapters on the content of contracts and what happens if something goes wrong with a contract. By the end of the chapter you should

- be able to define what a contract is
- understand the essential ingredients which are required for a contract
- be able to answer the questions following the two case studies at the end of the chapter.

1   What is a contract?

We all make contracts in everyday life:

- going to a supermarket and purchasing goods
- travelling by public transport
- going out for a meal
- reserving accommodation at a hotel
- ordering clothes from a catalogue
- employing or being employed either as an employee or an independent contractor.

It may well be that generally we are unaware of the contractual implications of these everyday transactions, but the law of contract is always there to be resorted to if things go wrong.

A contract can be defined quite simply as a legally binding agreement between two or more parties. Each party to the agreement commits itself to carry out some act or fulfil a promise at some time in the future. The importance of entering into a contract is that the commitment carries with it legal consequences. If one of the parties fails to act in accordance with the agreement or breaks a promise by failing to fulfil an obligation, then the other party – the 'innocent' party – can pursue a civil action for breach of contract, and if successful obtain a court order. The court order could order the payment of damages (i.e. monetary compensation) to the innocent party. Alternatively, but more rarely, an order may be made by the court directing a reluctant party actually to carry out the contract – this is known as an *order for specific performance*.

The vast majority of contracts are made by word of mouth only, and as a result are known as *oral contracts*. With contracts of a more complex nature, the parties may prefer to have the main points put into writing. In all but a few exceptional types of contract this is not necessary. Nevertheless many contracts (or the main terms of them) are put into writing, the reason being that should problems arise and the parties cannot agree as to who is responsible for what, it is usually much easier for the court to look at a written agreement and to decide upon its meaning than to have to listen to what the parties say was said at the time.

This is particularly important because the terms of contracts are often not quite as simple as they seem and their wording may have unexpected implications. To have some real idea of what we mean, try this exercise with a friend and look at the results.

   CASE STUDY 1

Step 1   Read this out loud to a friend as if over the telephone:

'I understand you telephoned because you wanted us to come and repair your television. We will be happy to do it. We have a call out fee of £35 and charge for the time spent at an hourly rate of £15. Someone will be round to have a look at it tomorrow morning.'

Step 2   Once you have finished reading it out ask your friend to make a note of what you have agreed.

Step 3   Then see how he or she would react to the following scenarios:

a) No one turns up until tomorrow at 12.50 p.m. Your friend was supposed to meet someone at 12.45 p.m. The engineer says that the company counts morning as 9 until 1 p.m and afternoon as 2 p.m until 6 p.m.

Consider whether your friend's expectation of before noon was appropriate. Does the fact that colloquially morning means before noon have any bearing on the relationship? Does the company policy as to what is meant by morning and what is meant by afternoon have any bearing on the relationship, particularly if your friend was not told of it?

b) The engineer who turns up has no parts with him and says he will come back the following day now that he has assessed the damage. When the bill arrives:

- there are two £35 call out charges, based, the company says, on the two trips to the house
- there is a charge for £15 × 5 hours even though the engineer was at the house for 20 minutes on the first day and 40 minutes on the second. The company says the rest is the charge for travelling time
- the result is a bill for a total of £145.

Your friend might well have expected a bill for £50. (The call out charge and the hour spent repairing the TV set.) What does your friend recall of what they were told about the hourly rate? Does that accord with what you know you actually said? Does the call charge apply twice, particularly if their engineer did not have the parts? Does your friend have to pay for the engineer's travelling time or just the time spent actually repairing the TV?

Even with a short conversation like this we can see two things:

- although at the outset the terms of an agreement may seem clear, it is not until something goes wrong, like the 'late' arrival of the engineer or the enormous bill, that you start to examine exactly what was meant by what was said
- you will be very lucky if two people's recollection of a conversation is exactly the same. Over time, when people have gone over things in their mind they will change (albeit not deliberately) small details of their recollection. After some time the parties' recollections as to what was said may be very different. How does a judge decide which version is the truth? The answer is that it is down to who the judge believes when the person gives their evidence. You might give an accurate account of what was actually said, but if your friend gives a more convincing account of a corruption of what was said, then your friend will be the one who is believed.

The net result of both these types of uncertainty is that whether or not a contract is required to be in writing, many are, in the hope of avoiding the uncertainties about who said what to whom. In day-to-day business situations people may not feel they have the time for written agreements and will rely on mutual commercial interest and common understanding to ensure compliance. However, even if a formal written contract is not the policy of your particular business, it is important to keep a written record of the most important agreed terms, just in case.

2 When does a contract exist?

2.1 'I have been hurt, therefore someone must pay': true or false?

The first hurdle that one needs to get over in looking at the law of contract is the natural inclination to say that if you have suffered some injury then someone must pay. Very often people will go to solicitors' offices or legal advice centres: it is clear that they have suffered some injury or that someone has let them down and they have suffered financial loss as a result. It is sometimes very difficult trying to explain to those people that however aggrieved they feel about the way someone behaved, in order to sue the person they must be able to establish a formal legal link between the injured person and the wrongdoer. This formal legal link is known as a 'cause of action', and in the case of contract law the first stage is actually to establish the existence of a contract at all.

Case Study 2

Consider the following situation:

You are the owner and manager of a new business providing PR and local advertising services to all types of businesses in your area. In order to try to win clients you arranged a champagne garden party and invited approximately 100 representatives of your target clients. The garden party was run by caterers and held in your own spacious garden. A close friend when chatting to you had agreed to provide the wine. He told you that he could get his hands on some really nice and reasonably priced champagne which he would deliver to your home on the Sunday morning and you could 'sort it out' with him later. He did not turn up and neither did the wine. As a result, instead of champagne you had to serve your guests a mixture of miscellaneous bottles of red and white plonk which you happened to have in the house. Needless to say, no new clients have emerged from the party and several who had actually agreed to use your services have since telephoned and asked to be removed from your books.

In this situation you will feel understandably aggrieved. The damage which you have suffered as the result of your friend's failure is quite clear (even if it might be difficult to quantify). After all, who is going to want to use a PR and advertising business that cannot even get its own advertising right? The problem for you though is that however much you have suffered, unless you can establish a legal link between yourself and the person who let you down you cannot sue. You may not be friends with them any more but that is not going to make up for what you may have lost financially. The problem with this situation is that there is no contract. This illustrates how important it is not to take for granted that first stage in contract law, that of establishing whether a contract was formed at all. In order to do that we need to look at the essential elements of a contract.

3   What are the requirements for a contract?

As we mentioned in Section 1, many contracts are made orally. There are some contracts which are required to be made in writing (for example contracts for the sale of land), but the vast majority may be made either orally or in writing. With most contracts there are three essential elements which must be satisfied:

- there must be *offer* and *acceptance*. In other words one party must have made a proposal in clear terms which the other party agrees to accept
- there must be *consideration*. This means in its simplest terms that each party must give something of value to the agreement. An offer by Mr Jones that he will do something for Mr Smith may be both an offer and an acceptance, but unless Mr Smith is doing something in return, it is not a contract at all but rather a promise made by Mr Jones. In English law simple promises, in all but a very few situations, cannot be enforced. With most business contracts this element is unlikely to present any problems. Most business transactions by their very nature involve consideration

- there must be an *intention* on behalf of the parties *to create a legally binding relationship*. In most situations where one is dealing with strangers or business people, this requirement will almost go without saying.

Imagine, however the following situation.

   CASE STUDY 3

I tell my sister that I will give her £10 if she mows my lawn on Saturday. She agrees. There is an offer, there is acceptance by her, there is even consideration by her in promising to mow the lawn and by me in promising to give her £10 for doing it. Now imagine that she does not turn up on Saturday. On Sunday I am having a lunch party and I really wanted the lawn to look nice. So I telephone a firm of garden servicers and they agree to mow it at Sunday rates of £50. The loss which I have suffered is the difference between what I agreed to pay my sister (£10) and what I have had to pay the garden services firm (£50), that is £40. Can I then sue my sister for £40? Her answer (and there is some merit in it) was that although there was offer acceptance and consideration there was no intention to create a legal relationship between us. It was an informal family arrangement that simply happened to have some of the elements required for a contract.

As we shall see, the question of intention can also be a significant issue in business situations where the parties to a purported contract want, later, to avoid being bound by their agreement.

---

4   Was there offer and acceptance?

The point at which a contract is usually formed is when an offer made by one party to the agreement (the *offeror*) is accepted by the other contracting party (the *offeree*).

If A says to B 'I will sell you my car for £3000,' and B responds by agreeing, providing there is an intention to create legal relations, a binding contract has come into existence; if either A or B were to change their minds, the other party could in principle sue for breach of contract. Even on a common sense basis we can see that the situation should be different if A were to say 'If I were to sell my car I would want at least £3000' and B were to reply by saying that he would give him £3000. A should not at that stage be bound to sell the car.

People do not normally talk in terms such as, 'I offer to sell you X for £Y' or 'I accept your offer.' The terminology is far more likely to be, 'You can have it for £Y' and the reply is likely to be 'OK' or even 'You're on.' It is obviously important therefore to be able to decide exactly what type of statement will constitute an offer, and in turn what will constitute an acceptance.

4.1   The offer

An offer is a definite undertaking by the offeror that he or she is prepared to be bound by the proposal if it is accepted by the offeree. A valid offer is a definite promise to be bound and on specific terms.

4.1.1   The offer distinguished from the vague statement

Vague statements which are incapable of precise meaning will not be capable of forming a contractual offer at all. Some statements which at first sight might appear vague could be made more certain by looking at them in the context of previous dealings between the parties. However, there are some statements which are of their very nature vague and so incapable of forming part of valid offer. For example in **Gunthing v Lynn (1831)**, an offer was dependent on a horse being 'lucky'. This was held not to be capable of being part of an offer as it was too vague.

4.1.2   The offer distinguished from the preliminary information or discussions

It is also important to distinguish an offer from a supply of information. Consider the following case.

⚖

In **Harvey v Facey (1893)**, the conversation went like this:

A: Will you sell us such and such? Telegraph your lowest cash price.
B: Lowest price for such and such £900.
A: We agree to buy such and such for the £900 asked by you.

It was held that no contract existed because no offer had actually been made. B's reply to A's enquiry was not an offer, but simply providing information. It was a statement of what B considered was a minimum price which he would accept if he were to sell. It was not a commitment to sell if A chose to buy.

4.1.3   The offer distinguished from an invitation to treat

An *invitation to treat* is an invitation to someone to make you an offer. You are effectively turning the tables on the other party and asking them to make the offer which you can then decide whether or not to accept. A common example of an invitation to treat is if you are out shopping and you see something in a shop marked at £2.50. The statement by the shop that the item is £2.50 is an invitation to treat. You can say you would like one of the items. You are the one making the offer. The shopkeeper then decides whether to accept your offer or not. He might for example say that he is very sorry but the price has been marked incorrectly and is in fact £12.50 and not £2.50. You would usually have no legal recourse against the shopkeeper and could not insist that he sell you the product for the marked price. The marked price was an invitation to treat, your response was an offer to buy, but on this occasion he has not accepted your offer.

Goods displayed in a shop window are an invitation to treat (**Fisher v Bell 1960**); goods displayed on a supermarket shelf are an invitation to treat (**Pharmaceutical Society of Great Britain v Boots Cash Chemist Ltd 1953**); and goods advertised generally in a newspaper or periodical will be an invitation to treat (**Partridge v Crittenden 1968**).

It is not always immediately clear whether an offer or an invitation to treat is involved. Consider the following two cases.

⚖

In **Gibson v Manchester City Council (1979)**, the council wrote to Gibson saying that they might be prepared to sell the house at a price of £x if he would be prepared to make a formal application to buy. Although this letter contained a price, it was held that it was an invitation to treat. The council was inviting Gibson to make an offer. For the council's letter to constitute an offer it needed at least to include a promise and there was no promise – only an indication that it might be prepared to sell at that price.

However in the more recent case of:

⚖

Blackpool and Fylde Aero Club Ltd. v Blackpool Borough Council (1990), the council issued invitations to tender (that is make offers) for a three-year licence to run pleasure flights from the airport. It was specified that tenders received after 12 noon on March 17 would not be considered. At 11 a.m. on March 17 the Aero Club's tender was delivered by hand to the council's letter box. Unusually the letter box was not opened that day. When it was opened the following day all the post was date stamped March 18. As a result of the date stamp the Aero Club's tender was not even considered and the contract was made with another party: When the facts came to light the Aero Club sued the council. The effect of the decision in the Court of Appeal was to say that there had effectively been a contract between the Aero Club and the council, that if the Club tendered in compliance with the specified terms then such a tender would at least be considered. It seems that the original invitation to treat by the council contained an offer to consider tenders which were appropriately submitted. The Aero Club had accepted that offer and a contract to consider the tender had been made. The decision is particularly surprising as the terms of the invitation to tender actually specified that the council did not undertake to accept the highest tender, or indeed any tender at all.

4.2 Termination or withdrawal of an offer

Once an offer is made it does not necessarily remain open indefinitely. The party who made the offer is usually in a position to withdraw it at any time before the offer is accepted. (Obviously an offer which has been accepted cannot be withdrawn because by the offer and the acceptance it has turned into a binding contract.) An offer can be terminated in various different ways.

4.2.1 Withdrawal prior to acceptance: Revocation

If the offeror withdraws the offer before it is accepted by the offeree, this is known as revocation. It is the most usual way of bringing an offer to an end. The usual everyday situation would be where you offer to sell your bicycle to your friend for £75. Your friend says that she will think about it and let you know. But before she gets back to you, you contact her and tell her that you have changed your mind and are not selling it. She cannot then accept the offer. She is too late, it has been revoked/withdrawn and no longer exists.

One of the most important factors to remember with revocation is that it must actually be communicated to the offeree. In the example above it would be no good you simply having decided that you no longer wanted to sell, but not actually telling your friend as much. At any time until you actually tell her that you have changed your mind she could accept your offer and a legally binding contract would be created. This principle is illustrated by the following case:

> **Byrne v Van Tienhoven (1880):** the events were as follows:
>
> October 1   A posted an offer to B
> October 8   A posted a revocation of the offer to B
> October 11   B received the offer from A and sent a telegram accepting the offer
> October 15   B posted an acceptance to A
> October 20   B received A's revocation of the offer.
>
> The rule which says that revocation must be communicated to the offeree had dramatic effects here. The rules said that the revocation took effect on the 20th when it was communicated to B and not on the 8th when it was decided upon by A. By the 20th the revocation was too late as the offer had already been accepted.

The rule does produce some apparently strange situations, but it also prevents offerors taking unfair advantage of market fluctuations.

Although revocation of an offer must be communicated to the offeree, it is not always essential that it is done by the offeror himself. If the offeree is informed of the withdrawal of the offer by a reliable third party that may be enough (**Dickinson v Dodds 1876**). The emphasis here is on the reliability of the third party.

4.2.2   Termination of an offer by lapse of time

An offer may come to an end after a lapse of time. The terms of the offer may be that it is to last for a certain length of time, in which case once that time has expired the offer will automatically come to an end. If no specific duration is stated, then the offer will terminate after a reasonable time. The problem is obviously what is meant by 'a reasonable time' and this will vary depending on the facts in each particular case. For example, I offer to sell you my car and a year later you purport to accept the offer; even if I have not, in the meantime, expressly withdrawn the offer, it is extremely unlikely that your purported acceptance will create a binding contract. In the absence of any other factors the court is likely to say that the original offer lapsed after a reasonable length of time – and certainly less than a year. For example, in:

> **Ramsgate Victoria Hotel Co v Montefiore (1866)**, A offered to buy shares in a company. Five months later the company purported to accept the offer. It was held that A's offer was only for a reasonable period of time and five months was, in this particular case, more than a reasonable period of time. The offer had lapsed and so could not be accepted.

4.2.3 Termination of the offer by the death of one of the parties

If the offeree dies, then the offer terminates automatically. If the offeror dies then the offer terminates unless it has been accepted by the offeree without knowledge of the offeror's death. Consider, however, the situation where the offer specifies that acceptance of the offer will not take place until it is communicated to the offeror. If the offeror is dead, then obviously the acceptance in the required form simply cannot be made.

4.2.4 Termination of the offer by the making of a counter offer

It is important to remember that in real life transactions the correspondence or discussions between the parties is often undertaken over a period of time and negotiations may involve a number of different suggestions being made by each party. If the original offer is not to be terminated, it is important that the offeree does not introduce any new terms when replying to an offer. The response must be acceptance or refusal of the offer. Any modifications of the original offer may be construed as a counter offer which will put an end to the original offer. For example in

---

Hyde v Wrench (1840)

- A offered to sell a farm to B for £1000
- B said that he would pay £950 for it
- A refused to sell for £950, whereupon B agreed to buy at the original price of £1000.

Given the state of the law at the time relating to contracts for the sale of land, if B had responded straight away by agreeing to buy for £1000, there would have been a binding contract between A and B. However, by saying that he would buy it for £950, B had, according to the court decision, made a counter offer which extinguished or revoked the original offer made by A. When A then rejected the counter offer, it was not open to B to accept the original offer – that had been terminated by the counter offer and could not be resurrected.

(If A had still wanted to sell for £1000 he could of course have agreed, but, unless he had expressly restated his original offer, it would have been a contract where B had made the offer and been the offeror and A had been the offeree and accepted the offer.)

The matter is of particular importance to businesses who have standard terms for their contracts. For example, an offer is made by A Company to sell something at a specific price and on standard terms, but B Company replies with a counter offer to buy the item at a different price and on B's standard terms. If A Company simply accepts B Company's offer, it is the standard terms of B Company which will apply to the transaction. The same principle was evident in:

⚖️

> **Northland Airlines Ltd v Denis Ferranti Meters Ltd (1970)**, where A offered to sell B an aircraft on certain specified terms, one of which was that a deposit of £5000 should be paid immediately on acceptance. B replied purporting to accept A's offer but failing to provide the deposit as specified. B's reply also specified a delivery date (a matter which was not mentioned in the original offer). It was held by the Court of Appeal that B's response was not an acceptance at all but was a counter offer. The counter offer therefore terminated the original offer and left A free to sell the aircraft elsewhere.

A further business case is:

⚖️

> **Butler Machine Tool Co Ltd v Ex-cell-O Corporation (England) Ltd (1979)**, where A offered to supply B with a piece of machinery. The offer included a price variation clause allowing A to alter the initial price in certain situations. B purported to accept the offer but did so making it clear that it was on B's own standard terms. B's own standard terms did not allow any price variation. A acknowledged the order but when the machinery was delivered A tried to claim an additional sum based on A's price variation clause.
>
> The issue was, did A's standard terms contained in the original offer apply or did B's standard terms apply? The Court of Appeal held that B had not unconditionally accepted the original offer. B had, instead, made a counter offer on their own standard terms which A had accepted. B's standard terms therefore prevailed.

It can be seen from these cases that if the offeree wants to discuss the terms of an offer he or she must be very careful indeed how it is done. If the discussions are such that they introduce new terms, they may be construed as a counter offer. This will terminate the original offer and leave the original offeror free to negotiate elsewhere. If the offeree does want to discuss terms, they must be sure that their response to the offer constitutes a request for information rather than a counter offer. If the response by the offeree is carefully worded so as to amount to a question as to whether the offeror would consider a slight variation on the terms of the original offer, then it may not constitute a counter offer and the original offer will survive the request (**Stevenson v Maclean 1880**).

4.2.5   Termination of the offer by failure to satisfy a preliminary condition

Imagine that A Company had offered to buy 200,000 stadium seats from B Company, providing that Manchester were successful in its bid in 1993 to host the Olympic games. The moment Manchester failed in its bid, the offer to B Company would come to an end.

4.3 Acceptance of the offer

The general rule is that the acceptance of an offer by the offeree must be communicated to the offeror. Without this actual communication there will usually be no contract. In:

> **Entores v Miles Far Eastern Corporation (1955)**, an offer was sent by telex from London to Amsterdam. The offeree in Amsterdam then telexed an acceptance. It was held that the acceptance took effect only when the acceptance was actually received by the offeror in London. Similarly in:
>
> **Brinkibon v Stahag Stahl (1982)**, the House of Lords approved the Entores decision and held that an acceptance by telex sent from London to Vienna created a binding contract only when the telex reached Vienna.

There are, however, two important exceptions to this general rule:

- where an offer is made to the world at large (for example an offer of a reward), then there is no requirement for any person wishing to accept the offer to communicate their acceptance to the offeror. All that they need to do is to act in accordance with the offeror's request. In:

> **Carlill v Carbolic Smoke Ball Co (1893)**, the company published an advertisement agreeing to pay £100 to anyone contracting influenza after using their patented medicine. Carlill bought the medicine and used it in accordance with the instructions and yet still caught influenza. Carlill claimed the reward but the company argued, among other things, that they were not obliged to pay as Carlill had not communicated her acceptance of the offer to the company. It was held that the purchase and use of the medicine in accordance with the instructions was sufficient acceptance despite the fact that it had not been reported to the company.

- if an offer is made and the offeror expressly or impliedly indicates that he or she expects the acceptance to be made through the post, then if the post is used acceptance takes place when the letter is actually posted (**Adams v Lindsell 1818**). This is the rule even though the offeror may not receive the acceptance until several days later and it might be delayed longer than that or indeed even lost completely. If the post is an acceptable method of acceptance, the only requirement is that the letter is properly addressed, stamped and is actually put in the post. When and whether it actually arrives has no bearing on the contract which was made at the time of posting.

This rule, known as the *postal rule*, can cause inevitable problems. The offeror may find himself bound by an acceptance which he knows nothing about. The contract is made when the letter is posted. He only knows about it when he receives the letter. For the commercial client this is obviously an undesirable situation, particularly when you bear in mind that the postal rule does not apply to the posting of a withdrawal of the offer.

✎   **CASE STUDY 4**

Your firm is in the business of buying up and reselling surplus and bankrupt stock. Six months ago you bought 200 orthopaedic beds (designed for hospital use) from a manufacturer who was going out of business. You have approached the local health authority (the LHA) but they say that they have a surplus stock of beds themselves and will not be purchasing any for at least 24 months. Three weeks ago you approached a chain of private nursing homes (the PNH) and offered to sell the beds to them for £500 each. On Thursday last week you received a telephone call from the LHA. There had been a fire at one of the hospitals and they needed to replace some beds urgently. They offered to buy the beds from you for £750 each. You immediately posted a letter to the PNH withdrawing the offer and then accepted the offer from the LHA. The PNH posted a letter on Friday accepting your offer; they received your letter withdrawing your offer on Saturday. On Monday you receive the letter from PNH accepting your offer.

Consider the chain of events:

1   The offer made by you to the PNH
2   The offer made by the LHA to you
3   The withdrawal of offer to the PNH posted by you (but not yet effective because the postal rule does not apply)
4   The acceptance by you of the LHA offer. Contract number 1 now exists between you and LHA
5   The acceptance by the PNH of your offer. Contract number 2 now exists between you and the PNH (the postal rule applies)
6   Your withdrawal of offer is received by the PNH (but is ineffective as a contract already exists between you and the PNH)
7   The receipt of the acceptance of your offer from the PNH. This has no effect on the contract as the contract was formed when the PNH posted the acceptance. It will, however, make you realise that you are now committed to two contracts to sell 200 beds each to the LHA and to the PNH. You only have 200 beds in total. The owner of whichever contract is not honoured will be entitled to sue you for the additional costs in buying similar beds elsewhere.

The postal rule was developed in the last century and is arguably inappropriate to today's commercial methods. Nevertheless it remains in existence, and while it does in the interests of commercial certainty, it must surely be of the utmost importance that parties:

- are aware of its effects
- specify in the offer that the postal rule shall not apply, and that the contract is made only when it is actually received by the offeror. It is easy enough for the offeree to be sure when the contract is made by using a guaranteed and recorded delivery post – if they so wish.

4.3.1   Acceptance subject to contract

When an offeree accepts an offer *subject to contract* it means that he or she neither accepts nor rejects the offer, but intimates that the two parties should negotiate a formal written contract presumably based on the original offer. This method is sometimes employed in preliminary negotiations where the main substance of the agreement has been negotiated, but both parties want to allow their lawyers to fine tune the procedural details and perhaps to be more specific about the precise terms of the otherwise general agreement. This approach is particularly relevant to business negotiations. In some cases businesses may then decide not to proceed with the proposed transaction and to stop short of an actual contract.

4.3.2   Acceptance of an offer in ignorance of the offer

At first glance this may appear impossible, but consider the following cases. In:

> **R v Clarke (1927)**, an informant gave information for which there was a reward offered. The informant, however, had forgotten about the reward. It was held that he was not entitled to the reward as he could not accept the offer of the reward when he was ignorant of it – and forgetting about it was the same as never hearing about it.

Compare this with:

> **Williams v Carwardine (1833)**; a reward was offered for information leading to the arrest of a criminal. X gave the required information, her motive being revenge rather than the reward. Nevertheless it was held that she could accept the reward; her motive for acceptance was irrelevant provided that she actually knew about the offer.

These situations, by their nature, tend to be rare in business situations.

4.3.3   Silence cannot constitute acceptance

An offeror may not insist that if an offeree does nothing in response to the offer the silence will amount to an acceptance. In:

> **Felthouse v Bindley (1862)**, A, having offered to buy a horse from B, wrote to B saying 'If I hear no more … I consider the horse mine'. B intended to accept but failed to reply. In the meantime the horse was mistakenly sold to someone else. It was held that no contract had been formed between A and B as the original offer had not been accepted.

The silence of the offeree could not constitute acceptance unless the offeree himself expressly stated that silence on his part should amount to acceptance.

5 Was there consideration?

In English law consideration is an essential requirement in almost every contract (the only usual exception being where the contract complies with particular formalities and is in a special form of document which satisfies the definition of a 'deed'). Consideration has been defined as:

> 'some right, interest, profit or benefit accruing to one party, or some forbearance detriment, loss or responsibility given, suffered or undertaken by the other' (**Currie v Misa 1875**).

In essence the consideration is the bargaining aspect of the contract, the quid pro quo; each party to the contract gives something and receives something in return. It can be seen from the definition that the idea of consideration can be either positive in doing something or providing something, or it can be negative in the sense of accepting some detriment or loss. In **Alliance Bank v Broom (1864)**, it was held that the bank had provided consideration (in return for a customer's promise) by agreeing not to enforce immediate repayment of the customer's overdraft which the bank was entitled to do.

The importance of consideration is in many respects that it usually prevents a simple one-sided promise from being unenforceable. It is agreements in the form of bargains which are enforceable as contracts.

5.1 Can consideration be performed before the contract?

One of the principles of the idea of each party bringing something of value to the agreement is that the thing of value should be provided at the time of or after the agreement. If you have already paid the money, or performed the act *before* the contract is entered into, you are bringing nothing fresh to the agreement. Consider what would be the position if the agreement had not been concluded. You would already have paid the money or done the act and could not then take it back or undo it. In:

> **Roscorla v Thomas (1842)**, A sold a horse to B for £30. A short time after the sale A volunteered the information that the horse was 'free from vice'. This proved to be untrue and B sued A. B was unsuccessful, as the consideration provided by B of £30 was paid prior to the statement by A. B provided no extra consideration to balance the statement made by A and the payment of the £30 could not count, as that consideration was past.

In a further example:

> **Re McArdle (1951)**, according to the terms of a trust, a woman was permitted to live for her life in a house which would ultimately belong to her children. While living there she made considerable improvements to the property. After the improvements were made the children agreed with the

mother that they would pay her for the improvements. It was held that the children were not bound by the agreement as it amounted to a promise by them for which the mother provided no consideration. She had already done the work so that brought nothing fresh to the bargain. The consideration was past.

One exception to the rule that *past consideration is no consideration* is that if a service is carried out at someone's request there may be an implied promise to pay for it. In:

Lampleigh v Braithwaite (1615), X, having killed a man, engaged Y to obtain a royal pardon for him. Y obtained the pardon and X then promised to pay him £100 for his services. It was held that X's promise was binding because a promise to pay could be implied into the original request, and the implied promise existed before the service was carried out.

So, for example, if you walk into a hairdresser and explain what type of cut you want, the hairdresser cuts your hair. You cannot then claim not to be liable to pay for the haircut on the basis that the hairdresser's consideration is past, as there is, in your original request, an implied promise to pay.

5.2 Who must provide the consideration and who can enforce the promise?

The general rule is that only the person to whom a promise has been made and who has given the consideration can enforce the promise. In other words it is usually only the parties to the contract who can actually enforce it against each other. So if A agrees that in return for B repairing his roof A will pay C (who is B's child) £3000, C may not usually sue A if the payment is not made. C has given no consideration. The right to sue on the contract belongs to B (**Tweddle v Atkinson 1861**). This is a problem which is often encountered in everyday personal and business situations. Think about some birthday presents which you have bought recently:

- The contract for the sale of the goods was between you and the retailer.
- You then gave the goods as a present to a friend.
- If something is the matter with the goods, it is not strictly possible for your friend to use the contract made between you and the retailer to enable him or her to make a claim against the retailer.
- There is a contractual link (known as *privity of contract*) between you and the retailer. There is no contractual link/privity of contract between your friend and the retailer.

This matter is often overlooked, either because the retailer may have a policy of ignoring the strict legal rules and looking instead for customer (and friend!) satisfaction, or your friend may, depending on the nature of the defect and what damage it has caused, be able to rely on some statutory provision. The fact remains, however, that if it comes to the crunch, bringing an action based on the contract which you made is not a possibility for your friend.

5.3   How much consideration must be given?

The rule in law is that *consideration need not be adequate but must be sufficient.* In other words the courts are not concerned that the consideration which the parties provide for the contract is of equal value, but it must be of some value.

The following case shows the consideration need not be of great value. In:

Chappell & Co Ltd v Nestle Company Ltd (1960), Nestle ran a special promotion in which a record could be obtained by sending off three chocolate bar wrappers and a small administration fee. A dispute over the payment of royalties and of copyright in respect of the record turned on whether they were being given away or whether there was a contract with some consideration involved. The House of Lords considered the question of whether or not the wrappers could be part of the consideration. Despite the fact that the wrappers were of little value and were actually thrown away by Nestle when they received them, the House of Lords held that they did form part of the consideration.

Sometimes the promisor will appear to be giving something of value, but on closer examination it transpires that the promisor is only agreeing to do something which he already has an obligation to do anyway. He is not therefore giving anything of himself to the bargain at all. The existing obligation may be in the form of a legal or public duty, in which case performing that duty cannot usually be consideration for a contract. In:

Collins & Godefroy (1831), A agreed to pay B a sum of money if he would give evidence for A in court. B was under a subpoena (a court order) to give evidence anyway and so he had done nothing for A over and above what he was in law bound to do.

Often the facts will need to be examined in some detail to ascertain what exactly one party is already bound to do and whether they are adding anything extra at all to the agreement. In:

Harris v Sheffield United FC (1987), the police were requested to maintain order at a match in return for the promise of an agreed sum of money. It was later argued that the police should not be entitled to the money as they were doing nothing more than their public duty which they were obliged to do anyway. However, on the facts it was decided that the police had been asked to provide extra services in excess of what they were required to do, and so had provided consideration for the payment.

The principle was thought to be similar where the parties are under a duty to do something as a result of an obligation under an existing contract between them. If a contract exists between A and B, and either party promises the other an additional reward if they merely complete their obligations under the contract, then theoretically the person to whom the promise was made cannot enforce payment of the additional reward simply because he has not done anything over and above what he was obliged to do under the already existing contract. The principle is illustrated by the two cases of:

Stilk v Myrick (1809) and **Hartley v Ponsonby (1857)**: in the first case two crew members on a ship deserted and the remaining nine were offered extra money to get the ship home. The money was not paid and it was held that the crew members could not enforce payment as they were doing nothing more than they were each contractually bound to do anyway. Nine sailors doing the work of 11 was not sufficient consideration. In the second, similar case 19 of the original 36 crew members remained. It was held that they could claim the additional sum as there was a sufficient difference between sailing the ship as they had originally contracted to do and sailing it with almost half the original crew.

It seems that the distinction between the two cases may now be less important following the case of:

William v Roffey Bros (1990): the situation here was that D engaged P to carry out some work on a block of flats by a certain date. The work had to be completed by that date or D would be liable on another contract to pay a financial penalty. It became clear that P would not be finished in time and so, anxious to avoid paying a penalty on his other contract, D promised P an extra £10,300 to finish on time. P did finish on time and claimed the 'bonus'. The argument made by D was that P was already bound to finish the work by the agreed date and so had provided no additional consideration for the payment of the bonus. It was held that P was entitled to recover the extra £10,300 even though he had done no more than he was obliged to do under the contract. It was sufficient that there was some benefit to D in avoiding the financial penalty on his other contract.

The case is difficult to reconcile with **Stilk v Myrick**. In practical terms it would seem that the sensible course for someone in D's situation would now be either:

- to build a bonus for completion on time into the original price of the contract, or
- to make it clear in the original contract that if P failed to carry out the work by the agreed date the claim for damages which D would make against P in respect of his breach of contract would include the amount of the penalty payable on his related contract with a third party.

5.4   Creating an alternative contract/Waiving rights under an existing contract

Agreeing to waive existing rights is also something which requires fresh consideration for it to be binding (**Pinnel's Case 1602**). Consider the situation where I owe you £100 which is due to be repaid next Thursday. If I say that I am unable to pay you but will pay you £90 on Thursday instead, you will not by accepting the £90 waive your right to the other £10. There is no new contract. I may have offered to pay you £90; you may have accepted, but I have brought nothing fresh to the agreement by way of consideration. I have done nothing over and above what was provided for in the original contract. The original contract (for the repayment of £100) therefore still stands. It is simply that you have performed part of your obligation. This rule is subject to three exceptions:

- acceptance of a lesser sum on an earlier date: if I offer to pay you £90 on Tuesday rather than £100 on Thursday and you accept, then that can be a new contract. I have provided some additional consideration for the new contract. I may have paid less but I have paid it earlier
- performance of the contract at a different place: if the original contract had specified that the £100 should be paid on Thursday in Birmingham, but at your request I pay £90 on Thursday in Leeds, then again I have brought something additional to the transaction by way of performing the contract in a different place from that which the original contract required
- adding something new to the contract: if you agree to accept £90 on Thursday, so long as I provide it in French currency, that may suffice to vary the original contract and to wipe out the requirement to repay the other £10.

On one level this case does not seem to be harsh, but consider the situation of Alan, who has borrowed £5000 from his friend. When the time comes to repay it Alan admits to his friend Tony that he does not have the money. He also tells him that his wife is ill and needs private medical treatment; he cannot afford to repay the loan and also borrow the money for the treatment. Tony tells Alan that he can forget the repayment of the £5000; it does not matter.

5.5   Promissory estoppel

On the basis of Pinnel's Case, Alan could do nothing if in 6 months time Tony insisted on repayment of the £5000. Tony may have agreed to waive the loan but Alan did not provide any consideration for Tony's agreement. The result seems very harsh. It is because of this harshness that the principle of *promissory estoppel* has arisen. This principle would have the effect of injecting some fairness into the agreement reached by Alan and Tony.

The principle is that if Tony promised Alan that he would not enforce repayment of the loan, intending Alan to act on the promise and if in fact Alan did so, to his detriment (taking on the additional loan which he could not afford), then even though Alan has provided no additional consideration, Tony will be *estopped* (that is prevented because of his own previous conduct) from claiming repayment of the loan contrary to his original promise. Consider one of the leading cases in this area:

> **Central London Property Trust v High Trees House (1947)**: In 1939 A let a block of flats to B. B subsequently found that, because of wartime conditions, he was having difficulty in subletting the flats and so finding it difficult to pay the rent. A therefore agreed to accept half rent for the period of the war. The discussion in this case made it clear that while A could reclaim full rent after the war, had he attempted to renege on the interim agreement before the war was over, he would have been prevented from doing so by promissory estoppel.

The principle of promissory estoppel is clearly an important one, although two limitations must be borne in mind:

- the effect of promissory estoppel is to *suspend* rights, not extinguish them. When there is a change in circumstances so that the reason for the promise ceases to apply, the original rights of the promisor become enforceable again. (So in our example, if Tony's fortunes took a turn for the better and he could afford to repay the loan for medical treatment and Alan's loan, Alan could enforce his rights again. He had not waived them forever.)
- promissory estoppel can only be used to prevent one party from enforcing existing rights in a situation where it would be unconscionable. It does not create any new rights.

A good business example of the type of situation where this might arise was found in:

> **D & C Builders v Rees (1965)**, where A, a small building company, completed work for B, but B failed to pay. Eventually A, who desperately needed the money, agreed to accept a smaller sum. This smaller sum was accepted because B had made it clear that if they did not accept the smaller sum they would get nothing. A later sued B for the balance. The issue was whether B could rely on promissory estoppel to resist having to pay the outstanding balance. The Court of Appeal found against B because they said that A had been effectively forced to accept the reduced offer.

6 Intention to create legal relations

An agreement, even though you may be able to identify offer and acceptance and consideration, will not be a legally binding contract unless there is an intention to create legal relations. The test of intention is objective. In other words you do not look at what those particular parties themselves intended, but rather at what two hypothetical and 'reasonable' parties would have intended in the circumstances. The task of deciding whether there is the intention to create legal relations or not is made easier by certain presumptions. These presumptions allow the court to presume that the intention did exist in certain likely situations. The nature of a presumption, however, is not that it is conclusive. It simply indicates the approach which the court will take to the matter in the absence of any convincing evidence to the contrary.

6.1 Commercial agreements

In the case of commercial transactions the courts will usually presume that there was an intention to create legal relations. There would need to be clear evidence of contrary intention for this presumption to be negatived. In:

Rose and Frank Co v JR Crompton & Bros (1923): A and B entered into an agreement whereby B would have the sole agency to demonstrate A's goods in the UK. Both parties entered into a written agreement and signed a document which included the clause '... the arrangement ... shall not be subject to the legal jurisdiction in the law courts either of the United States or of England ...' The House of Lords decided that the purpose of that clause was to make it clear that each was relying on the other's good faith and did not intend to create a legal relationship which could be enforced through the courts. There was clear offer acceptance and consideration. The element which was lacking was the intention to create legal relations. Without the 'honourable pledge' clause doubtless this would have been a contract, but the existence of that clause effectively negatived any intention to create legal relations.

The negativing of the intention to create legal relations must, however, be clear. In:

British Steel Corporation v Cleveland Bridge and Engineering Company Ltd (1984), A asked B to act as subcontractor for A in a large tender for which A was bidding. A did not want to commit itself until the tender was won and so A sent a 'letter of intent' to B saying that B had been chosen and asking B to do some preliminary work. But the letter made it clear that a contract would have to wait until the tender had been won. When B tried to claim for the preliminary work, it was held that, despite the wording of the letter, the request for B to do the initial work could constitute a contract.

6.2 Agreements between family and friends

If an agreement is reached in a domestic situation between relatives or friends, there is a presumption that there was no intention to create legal relations (see Case study 3). Neither party in these types of situation would usually expect the courts to intervene to enforce the agreement. Obviously the nature of the relationship between the parties must be looked at fairly closely in each particular case. In:

⚖

Merritt v Merritt (1970), Lord Denning said that a distinction must be drawn between the situation where the parties are living together amicably: 'In such cases their domestic arrangements are ordinarily not intended to create legal relations,' and where they may be separated: 'It is altogether different when the parties are not living in amity but are separated, or about to separate. They then bargain keenly. They do not rely on honourable understandings. They want everything cut and dried. It may safely be presumed that they intend to create legal relations.'

6.3   Was there genuineness of consent?

As we have seen, the essential ingredients of a contract are the existence of an agreement (offer and acceptance), the giving of some value to the agreement (consideration) and the importance which the parties attach to the agreement (intention to create legal relations). One final element of the contract is that the agreement should be entered into freely. Two parties may have provided all the elements for a contract, but if one party has been *forced* into the contract the courts may not enforce it. In:

⚖

Atlas Express Ltd v Kafko Ltd (1989), a small company (K Ltd) contracted to supply goods to Woolworths. The contract with a major retailer was of considerable importance to the company. K Ltd then contracted with a road haulier to deliver the goods to Woolworths. After the first deliveries the hauliers realised that the size of the loads was different from what had been estimated and therefore the price which they were charging for delivery was too low. The haulage company sent a van to collect the next load and gave the driver instructions not to collect unless K Ltd agreed to vary the contract to include more favourable terms for the haulier. K Ltd agreed because they were desperate that the delivery should be sent so they would not lose the contract with Woolworths. The High Court held that K Ltd's agreement had been obtained by *economic duress* and the new contract could not therefore be enforced.

It is important to note, however, that contracts made under economic duress, where the agreement is not genuine, must be acted upon quickly. If the party who suffers the coercion delays in applying to the courts, they may find that they cannot get out of the contract. If they continue with the contract even after the original duress has passed they may be regarded as having confirmed the contract and their agreement to it (**North Ocean Shipping Company Ltd v Hyundai Construction Company Ltd 1978**).

6.4   Statutory provisions

There are other situations where statute may prescribe that the particular type of agreement should not give rise to a legally enforceable contract. An example of this is contained in Section 179 of the Trade Union and Labour Relations Act

1992, whereby collective agreements reached between employers and trade unions are not intended to have the status of contracts. The terms of such agreements will only usually become legally binding when they are incorporated into each individual's contract with his or her employer.

7 Capacity

There are some situations, however, where the basic rules suggest that a contract was formed, but the other party has not performed the contract, and yet you *cannot* sue anyone because there is some fundamental problem which prevents you from doing anything about their failure to perform the contract. One such case is capacity.

In normal circumstances there will be no problem with regard to the capacity of the contracting parties. In other words most people and organisations can enter into whatever contracts they wish and will, in consequence, be bound by the terms of the contract.

Business people should however be aware of the special care which should be taken with regard to:

- children (someone under the age of 18 years, referred to as a *minor*)
- mental patients
- drunkards
- companies

as they are exceptions to the general rule and special provisions apply. There are some circumstances in which an apparently valid contract cannot be enforced against them.

7.1 Minors

A minor is a person who is under the age of 18. The terms children, infant and minor are often used interchangeably in this respect.

If a contract is made with a minor and, for whatever reason, a problem arises, then the other party may be left unable to sue either the child or the child's parent(s).

The law is extremely favourable to minors. The general rule is that if a minor enters into a contract with an adult, then the minor can enforce the contract against the adult but the adult is unable to enforce the contract against the minor. Such a contract would only become enforceable against the minor if he or she decided to confirm the contract on or after reaching the age of 18. This general rule is applicable to all contracts except:

- contracts for necessaries
- contracts of employment if on the whole it is to his/her advantage
- contracts of continuing obligation/voidable contracts.

We need to look at each of these in turn.

7.1.1   Contracts for necessaries entered into by minors

'Necessaries' are defined by section 3 of the **Sale of Goods Act 1979** as 'goods suitable to the condition in life of the minor and to his actual requirements at the time of sale and delivery'. This definition also covers services, and if the minor is married it includes necessary goods and services required by his/her family. The definition is obviously problematic. It is difficult for the courts to decide which goods/services are necessaries and which are luxuries. Nor is the case law in this area very helpful.

In **Nash v Inman (1908)** a wealthy undergraduate at Trinity College Cambridge bought a quantity of clothing including 11 fancy waistcoats. His father confirmed that although such clothes were suitable to his station in life he was nevertheless well supplied with such clothes already. It was held that the goods were not necessaries; the consequence was that the supplier tailor could not recover the price of the clothes supplied. The onus, it was said, was on the tailor to show that the boy was not adequately supplied.

The whole area is fraught with difficulty. How could the tailor be expected to know whether the boy was adequately supplied or not? Indeed what on earth is meant by the definition of goods *suitable to the condition in life of the minor*? Dealing with a minor must be regarded as a minefield for most business people.

7.1.2   Contracts of employment with minors

A minor is bound by a contract of employment or apprenticeship if, taken as a whole, it is for his/her benefit. It is in effect treated similarly to contracts for necessaries.

In **De Francesco v Barnum (1890)** a girl was apprenticed to a dancer. Her contract of apprenticeship contained very onerous terms: she was entirely at the disposal of her master; she would only be paid if he elected to employ her; she was not allowed to marry during the apprenticeship; he could terminate her employment at any time; and she could not take other employment without his consent. It was held that the terms of her employment were unduly burdensome and so the contract was invalid and the minor was not bound by it.

The age limit of 18 and the anomaly of contracts with a minor may well produce some problem areas. Most contracts of employment nowadays will be fair and of benefit to the minor. The world of pop music, though, might find that some of its contracts, while surviving dispute with those who contracted with them at the age of 18 or over, might not survive so well with a 16-year-old pop star who, their career having taken off, two years later seeks to get out of the long-term contract.

7.1.3   Voidable contracts entered into by minors

Examples of such contracts are contracts to acquire shares in companies, partnership agreements, or contracts to acquire interests in land. The essence of such agreements is that the minor acquires a continuing/enduring benefit to which certain obligations attach. The consequences of a minor entering into such a contract are that it is binding on him/her unless he/she repudiates the contract either before, or within a reasonable time of, reaching 18 years of age.

It should be noted that if the minor has paid money under the contract prior to avoiding the contract, he/she cannot recover the money already paid unless he/she has not yet received any benefit under the contract.

In **Steinberg v Scala (Leeds) Ltd (1923)** a minor applied for shares in a company. Once they had been allotted to her she repudiated the contract. It was held that she was entitled to back out of the contract and so would not be liable for the balance of the purchase price which she still owed. She could not however claim back what she had already paid since she had received some benefits such as the right to vote at meetings and to receive dividends on the shares.

From what we have seen it should be clear that dealing with a minor is a risky business and often dependent on whether or not the minor changes his mind. A crumb of consolation is offered to those who are caught out in such contracts. Section 3 of the **Minors' Contracts Act 1987** confers the power on a court to order the minor to return property which has been unfairly acquired under a contract.

7.2   Mental patients

If a person's property is placed under the management of the *Court of Protection* under the Mental Health Acts, the court or someone appointed by it retains complete control of that property. The mental patient has no capacity to enter into any contract relating to that property.

7.3   Temporary mental illness/incapacity through drink or drugs

If a contract is entered into by someone while they are suffering a temporary mental illness or are drunk or under the influence of drugs, the contract will nevertheless be valid. It will only be invalid if the person can prove that he/she did not understand the nature of the contract *and* that the other party ought to have realised their condition and lack of understanding of the contract.

Even a contract which might initially have been invalid on this basis can be made valid by confirmation by the person at a later time when they can understand what they are doing.

7.4 Companies

If a company is created by statute then that statute will dictate what the company can or cannot do. A company created by *Royal Charter* has all the powers that an individual has to enter into a contract.

A company registered under the Companies Acts is, in theory, limited to entering into contracts which are permitted in its *Memorandum of Association*. (This is one of the documents which is required to be filed at Companies House when a company is created.) Companies have always been able to enter into contracts which are outside the powers contained in the Memorandum of Association. The questions which arose if a contract was outside their powers were:

- Could the contracting party force the company to go through with the contract? The answer prior the **Companies Act 1989** was usually no.
- Could the shareholders do anything about the unauthorised contract? The answer to this was usually yes. They could prevent it being performed and penalise the director responsible.

In practice, since the 1989 Companies Act, usually any contract which a company enters into can be enforced against it. (The shareholders nevertheless can still penalise the director responsible.)

These are all instances where the other party to the contract is not regarded as having legal capability or responsibility to be bound by the contract.

Summary

A contract is *a legally binding agreement between two or more parties.*

A contract is only created when four essential ingredients are satisfied:

- *offer and acceptance*: one party makes a clear proposal which the other party accepts
- *consideration*: each party must give something of some value to the agreement
- *intention to create a legal relationship*: both parties must intend to create a legally binding relationship on the basis of which they may be able to sue and be sued
- *genuineness of consent*: neither party must be coerced into entering into the agreement
- *capacity*: the law excludes some groups from making contracts with or having contracts enforced against them.

Some of the key issues discussed in this chapter are summarised on the diagram on the next page. You may find this useful to consolidate what you have learned.

Now read through these two case studies and answer the questions which follow. Use the summary and diagram as a guide to reading the chapter again on any points on which you are unclear.

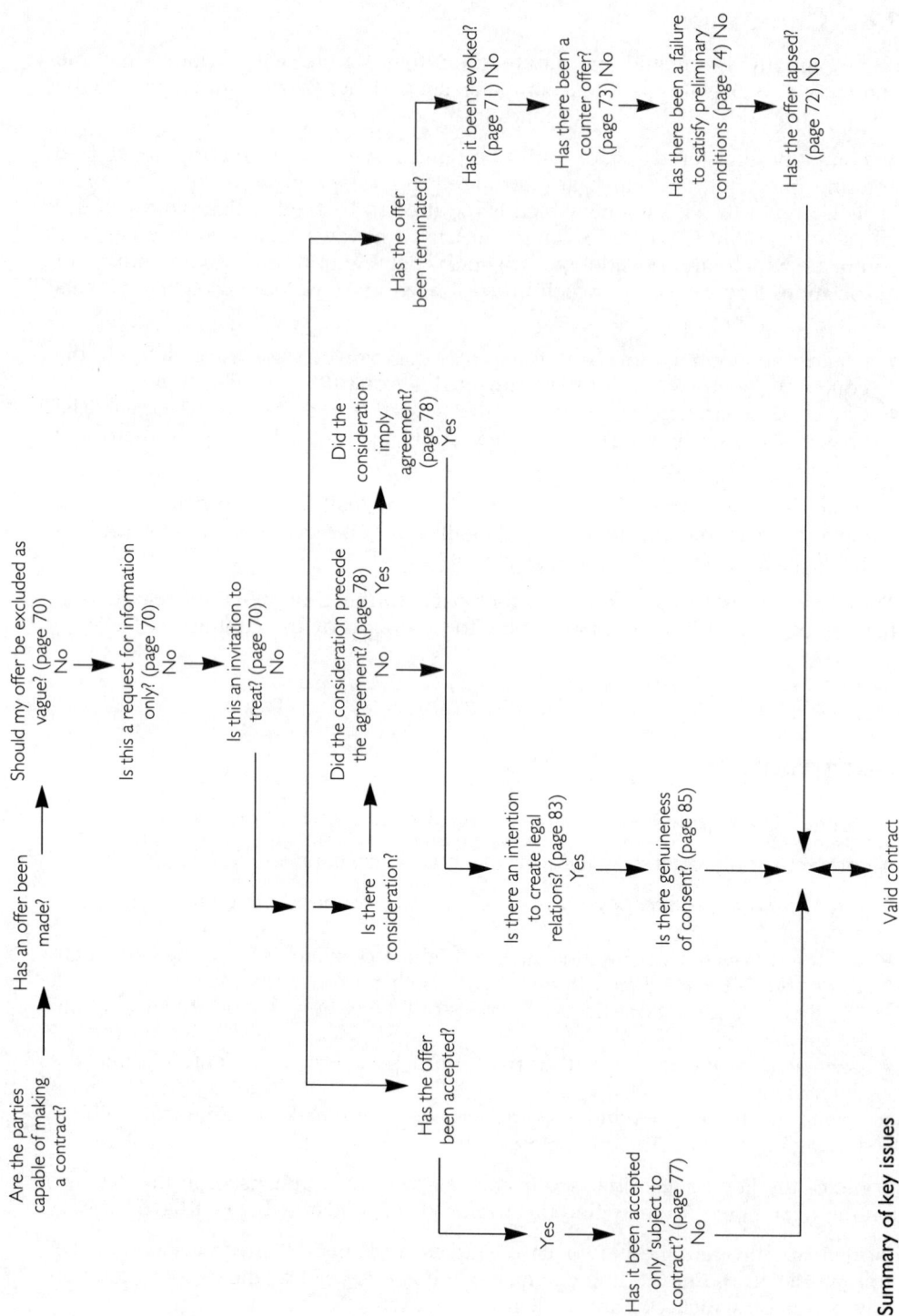

Summary of key issues

CASE STUDY 5

Your firm has recently invested in a new computer hardware system. You had decided to try and the sell the old system. You mentioned this to a supplier, Mr Jones, who was in the office. He asked whether you would be prepared to sell it for £2500. You said that you were not sure. The following day you decided to advertise the system for sale in the local paper. The advert reads:

Zomega 6098 system perfect working order £3000. Tel 987456

Mr Jones saw the advert and rang saying that he would pay £2700 for the system and could give you a £500 cash deposit until funds cleared in his bank account. You told him that you wanted to see what other responses the advert produced and would get back to him. You received no other responses so you telephoned Mr Jones and asked him whether or not he would be prepared to increase the deposit to £1000. Mr Jones said no, that he could only pay £500 in advance. You telephoned him today to say that you would agree to his terms. He told you that he had written to you yesterday withdrawing any offer which he might have been regarded as having made.

1 What is the nature of the original discussion between yourself and Mr Jones? Is it an offer to buy made by Mr Jones, or is it simply a preliminary enquiry?

2 What is the nature of the advert? Would you be bound to sell the system to someone who was prepared to pay the full asking price?

3 What is the status of Mr Jones' suggestion that he will pay £2700?

4 If Mr Jones' proposal to pay £2700 were regarded as an offer, would your response count as a rejection of the offer which would put an end to it?

5 If Mr Jones' proposal to buy were regarded as an offer, would your enquiry about the deposit be considered a request for information or a counter offer which extinguished his original offer?

6 If there was an offer by Mr Jones, does your last telephone call constitute an acceptance?

7 If there was an offer by Mr Jones, would his revocation of the offer yet be effective?

 CASE STUDY 6

You are an employee of a catering business. Your boss, Brian, telephoned you last week to tell you that a new and important rush order had come in. He asked you to work two extra days even though they were in fact agreed with him as holiday. You agreed to work one day on the basis that he pay you double time. Your colleague James heard about the new order and, without being asked, went in to work on his day off. At the end of the day Brian noticed that James was there and told him he was grateful and would pay James at the usual rate. Brian's mother had also, at his request, lent a hand for the day.

Brian's costings for the rush order now appear to be in error and he has said that he cannot afford to pay anyone anything for the extra day's work.

1 In your case, has there been an offer and acceptance?

2 In your case, are you providing sufficient consideration?

3 In your case, would it make any difference if Brian reminded you that one of the original terms of your employment was that you would be flexible in your working in response to the needs of the business?

4 in James' case, was there at any time an agreement between James and Brian? Did the provision of consideration come before or after any agreement? Would it make any difference if Brian and James had had their conversation at the start of the day?

5 In the case of Brian's mother, if payment was not mentioned in the original request, was there consideration? Even though the consideration may have been performed without any mention of payment, was there a reasonable expectation that she should be paid? Would it make any difference if she had helped out before and been paid?

6 In the case of Brian's mother, does the fact that they are related mean there was no intention to create legal relations and so no contract?

Once you are clear on the key ingredients governing the existence of a contract we can now look in more detail at the actual terms of a contract in the next chapter.

9 What are the terms of a contract?

Objectives

> By the end of this chapter you should:
>
> - understand what is meant by an express term of a contract
> - understand how terms can be implied into a contract
> - understand the difference between different types of contractual term
> - realise when terms may be excluded from a contract for being unfair.

1 What are the terms of the contract?

This may seem like a very unnecessary question indeed. Most contracts we enter into are so straightforward that we don't need to think about the actual terms of the contract at all. In the last chapter we looked at the existence of a contract. We looked at what components are required for us to actually be able to say that a contract exists between two particular people. Now we need to look at a particular contract and see what its terms are. A contract could be very simple indeed. You could, for example, go into a record store and see a CD that you want. You ask for it at the checkout, offer the money and pay for it. You then take it home. Clearly there was a contract made between you and the store. Remember the last chapter …

- the store's display would be an *invitation to treat* (an invitation to you to make them an offer)
- your asking for the CD at the cash desk and offering the cash was an *offer*
- their accepting the money was *acceptance*
- the *consideration* was provided by your giving them the money and their giving you the CD
- the *intention to create legal relations* would be implied given the commercial nature of the transaction.

So we know that there is a contract. But do we know anything more detailed about the actual terms of the contract?

What if you get the CD home and discover that the wrong CD had been put into the cover? Or what if you get the CD home and discover that there is a fault on it which makes one track unplayable?

If your problem were that it was the wrong disc in the cover you could point to your express request for that particular CD to say that it was part of the contract.

93

You could say that part of the contract itself was that they should provide you with that particular CD. It was an *express term* of the contract. The matter of the fault on the track might seem less straightforward. The matter of the condition of the CD was not actually discussed by you at all. If you are able to pursue this matter with the store it will not be on the basis of any express term of the contract but rather on what terms will be *implied* into the contract.

This illustration introduces us to the idea of *express and implied terms* of the contract. The situation, however, may be even more complicated than this. Consider the following case study.

  CASE STUDY 1

You decide to buy a new television. You go to a local electrical retailer. Having looked at a number of TVs you see a 'Matawi' TV which looks to be what you want. You are approached by a sales assistant who asks if you need any help. You ask whether the television is compatible with your rather aged video recorder and are told it is. You ask whether they will deliver within the price and they say they will. So you agree to buy it and you give them a cheque for the full amount. As the assistant hands you the till receipt she says that she hopes you enjoy your new television and that of course it will work with any standard remote control unit which is always useful if you lose the original unit.

Consider how you would feel about the following situations:

- The television is not delivered within the next week. You telephone the store to find out why and are told that they only have fortnightly deliveries to your area and it will be another week coming. You are particularly upset as the world series of table tennis was due to be shown this week and you wanted to watch it.
- When the television arrives you discover that it is not a 'Matawi' but a very similar 'Cameron' TV.
- When the television arrives it is the right TV but you discover that it is not colour. You telephone the shop who ask you what you expected for the price. Their range of colour TVs started at over £100 more than you paid.
- The television is not compatible with your video recorder.
- Two weeks later a friend's dog chews and destroys the remote control unit. You buy a standard replacement only to find that it will not work with your TV.

---

1 Now that you have considered how you feel, what would your reaction be if you were the manager of the store? Which of the customer's complaints do you think you should take seriously?

2 Obviously good business sense says that you may want to appease this customer more than you are legally obliged to. It may be worth while to give in to this customer in order to keep them happy. But if the policy of the company is not to give refunds, exchanges or compensation except where you are legally obliged to, what is the situation?

Regarding the delivery date

Was the company's agreement to deliver a term of the contract? The answer surely is yes. It is something which you checked before you agreed to buy and which was part of the bargain. It was part of the *consideration*.

Was it part of the contract as to *when* they would deliver? Certainly there was no *express* term or condition but common sense says that it must be delivered within a reasonable time. Waiting a year for delivery of a new television surely could not be reasonable! But is waiting two weeks unreasonable and who would decide what was reasonable and what was not? The term that delivery would be within a *reasonable* time is what would be called an *implied* term and the courts would interpret what would be reasonable in the particular circumstances. The courts are not deciding matters for the parties, they are simply stepping in with a commonsense solution by implying a term of the contract where the parties had not considered the particular point. The contract might otherwise be made ridiculously unworkable because of a small omission. The courts by applying their own common sense and by implying a term are making the contract workable again.

Regarding the television being a Cameron make rather than a Matawi

The contract was for the purchase of that particular type of television. The shop is in breach of contract by not providing the type of TV which they contracted to provide. The only likely and possible exception to this is if you in fact signed a written contract which included an *express term* allowing the store to substitute a TV of similar standard to that originally contracted for. This is the type of clause commonly included in the small print of package holiday contracts which allows the tour company to alter the accommodation to a different hotel or apartment to the one you had selected from the brochure.

Regarding the television not being colour

There was no discussion between you or the sales assistant as to whether it was a colour television. Assume that there was simply a sign in the shop saying 16 inch television and no other description. You may have assumed that the television was colour but the shop never suggested it was. There was no *express* term of the contract. There is no reason why the courts should imply a term into the contract. The contract for the television which turns out to be black and white is not unworkable, it is simply not what you expected. But the matter is nothing more than your mistake. It is your problem; if it was so important you should expressly have checked with the sales assistant.

Regarding compatibility with your video recorder

You took the precaution of checking with the assistant that the television was compatible with your video. There are two possibilities. It may be that it is regarded as having been an *express* term of the contract that the TV was compatible. The fact that it is not, means that the store is not honouring the terms of the contract by providing a compatible TV. They are said to be in *breach of contract*. Alternatively it might be said that the contract was simpler than this and that there was no actual term that it would be compatible with the video. Instead the statement may be regarded as a *representation* which may under certain circumstances, and if it is inaccurate, entitle you to sue the store.

The distinction between these two concepts is not always an easy one to grasp but whether it is classified as a *misrepresentation* or a *breach of contract* may affect your entitlements if you need to pursue the matter through the courts.

Regarding the remote control

There was certainly some express discussion between you and the sales assistant about the use of a standard remote control unit with that particular television. But what about the timing of it? When was the contract created? When the cheque was handed over and accepted. That is the point where there has been *an offer, an acceptance, consideration and an intention to create legal relations*. The conversation which comes after that is just that: it is a conversation, it is not preliminary to nor part of the contract.

Consider what we looked at in the last chapter about varying the contract after it has been made. In order to vary the contract or create a new one there must be some additional consideration. What additional consideration did you provide for the remark about the remote control? Answer: nothing. You had agreed to buy the TV without even considering the question of what would happen if the remote control unit were lost. The statement made by the sales assistant means that you are now disappointed but it does not form part of the contract at all and there is nothing you can do about the matter now.

2   The different types of statement

From this case study we can see that in looking at the discussions surrounding a contract we have to consider various things.

If we consider there is an *express statement* which covers our complaint there are three possibilities:

- it may be regarded as a *representation* made before the contract which might, if it is incorrect, entitle you to sue on the basis of *misrepresentation,* or
- it may be regarded as an *express term of the contract*, or
- it may amount to *nothing* other than conversation which gives you no legal rights at all against the person who made the statement.

We may however look at the transaction and decide that there wasn't actually any discussion about the particular point. If there was no discussion of the matter then we may find that we have no legal rights against the other party to the contract. Nevertheless it may be that our gut reaction says that to leave us with no rights at all is unfair. It is in these types of situation that the courts or Parliament may intervene and *imply* a term into the contract. So *implied terms* of the contract may come from two sources:

- the courts may decide to imply a term. Usually this is in order to make an otherwise straightforward contract workable when there is one particular aspect which was not fully considered by the parties
- Parliament may imply a term into the contract in the form of a statute or other legislation. Usually these provisions are designed to protect the consumer against unfair terms in contracts prepared by unscrupulous business people.

3 What is the status of an express statement?

It is obviously of vital importance to anyone entering into a contract to know exactly what the contract commits them to. They need to know what they are entitled to expect of the other party and what the other party can expect of them. People rarely, if ever, enter into contracts simply by making an offer and it being accepted. Usually there is some discussion about the product first. For example, if you go to buy a car your conversation is unlikely to be limited to how much it is. The buyer will want to know the type of car (although that may be self-evident); the buyer will want to know the age of the car; whether it has any defects; and, if they want to buy it, whether it will be delivered and if so when. These various points may be negotiated orally or in writing. There are three possibilities for statements made during these negotiations:

- they may be regarded as *express terms* of the contract
- they may be regarded as *representations* which would entitle the buyer to sue if they are inaccurate
- they may be regarded as *representations* which are not part of the contract itself and which do not entitle the buyer to sue on any other basis, even if they are inaccurate.

We need therefore to look at three things:

- we need to decide what counts as a statement or representation. Some parts of a conversation are so inconsequential that to base legal liability on them would be practically impossible, even if they are part of negotiations leading up to a contract
- we need to decide whether or not a statement or representation is part of the contract itself and whether the innocent party could sue for breach of contract
- if the statement or representation is not a term of the contract we need to decide whether it is a statement about which the innocent party can do nothing or whether it amounts to a 'misrepresentation' – a formal legal concept which would entitle an innocent party to sue even though the statement was not part of the contract itself.

3.1 What counts as a statement/representation?

In order to decide whether a statement could be a contractual term or a misrepresentation we first need to decide whether it was a *serious* statement at all. Some things may be said in the course of a pre-contract negotiation which were not intended to be taken seriously and simply amounted to sales talk. These frivolous statements are known as *trader's puffs* and usually no legal liability is involved. For example, in the sale of a car a salesperson might say that it 'goes like a bomb'. Such a statement is obviously not meant to be taken literally and relied upon. (Quite apart from anything else you would find it very difficult indeed to go to court and explain exactly what the salesman meant and how the vehicle did not measure up to the statement.)

3.2   Is a statement a term of the contract?

In order to know on what basis you might be able to sue the other party you need to be able to distinguish statements which are *express terms* of the contract from those which are simply representations made before the contract is entered into and which might amount to a *misrepresentation* on which you could sue the other party.

It may be very difficult to tell which is which. During the course of creating the contract there may be a number of matters discussed. It is obvious to both parties that some of those statements would be relied upon by the other party in deciding whether or not to enter into the contract. But do they actually form part of the contract?

There appears to be no hard and fast rule as to whether a statement is a representation or a term of the contract. A statement which starts its life as a representation in pre-contract discussions may 'harden' into a contract term. It is a question of intention. The test though is objective in that one doesn't look at what those particular contracting parties intended but rather what two 'reasonable' people in the same position would intend. Would two 'reasonable' people have thought that they were pre-contract representations or part of the contract itself?

In trying to reach this decision there are a number of guidelines which we can bear in mind.

3.2.1   The strength of the statement

Two cases where similar types of statements were made illustrate this principle. The statements were of similar type but of different strength.

In **Ecay v Godfrey (1947)** a contract was entered into for the sale of a boat. Prior to the contract the seller informed the buyer that the boat was sound but nevertheless he suggested that the buyer should have it examined. The court considered whether the statement was an express term of the contract or a pre-contract representation which, if all the requirements were satisfied, might amount to misrepresentation. The court held that the statement was a representation. Had it been a term of the contract the buyer, on later discovering that the boat was unsound, could simply have sued the seller for breach of contract. Given however that the court decided it was not a term but a pre-contract representation, the buyer would be left trying to rely on the quite complicated rules of misrepresentation in order to successfully sue the seller.

In **Schawel v Reade (1913)** the seller of a horse, in order to prevent the buyer from discovering a defect, stated that it was sound and that it did not need examining. This statement as to soundness was held to be an express term of the contract.

3.2.2   The importance of the statement

Here one has to consider the importance of the statement to the person to whom the statement is made. The greater the significance of the statement the more chance there is of it being regarded as a term of the contract.

In **Bannerman v White (1861)** the potential buyer of a quantity of hops emphasised that it was absolutely essential to him that the hops should not have been treated with sulphur. The seller expressly stated that no sulphur had been used in the production of the hops. The buyer bought the hops and subsequently discovered that they did contain sulphur. It was held that the statement by the seller as to the absence of sulphur was intended to be a term of the contract, and that because the seller had breached the contract the buyer was entitled to send the hops back and sue the seller.

3.2.3 The relative knowledge of the two parties

The general principle here is that a statement made by someone with expert knowledge to someone without such knowledge is more likely to be regarded as a term of the contract than a similar statement made by a layman to an expert. A comparison of two cases illustrates this.

In **Oscar Chess Ltd v Williams (1957)** an individual sold a car to a car dealer and in all innocence described it as a 1948 Morris when in fact it was a 1939 model worth considerably less. The Court of Appeal held that the statement as to the car's age was a representation and not a term of the contract because the buyers, being car dealers, had greater expertise than the seller and were in a better position to discover the true age of the car.

In **Dick Bentley Productions Ltd v Harold Smith (Motors) Ltd (1965)** the same rationale applied. Here a car dealer sold a car stating that it had only done 20,000 miles since the fitting of a replacement engine. In fact it had done 100,000 miles. It was held that the statement as to mileage was a contract term. The seller being a car dealer was in a better position than the buyer to discover the true mileage of the car.

3.2.4 The form of the contract

If the oral negotiations entered into by the parties are followed by the drawing up of a written contract, then the absence of the statement from the written contract may indicate that it was intended to be a representation and not a term of the contract. For example in

Routledge v McKay (1954) the parties to a potential contract discussed the possible sale and purchase of a motor cycle on 23 October. The seller innocently told the buyer that it was a 1942 model whereas in fact it was a 1930 model. A week later a written contract was drawn up and signed by the parties. Nowhere in the written contract was there any reference to the date of the model. It was held that the oral statement made on 23 October was a representation and not a contract term.

3.3   If the statement is a representation rather than a contractual term does it amount to misrepresentation?

We have already seen that there may be some statements/representations made in the course of pre-contract negotiations which do not entitle the innocent party to sue the party who made the statement. If the statement is not a contract term then in order for the innocent party to be able to sue they must show that the statement was a *misrepresentation*.

The essence of misrepresentation is that the statement must be

- a *false* statement of *fact*
- which *induces* the innocent party to *enter into the contract*.

3.3.1   Statements of fact distinguished from statements of opinion

The first thing therefore that we need to do is to look at the statement and decide whether it is a statement of fact or of opinion. If the statement is opinion then the innocent party, however aggrieved they may feel, cannot sue for misrepresentation. Again we have to look at whether a reasonable person would consider the statement to be fact or opinion. Some matters are relatively straightforward. If I agree to sell you a personal stereo cassette player and I say that it has 'great tone', that is likely to be a matter of opinion. My idea of 'great tone' may be entirely different to yours, and your idea of 'great tone' may be entirely different to anyone else's. If on the other hand I say that the cassette has auto rewind that is a statement of *fact*. If there is no auto rewind I have made a *false statement of fact*. The first limb of misrepresentation is satisfied.

Both these statements are relatively easy to deal with. Some statements are less easy to categorise as fact/opinion. To describe a property as 'desirable commercial premises' sounds at first hearing like a statement of opinion. Who can say whether premises are 'desirable commercial premises'? Consider though if the facts show that there is a prohibition on using the premises for anything other than a house. The change in the facts means that the premises are not 'desirable *commercial* premises' and the statement could be one of *fact* rather than *opinion*.

3.3.2   Statements of fact distinguished from statements of future intention

For a false statement to amount to a misrepresentation it must relate to an existing fact. A statement of intention as to future conduct may not amount to a misrepresentation if the promised conduct never occurs owing to unforeseen circumstances, or perhaps even a change of mind. If however the intention never really existed, even at the time the statement was made, that may amount to misrepresentation.

Imagine I enter into a contract with you to borrow £500 from you on terms that it will be repaid in a year's time. In order to persuade you to lend me the money I say that I want to use it to build a tennis court to which the public will be allowed access. If I do intend to use it for that purpose but I am frustrated by being unable to secure planning permission, then my representation of future intention is unlikely to be a misrepresentation so that you could not sue me.

If however I never actually intended to build the tennis court but was borrowing money in order to pay off my credit card bills, that could be a misrepresentation. It would amount to a false statement of fact as to the state of my mind at the time, which, according to Lord Justice Bowen, could be 'as much a fact as the state of [my] digestion'.

3.3.3 Can silence be a statement of fact?

The general rule is that silence is not misrepresentation. The usual idea is that if you say nothing at all about the state or condition etc of an item you are selling, then it is up to the buyer to look out for himself: the idea of 'let the buyer beware'.

This general rule is just that though. It is a general rule to which there are exceptions. Telling a half truth which although technically accurate gives a misleading impression could amount to misrepresentation by silence. We all know how to do it and have probably been caught out doing it at some stage in our youth. It is politely called being economical with the truth. It means making a true statement in such a way as to effectively disguise the true picture. The intention of telling that particular piece of the truth is to give a false impression as to the overall situation. An example of this was the case of

> **R v Kylsant (1931)** where a company stated in its share prospectus that a regular dividend had been paid during the Depression years. This statement was technically true but it gave the impression that the company was profitable during the Depression. In fact the dividends had been paid from saved up pre-Depression profits. The statement although technically true was a half truth which could amount to a misrepresentation to investors.

The other time when silence can amount to misrepresentation is when a statement is made which is true at the time but then circumstances change and the statement becomes untrue. To remain silent in that situation could amount to misrepresentation. For example in

> **With v O'Flanagan (1936)**, negotiations for the sale of a medical practice were taking place. The seller stated that the practice was worth £2000 a year. This statement was true at the time but four months later, due to the seller's illness, the value of the practice had declined to virtually nothing. It was held by the Court of Appeal that the seller's failure to update the situation amounted to a misrepresentation.

There are also certain situations where the courts will apply the principle of 'utmost good faith'. The parties are required either by the courts or by statute to make full disclosure of any material facts. In other words silence *can* amount to misrepresentation. This would, for example, apply to contracts between business partners and most commonly to insurance companies. It is not sufficient when applying for insurance simply to answer accurately all the questions asked of one. There is also an overriding duty to disclose anything which might affect the insurer's decision to give insurance cover.

3.3.4   Has the misstatement induced entry into the contract?

Once you have established that the false statement is one which is capable of being a misrepresentation, you then need to show that it does amount to misrepresentation by showing that the innocent party relied on the statement and that it induced them to enter into the contract.

The innocent party must have relied on the statement. If the person to whom the statement was made carries out their own investigations regardless of the statement having been made, then they are unlikely to be able to say that they relied on the statement.

Imagine, for example, that you go to buy a car. The seller tells you how wonderful the car is, says that it has not been in an accident and that the engine is completely sound. You hear what he says but then ask a friend who is an engineer to go and check the car over for you. Your friend does a bad job and does not check the car properly. He tells you that what the seller has told you is true. In fact it is untrue. The car has been involved in a major accident and the engine is in very poor condition. You are unlikely to be able to sue the seller on the basis of misrepresentation. He made false statements of fact but you did not rely on them in entering into the contract. You relied on what your friend reported. You cannot sue the seller. Unless you want to try and sue your friend you may be left without any comeback at all.

This principle does not however place any obligation on the buyer to make their own enquiries. Ironically, if you had taken the seller's word for it and not asked your friend to check the vehicle you might have been successful in suing the seller for misrepresentation.

✎   CASE STUDY 2

You are the owner of an industrial waste disposal site which you bought last year from Excreta International Inc. At the start of negotiations for the sale the representative of the selling company assured you that there was no other licensed waste disposal site within a 50 mile radius. The turnover of disposal fees he said grossed £300,000 a year. He said at the time that you could inspect the books if you wished. He also told you at the time that the licence fee payable to the local authority was £5000 a year. At the time of the purchase you made informal enquiries of a friend who is in the same line of business to see if he thought the price appropriate and the operation viable.

Since purchasing the site you have received a notice from the council demanding an annual fee of £8000. When you question the local authority they tell you that Excreta International Inc. were advised at the outset that the licence fee was on a sliding scale rising from £2000 in the first year of its operation to £10,000 within five years. Since the time you purchased your site, a new site has been licensed less than 10 miles away and the licence was granted several months after you had started negotiations to buy the site but before the contract was concluded. You have also recently been told by an employee that the gross disposal fees never exceeded £250,000 in any year.

In this situation you understandably feel that you have been 'sold a pup'. But in order to examine whether or not you have any rights against Excreta International Inc. you need to impose some structure on the problem.

Firstly you need to consider what the factors are about which you are unhappy. Let's call these your 'grievances':

a) the fact that you were led to believe that the gross fees were 20% higher than you now believe that they were
b) the fact that the licence fee is higher than you expected
c) the fact that yours is not the only site within a 50 mile radius.

Secondly you need to consider whether any of these matters were *terms of the contract* (assume for the purpose of this case study that they were not).

Thirdly you need to consider whether the seller might be liable for *misrepresentation*. You need to consider whether there was a *misstatement of fact* which *induced* you to enter into the contract. You need to consider this in respect of each of your grievances.

a) Consider:

- Was there a misstatement of fact? Answer: if the information which you have is correct – yes.
- Did it induce you to enter into the contract? The answer to this lies in your own mind. Well did it? Was it one of the factors which persuaded you to buy the site?
- Does it matter that you were offered the books but did not look at them. The answer to this is yes and no.

We have seen that there is no actual obligation on you to check the books. Therefore failing to check them does not in theory exclude you from being able to claim misrepresentation. On the other hand consider what would happen if the matter came to court. The seller's lawyer would be trying to show that although his client's statement was incorrect, it could not amount to misrepresentation as you had not relied on it on entering into the contract. The line of questioning which he or she will follow is likely to be:

'So the matter of the gross fees was obviously very important to you. You might not have entered into the contract in the first place had you known the true level of fees? You really expect us to believe that it was of such importance to you when you did not take the precaution of checking what the seller said, even when the books were offered to you?'

Here you can see that although being offered sight of the books does not preclude you from claiming misrepresentation, in practice it is likely to weaken your case and make a successful claim less likely.

b) Consider:

- Was there a misstatement of fact? Answer – no. At the time the statement was made it was correct. The real complaint is not the statement but the silence regarding the change in the fee. So could this silence constitute a misstatement of fact? Clearly the seller knew about the increasing fee. Clearly the effect of the omission to tell you about the increases was to distort the real picture. It may well be one of those few occasions when silence could constitute a misstatement of fact.

- Did it induce you to enter into the contract? Again the answer here lies in your own mind and also whether you made any other checks to discover that the, licence fees were variable.

c) Consider:

- Was there a misstatement of fact? If at the time the statement was made there was no other licence granted the statement was technically true. If the granting of the new licence and the opening of the new site had taken place *after* the contract was concluded it would simply have been 'tough luck' on you the buyer. But the licence was applied for and granted before the contract was concluded. Again the seller's silence could amount to a misstatement of fact. The seller made a statement which was true at the time but became untrue before the contract was concluded. There is an obligation on the seller to update that information.
- Did it induce you to enter into the contract? Again the answer here lies in your own mind and actions. If you had relied either on your enquiry of your friend as to the likelihood of another licence being granted nearby, or on your own enquiries of the local authority itself, then you may be prevented from claiming that you *relied* on what the seller told you. Rather you would have relied on other erroneous information.

3.4 Does the timing of a statement have any bearing on its status?

We have already touched upon this but it is an area which seems to cause considerable problems to students and so is considered worthy of separate treatment and reiteration.

We have looked at statements made by the other party to the contract and asked whether they are

- contractual terms or
- misrepresentations or
- false statements which may make you feel aggrieved but which give you no right to sue the other party to the contract.

What relevance does the timing of a statement have on its status?

3.4.1 Statements made before the contract is made

Statements made before the contract is concluded may amount to any of the three types of statement: contractual terms; representations in respect of which the innocent party may be able to sue for misrepresentation; or simple statements that have no legal status.

The precise timing of the statement may have some bearing on the objective test of whether the statement is a term of the contract itself or simply a representation made in negotiations leading to the making of the contract. One may say that the timing of the transaction reflects the intention of the parties as to what would or would not be the actual terms of the contract.

3.4.2   Statements made after the contract is made

A statement made after the contract is made cannot be a misrepresentation. Remember that one of the requirements is that the misstatement of fact must *induce* entry into the contract. It cannot possibly do that if it is not even made until after the contract is created.

A statement made after the contract is made cannot be a contractual term either. Consider the example earlier in this chapter about the TV and the sales assistant's statement that you could use any standard remote control unit with it. That statement could not be a misrepresentation because it was made after the contract itself was made. It could not be a term of the contract as it came too late. Remember the issue of consideration and variation of the contract once it is made. If the contract is to be amended, added to or in any way varied, each party must bring some fresh consideration to the agreement. A simple statement, albeit incorrect, by one party after the contract was made usually has no legal effect at all.

This point about whether a particular statement is 'in time' to form part of the contract is most usually encountered in the business situation where a standard notice tells customers/clients the procedural terms of the relationship between the parties. Anyone who wants a particular term in a contract must be sure to make sure that the matter is mentioned *before* the contract is made. Some cases illustrate the point quite nicely.

Olley v Marlborough Court Ltd (1949) concerned a guest in a hotel. The hotel sought to avoid paying compensation to the guest by relying on a list of conditions relating to their obligations which was displayed on the back of the hotel bedroom door. The hotel was unsuccessful because the court held that the contract had been made in the hotel lobby when the guest booked in. The 'conditions' on the back of the door were not seen by the guest until after the contract had been made. They could not therefore be terms of the contract. They were simply statements with no legal status at all.

Similarly in **Chapleton v Barry UDC** the supposed statements which were claimed to be terms of the contract came too late after the contract was made to count as terms at all.

In **Chapleton v Barry UDC (1940)** the facts were that the council left a pile of deckchairs next to a sign which told passers-by the prices for the hire of the chairs and invited them to take a chair and obtain a ticket from the attendant when he came round. A man took a chair and sat on it. Later the attendant came round, collected the money, and gave the man a ticket. The deckchair collapsed under the man and injured him. The council claimed not to be liable because it said on the back of the ticket that they accepted no liability. Amongst other findings the court found that what was written on the back of the ticket could not amount to terms of the contract as the contract was made when the man took the chair and sat on it, at the same time incurring the contractual obligation to pay its hire.

4   Types of contractual terms

So far we have been looking at whether or not a statement is a term of the contract at all. But once we have made the decision that the statement is an *express term* of the contract we then need to decide what *type* of term it is. The fact that it is a term of the contract at all means that if the statement is false the person who made the statement can be sued for breach of contract. The type of term, or in other words its importance, will determine what rights or remedies the innocent party may be entitled to.

So far this may sound unduly academic but the practical effects are far from that. What type of term the other party has broken may decide whether you can get out of the contract (called 'rescission') and claim compensation (called 'damages') or whether you must go through with your part of the contract but may get some compensation.

Imagine that you have bought a car. You discover that it has previously been in a serious accident. You are very concerned about safety and on finding out about the accident you would like the garage to take the car back and give you your money back. Assume there was a contractual term that the car had not been in a major accident. What type of term it is may determine whether you are entitled to return the car or whether you must keep what you consider to be an unsafe vehicle and simply accept some monetary compensation.

Broadly there are three types of contractual term:

- the condition
- the warranty
- the intermediate term.

This latter term is the subject of some discussion but is really a compromise according to the facts. The courts have introduced it to allow themselves to say that a particular term may be a *condition* in one factual situation and yet a *warranty* in a different situation.

4.1   Conditions

A condition is the more important of the types of contractual term. Breach of a *condition* would entitle the innocent party to bring the contract to an end *and* claim damages.

4.2   Warranties

A warranty is a less important term of a contract. Traditionally it was thought of as being subsidiary or peripheral to the main purpose of the contract. If one party did not comply with a warranty, the innocent party would be entitled to damages but not to refuse to go through with their part of the contract.

4.3 Deciding whether a term is a condition or a warranty

Whether a term is a condition or a warranty depends very much on the state of affairs existing at the time of making the contract, including the practical effect of failure to comply with that particular term on the contract as a whole. Two cases are traditionally used to illustrate the difference between a condition and a warranty. They are useful illustrations since both cases deal with the failure of an opera singer to turn up on a date agreed in the contract.

In **Bettini v Gye (1876)** the singer had contracted to turn up six days before performances started in order to rehearse. The singer turned up three days late but in time for the performances.

In **Poussard v Spiers (1876)** the singer contracted to turn up for the performances. Five days before the first performance she was taken ill and it was clear she would be unable to attend.

In the first case (**Bettini v Gye**) the provision requiring the singer to turn up on time was held to be a warranty. The contract could still be effective. The employer was not entitled to dismiss the singer, only to damages for the failure to attend the earlier rehearsals as promised. In the second case (**Poussard v Spiers**) the provision requiring the singer to turn up on time was held to be a condition and the singer's failure to comply with it entitled the employer to terminate the contract and to hire another singer.

The term that was breached in each case was a provision requiring the singer to turn up at a particular time. Clearly though the courts must have looked at the term in the context of the contract as a whole and the difference in the two contracts accounts for the difference in the classification of the terms.

It seems now that the courts have in fact gone further than this. Not only will they look at the particular term in the context of the contract as a whole but they may also look at the nature and effect of the breach in deciding whether the term is a condition or a warranty. These 'in-between' terms can be either warranties or conditions depending on the effect of the breach. The courts basically wait and see how bad the damage is before classifying the term.

This type of intermediate term was looked at in the case of

Hong Kong Fir Shipping Co Ltd v Kawasaki Kisen Kaisha Ltd (1962). A shipowner had expressly promised that a ship was seaworthy. What was actually stated was that the ship was 'in every way fitted for ordinary cargo service'. The agreement was to charter the ship for two years. In fact the engines were defective and the result was that the charter was delayed for four months of the two year total. The question was: was the term as to seaworthiness a condition or a warranty? If it was a condition then the charterer could repudiate the contract, charter a ship elsewhere and claim damages on top. If it was a warranty the charterer must go through with the contract but would be entitled to damages for the delay.

In the Court of Appeal they recognised that it was difficult to categorise this term as either a condition or a warranty. Even if you looked at the contract as a whole and put the term into the context of that whole contract, how *important* the term was might depend on *how* it was breached and what the practical effects of the breach were. Lord Justice Diplock said of such terms:

> '... all that can be predicted is that some breaches will, and others will not, give rise to an event which will deprive the party not in default of substantially the whole benefit which it was intended that he should obtain from the contract; and the legal consequences of the breach of such [a term], unless provided for expressly in the contract, depend on the nature of the event to which the breach gives rise and do not automatically flow from a prior classification [of the term] as a "condition" or a "warranty" ...'

In the particular facts of the case it was decided that, as the charter still had 20 months to run, the breach in question had not deprived the charterers of substantially the whole benefit that it was intended to have by the contract and so they were not entitled to terminate the contract. In other words this *intermediate* term was on the particular facts determined to be like a warranty. If the effect of the breach had been to put the ship in dock for 18 months it might have been considered to be like a condition.

5   Implied terms

Express terms are terms expressly stated either orally or in writing by the parties to the contract. They reflect what the parties have actually agreed upon.

Implied terms are terms 'injected' into the contract from some outside source. They may refer to aspects of the contract which the parties or a party had never considered or perhaps overlooked. They may on the other hand simply confirm what was intended by the parties but which they had never bothered to express.

Terms can be implied into a contract in three ways:

- by common law (in other words the decision of the courts)
- by custom (again it is the courts' responsibility)
- by statute.

5.1   Terms implied by common law

The courts will sometimes imply terms into a contract in order to give effect to what the parties must have intended. The implication of such terms is literally to make the contract work – to give it what is known as *business efficacy*. In the words of Lord Justice Mackinnon in **Shirlaw v Southern Foundries Ltd (1939)**, usually:

'that which in any contract is left to be implied and need not be expressed is something so obvious that it goes without saying; so that, if, while the parties were making their bargain, an officious bystander were to suggest some express provision for it in their agreement, they would testily suppress him with a common "Oh, of course!"'

This principle of giving business efficacy to a contract is sometimes referred to as the doctrine of 'The Moorcock' after a leading case of that name.

In **The Moorcock (1889)** there was an agreement whereby one party was allowed to unload his ship at the other party's wharf. It was known to both parties that inevitably at low tide the ship would settle on the river bed. However there was nothing expressly stated in the contract that the river bed was safe and would not damage the ship. Whilst unloading the ship was damaged when it settled on a ridge at the wharf at low tide. Could a term be implied into the contract that the wharf owner undertook that the river bed was suitable and reasonably safe for the shipowner to moor his ship. Such a term was implied by the court and since the wharf owner was in breach of this term he was liable to pay damages to this shipowner.

Many business contracts are subject to established terms implied by common law. In contracts of employment, for example, both employers and employees have imposed upon them various implied terms. Amongst other things it is implied that an employer will provide a safe system of work for his/her employees and that an employee will obey reasonable orders and owes a duty of good faith to his/her employer. These particular implied terms are well established but the court can always introduce new ones to fit the facts of a particular case. They are using their own common sense – or the 'officious bystander test'.

5.2 Terms implied by custom

Terms can be implied into a contract by virtue of local custom relating to a particular trade.

In **Hutton v Warren (1836)** a tenant was given notice to quit by his landlord. A term was implied into the agricultural lease that the tenant was entitled to be compensated for the seeds and labour expended on the land. Such an implication arose as a result of custom which was automatically incorporated into all such contracts unless there was an inconsistent express term.

5.3 Terms implied by statute

Terms may be implied into a contract by statute. The best known examples are the terms implied into contracts for the sale of goods by virtue of sections 12–15 of the **Sale of Goods Act 1979** as amended by the **Sale and Supply of Goods**

Act 1994. Originally some of these terms were implied by common law but have now been incorporated into statute in a 'tidying up' operation. Many of the terms were previously implied by common law. That is why some of the cases which relate to the 1979 Act pre-date it. They are still, however, good examples and authorities on the particular points.

The sections are all really designed to make sure that the consumer gets what they think they are getting. First of all we need to consider exactly which contracts the Sale of Goods Act will cover. It is then perhaps most useful to look briefly to see what the main sections do and to look at each section in turn in more detail.

5.3.1   Contracts covered by the Sale of Goods Act

A contract for the sale of goods is defined by the Act itself as 'a contract by which the seller transfers or agrees to transfer the property in goods to the buyer for a money consideration called the price'.

A contract for the sale of goods is a contract of the types that we have looked at in the last chapter. Usually the general legal principles relating to contracts are applied alongside the rules contained in the Act. The only time they will not apply is if they are actually inconsistent with the Sale of Goods Act.

The definition of a contract for the sale of goods also mentions the word 'price'. The consideration for a contract for the sale of goods must always be at least partly in money. This stipulation excludes from the ambit of the Act contracts whereby goods are exchanged for other goods (contracts of barter). Contracts of *part exchange* are however covered by the Act.

So for example consider the following situations:

a) Desmond enters into a transaction whereby he agrees with Tony to exchange his bicycle in return for £20
b) Martina agrees with Tod that she will sell him her new tennis racquet for £5 and his chess set.
c) Alison and Natasha agree that in return for Alison giving Natasha a crystal vase, Natasha will give Alison two video tapes.

Of these examples a) and b) are covered by the Act, c) is not.

5.3.2   The provisions of the Sale of Goods Act in outline

The most commonly known provisions of the Sale of Goods Act are probably the following:

- **section 12** inserts into contracts an *implied term* that the seller has the *right to sell* the goods
- **section 13** inserts into contracts an *implied term* that the *goods correspond to any description* of them, or *if sold by sample* that the *goods correspond to the sample.*
- **section 14** inserts into contracts an *implied term* that goods sold are of *satisfactory quality* and *fit for the purpose for which they were intended.*

5.3.3   Section 12 of the Sale of Goods Act 1979

Section 12 states among other things that there is an implied condition in all contracts for the sale of goods that the seller has the right to sell the goods. Therefore if the goods are stolen, the seller will be in breach of a condition and liable to the buyer for the full price of the goods. (The practical problem with this provision of course is that it may be difficult or impossible to trace the seller!)

In **Rowland v Divall (1923)**, after the buyer had been using a car for four months the police took it away because it had been stolen before coming into the seller's possession. The buyer, deprived of his car, took action to recover the full price and succeeded because there was a breach of section 12 (or rather its earlier equivalent!). The seller, although unaware of the fact at the time of the sale, did not actually own the vehicle and therefore the buyer received nothing valuable from the contract. The court said that there had been a complete failure on the seller's part to provide the agreed consideration, therefore he was obliged to repay to the buyer the whole of the purchase price.

5.3.4   Section 13 of the Sale of Goods Act 1979

This section provides that where goods are sold by description there is an implied condition that the goods must correspond to the description. (Furthermore if the sale of goods is by sample as well as by description then both must correspond.) If there is a breach of section 13 the buyer is entitled to reject the goods even though he suffers no real damage.

In **Re Moore and Landauer (1921)** X agreed to buy 3,000 tins of fruit from Y. It was agreed that the fruit was to be packed in cases of 30 tins. When the fruit was delivered, half the cases contained only 24 tins but all 3,000 tins were delivered. Despite an arbitrator's finding that there was no difference in value between the tins packed as they were and as they should have been, nevertheless X was entitled to reject the entire consignment as there was a breach of section 13.

It should be noted, however, that because of section 15A of the Sale of Goods Act 1979 (which was added by the Sale and Supply of Goods Act 1994), where a buyer is not dealing as a consumer and a breach of a term in sections 13, 14 or 15 is so slight that it would be unreasonable for the buyer to reject the goods, the breach is not to be treated as a breach of condition but may be treated as a breach of warranty. So, if the same situation arose today the decision would probably be different.

Deviation from description may, in any event, occasionally be so minute as to be insignificant. In situations like this the courts may apply what is known as the '*de minimis*' rule. The rule allows the courts to say that a breach of contract is so trifling as not to be worthy of the award of compensation. However the principle is not applied lightly and each case has to be taken on its merits.

⚖

> In **Arcos v Ronaason (1933)** A agreed to sell to R a quantity of staves half an inch thick. Only 5 per cent of the staves were the correct thickness but nearly all the rest were less than 9/16ths of an inch thick. An arbitrator confirmed that the staves were merchantable (satisfactory). Nevertheless the court said that there was a breach of section 13. The court emphasised that 'a ton does not mean about a ton, still less does half an inch mean about half an inch'.

5.3.5   Section 14 of the Sale of Goods Act 1979

This provision, unlike the previous two which we have looked at, only applies where a seller sells goods in the course of a business. The definition section of the Act says that 'business' includes a profession and the activities of any government department or local authority. It is clearly wide ranging but clearly what will not be covered is an individual selling their own possessions rather than commercial products.

This section implies a term that the goods will be of *satisfactory quality*. Further it provides that where the buyer expressly or impliedly makes known to the seller any particular purpose for which the goods are being bought there is an implied condition that the goods supplied under the contract will be *reasonably fit for that purpose*.

Looking first at the question of satisfactory quality under section 14(2). Let us say that you go and buy a pair of walking boots. On getting the boots home you discover that the soles on the particular pair which were packed up for you are coming away from the uppers. You would return them to the shop. Your complaint would be that they are not of satisfactory quality. If you buy walking boots they must at the very least start out life fit for their job.

Consider also what might happen when you take the boots back to the shop. They may say that they are very sorry and that they will have them mended for you. Even if they have a repairing cobbler in the store you are still not obliged to accept this as a solution. It is irrelevant that the goods can be made of satisfactory quality quickly, easily and cheaply. Because they are of unsatisfactory quality to start with you are entitled to return them and to receive your money back.

The goods must not only start their 'life' of satisfactory quality but they must also remain satisfactory for a reasonable time. Imagine that the boots that you bought did not appear faulty when you got them home but on your first weekend away the stitching comes undone and the soles begin to separate from the uppers. You might not expect them to last forever but certainly more than one weekend. They were not after all sold to you as 'disposable' walking boots. Nor were they sold to you as lightweight beach shoes – whose durability might be limited in tough walking terrain! Your complaint would again be based on section 14(2) and on the fact that the boots were not of satisfactory quality.

There are two important limitations to section 14(2). The provision as to satisfactory quality does not apply where

- the defects were drawn to the buyer's attention prior to the purchase. So, for example, where goods are marked in a shop as 'Slight Seconds' it is up to the buyer to check the particular item carefully to make sure that they are satisfied with any defect. Returning a garment later saying that the stitching has come undone is likely to receive short shrift in this situation
- the buyer has examined the goods and that examination ought to have revealed the defect. A few stores actually include on the receipt a statement to be signed by the buyer saying that they have examined the goods and that they are in satisfactory condition. Clearly one would not be expected to start taking a product apart during such an inspection but the clause might prevent you from returning a product with a readily visible defect.

Secondly we need to consider the matter of *fitness for purpose*. Section 14(3) provides that where a seller sells goods in the course of a business and the buyer expressly or impliedly makes known to the seller any particular purpose for which the goods are being bought, there is an implied condition that the goods supplied under the contract will be reasonably fit for that purpose.

As with the satisfactory quality provision the seller must be selling in the course of a business but, in addition, the buyer must expressly or impliedly communicate to the seller the purpose for which the product is being bought.

In **Frost v Aylesbury Dairy (1905)** a woman was infected with typhoid from milk supplied by the dairy. The Court of Appeal held that the dairy knew, *by implication*, the purpose for which the plaintiff bought the milk. That was for domestic purposes and clearly the milk was not fit for that purpose.

In **Griffiths v Conway (Peter) Ltd (1939)** a person who had a particularly sensitive skin bought a tweed coat. After wearing the coat the person contracted dermatitis. The evidence was that a person with normal skin would not have suffered from the coat. The seller in this case was not however held liable as the particular purpose (i.e. to be worn by someone with a sensitive skin) had not been made known to them before the sale.

The other matter to bear in mind is that the statute says the goods must be *reasonably* fit for the purpose. It does not say they must be absolutely fit.

In **Heil v Hedges (1951)** a person bought pork chops from the seller. The buyer did not cook the chops completely. The chops contained a parasitic worm which made the buyer ill. The evidence was that had the chops been properly cooked the worm would have been killed and would have caused the buyer no harm. Here it was held that the seller was not liable as the chops were *reasonably* fit for their purpose.

The buyer will also be precluded from relying on this provision as to fitness for purpose where it is apparent that:

- either the buyer is not relying on the seller's skill or judgement
- or it is unreasonable for the buyer to rely on the seller's skill or judgement.

5.3.6 Section 15 of the Sale of Goods Act 1979

This section relates to the situation where goods are sold by the seller providing a sample of the goods before the contract is made and later providing the bulk of the order. The provisions say that:

- the bulk must correspond to the sample. This would prevent, for example, a grocer from displaying, say, raisins which look plump and juicy but when you open the pre-packed bag you discover that the contents are shrivelled up and simply not comparable with what was displayed in the shop
- the buyer must have a reasonable opportunity of comparing the bulk with the sample.

If the buyer is afforded an opportunity to inspect the goods, then, whether they make the inspection or not, they are assumed to have accepted the condition of the bulk product as if they had actually made the inspection. The buyer who, in this situation, declined the opportunity to inspect would not be able to complain that the bulk did not correspond to the sample. They could not bring any proceedings under section 15 but might, if the goods were so poor as to be not of *satisfactory quality*, be able to bring proceedings under section 14.

✎   **CASE STUDY 3**

Last week you called at a local chemist and bought the following products:

- a bar of Sensa soap – which was described as being suitable for sensitive skins
- a packet of Curly Top home hair perming solution
- a new hair brush
- a packet of razor blades.

Since your visit you have used both the soap and the perm solution. The soap caused a bright red allergic reaction on your face. Later that week when using the perm solution you experienced a similar reaction on your face and scalp.

When you used the hair brush the handle broke and when you tried to use the razor blades you discovered that they were so blunt that they would not cut through even fine hairs.

You have undoubtedly suffered considerable damage and been fobbed off with some shoddy goods but do you have any redress?

Consider how you would answer the following questions.

---

1 Are there any express terms of the contract which have been breached?

2 Are there any implied terms of the contract which have been breached?

Express terms

The contract was probably a very simple one. There was an invitation to treat by the shop. You offered to buy the products when you took them to the counter. The offer was accepted when the chemist took your money. There is no written contract and little or nothing may have been said between you and the chemist. There are probably *no express terms* at all for you to refer to.

Implied terms

Regarding the soap
The soap was described as being for sensitive skins. Even if your skin is fairly sensitive you could expect it not to cause such a reaction given its description. Section 14(3) of the Sale of Goods Act says that the goods must be reasonably fit for the purpose for which they were intended. Your argument would be that the description of the goods made the purpose self-evident, that your skin is sensitive and it was not suitable for you to use. The only limitation, remember, is that the goods must be *reasonably* fit for the purpose for which they were intended. If it could be shown that your skin is exceptionally sensitive then the chemist might argue that the soap was reasonably fit for sensitive skins but not for rare and extreme levels of sensitivity such as yours.

Regarding the perm solution
The perm solution must again be *reasonably* fit for the purpose for which it is intended. The product may have been suitable for use by someone without a sensitive skin. The chemist could argue that the product was reasonably fit for use by most people. Unless you made your skin condition known to the chemist you may have little or no redress.

Consider though how different the situation might have been if you could show that the perm solution caused a similar reaction on one of your friends who had a normal skin.

Regarding the hair brush
The hair brush might still be usable for its purpose after the handle has broken. The point though is that you bought a hair brush with a handle. The handle could not withstand ordinary use and so your argument would be that it was not of satisfactory quality.

The situation might however be different if the handle had broken after six months. No one would reasonably expect it to last for ever.

Regarding the razor blades
The razor blades which would not cut from the outset would be neither of satisfactory quality nor reasonably fit for the purpose for which they were intended. (What other purpose than to cut would be likely to be intended for razor blades?)

The problem with this situation is always going to be one of degree. Exactly how sharp must the blades be in order to satisfy section 14 of the Sale of Goods Act?

5.3.7   The Sale of Goods Act 1979 and the Supply of Goods and Services Act 1982

So far we have looked at the law relating to the sale of goods contained in the Sale of Goods Act 1979. As we saw, the Sale of Goods Act will only apply where *goods* are sold for money. The Sale of Goods Act does not apply to obtaining goods by barter, nor does it apply to goods on hire or hire purchase, nor to the provision of services.

The **Supply of Goods and Services Act 1982** goes some way towards remedying the situation by implying terms very similar to those in sections 12–15 of the Sale of Goods Act into contracts for the supply of goods and services.

Sections 2–5 apply to contracts for *work and materials* and *barter* under which a party acquires ownership of goods.

Section 2 implies a condition that the transferor has the right to transfer the goods.

Section 3 implies that where goods which are the subject of the contract are described, the goods supplied will correspond to the description.

Section 4 corresponds to section 14 of the Sale of Goods Act. The goods must be of satisfactory quality and reasonably fit for their purpose.

Section 5 corresponds to section 15 of the Sale of Goods Act dealing with sale by sample.

5.3.8   The supply of goods and services and contracts for hire

The Sale of Goods Act did not cover contracts for barter but neither did it cover contracts for the hire of goods. Section 6 of the Supply of Goods and Services Act defines an agreement for hire. Sections 7–10 mirror sections 2–5 but apply to contracts for hire.

5.3.9   The supply of goods and services and contracts for services

A contract for services is defined in section 12 as 'a contract under which a person ("the supplier") agrees to carry out a service'.

The provisions apply both to contracts where a service alone is provided, e.g. shoe repairing, and to where both a service and the transfer of some goods is involved, e.g. the supply and installation of double glazing.

Section 13 implies that where a supplier is acting in the course of a business he or she will exercise reasonable skill and care in carrying out the service. For example, if you take your lawn mower to be repaired and when you get it back it cuts badly and the engine keeps cutting out, then the repair would seem to have been carried out in breach of section 13.

Section 14 implies a term that, where the supplier is acting in the course of a business and there is no fixed time stated in the contract for the service to be carried out (nor can it be determined by reference to any previous transactions), the supplier will carry out the service within a reasonable time.

For example, imagine that I take an electric shaver to be repaired and the repair is a minor one. If the shaver is still waiting to be repaired six months later, then (quite apart from the state of my beard!) there is almost certainly a breach of section 14.

Section 15 implies a term as to the cost of services. Sometimes you will ring up and ask, say, a plumber to call and you will discuss the fee. Other times you may previously have used the same tradesman and you know what their fees are. Occasionally though you may employ someone to do some work without discussing the price. For example, if a storm takes some slates from the roof of my house it is conceivable that, anxious to avoid further damage, I ring up a roofing contractor and simply ask them to see to the job as quickly as possible. The roofer is entitled to be paid a reasonable rate for the work done.

One example of this section in operation is the case of

British Steel Corporation v Cleveland Bridge and Engineering Company (1984). In this case work had started before all the final details of the contract were agreed. Both parties fully expected that a contract would be finalised. When the negotiations broke down and no contract was entered into, the supplier was entitled to be paid a reasonable rate for the work already undertaken.

6 Unfair contract terms/exclusion clauses

Obviously if a business person does their homework properly they will know about all their responsibilities to the person with whom they make a contract. They will know that, in the event of things going wrong, they may be sued on the basis of:

- statements made before the contract was entered into, or
- express terms of the contract, or
- terms implied into the contract by the courts, or
- terms implied into the contract by statute.

Bearing all this in mind some business people might prefer to limit their liability to the customer. They might think of doing this by including some *express terms* in the contract which say that they will not be liable if X, Y or Z were to happen.

This tactic is a common enough one. The small print in many contracts is full of such conditions which attempt to limit the rights of the customer. Usually the party relying on the clauses is in a stronger bargaining position than the person with whom they are contracting. Very often these express terms are not freely negotiated. The business person will say to the lay person that they can enter into the contract on the standard terms. There is often no room for negotiation. The customer must look at the terms on a 'take it or leave it' basis. Sometimes in these types of situation the term is obviously unfair. In this situation the **Unfair Contract Terms Act 1977** may provide the consumer with some redress. The

Act does not *imply* terms like the Sale of Goods Act which we have just looked at. What it does do though is to limit the effect of some of the *express terms* which a business person might put into a contract and which might result in considerable unfairness to the customer.

The Unfair Contract Terms Act often provides a solution where one's gut reaction to the situation was that there was unfair advantage being taken by the business person of the consumer's lack of legal knowledge. It often applies where we would say 'That's not fair!'

An exclusion clause (or exemption clause) is an express term of a contract whereby one party attempts to exclude liability that might arise in the future should unforeseen circumstances arise. For example, if that party finds himself unable to honour the contract or the contract is performed but results in one party suffering some loss or being injured.

6.1   How do exclusion clauses become part of the contract?

We have seen that exclusion clauses are express terms of the contract. They are usually contained in documentation and are seldom part of any oral negotiation. The terms could be included in the contract in two ways:

- by signature of acceptance, or
- by notice.

6.1.1   Exclusion clauses included in a contract by signature

If a person signs a document he is likely to be agreeing to the terms contained in that document. This is the case even though he may not have bothered reading the document (**L'Estrange v Graucob (1934)**). How many times have we all, even lawyers, simply signed a document where the salesperson makes a cross for your signature? You may well be in a hurry, there is a lot of small print, you feel you are holding up other customers, or the salesperson appears impatient, and what's more you know they wouldn't agree to change the standard terms especially for you anyway! Despite how commonly it may be done it really *is* so important to read the small print. Once your signature is on the document you may find the terms of the contract which you have agreed to are not at all what you expected.

One of the few occasions when a person may be able to escape being bound by contractual terms that they have signed is where a person signs a document but has been actively misled as to the contents.

In **Curtis v Chemical Cleaning and Dyeing Co (1951)** a clause contained in a document excluded liability for 'any damage however arising'. The defendant's employee had told the customer that the terms excluded liability only for particular types of damage. The court held that the company could not rely on the clause to exclude liability for damage other than the types which the customer was told about.

6.1.2 Exclusion clauses included in a contract by notice

An exclusion clause can become part of a contract by notice. This will only occur if the party subject to the clause was:

● either aware of the clause
● or reasonable steps were taken to bring it to the attention of the party before the contract was made.

There are two factors of importance here. There is the question of timing again.

If the notice of the term comes after the contract is made it can have no effect on the relationship between the parties at all. It may purport to be a term of the contract but it cannot actually be one if it comes too late. We looked earlier (at section 3.4.2) at the cases of **Olley v Marlborough Court Hotel** and **Chapleton v Barry UDC**. These are often relevant to exclusion clauses. If a term purports to exclude liability but doesn't actually form part of the contract at all we need consider it no further. The situation might however have been different if, for example, in **Olley v Marlborough Court Hotel** the terms which were on the back of the hotel bedroom door had been drawn to the attention of the guest in the hotel lobby at the time the contract was made; or in **Chapleton v Barry UDC** if the terms had been clearly displayed on the board which invited the visitor to take a deck chair and pay the attendant when he came around.

The next factor to consider is whether sufficient steps were taken to bring the condition to the party's attention before the making of the contract. The business person who 'hides' conditions in an attempt to make sure that the other party is bound by them, even though they have not seen them, is likely to receive short shrift from the courts.

The general principle is that the party seeking to rely on the clause must take reasonable steps to bring the term of the contract to the other party's attention.

Deciding whether or not *reasonable* steps have been taken will mean taking into account all the circumstances of the particular case.

In an early case Lord Justice Mellish distinguished between two types of document. He said that there were some types of document in which a party might expect to include conditions (perhaps a modern-day example might be a leaflet containing information about the provision and times of sports classes at a leisure centre). There were, he said, other types of document in which they would not expect to include conditions (perhaps a modern-day example might be publicity sheets handed out to a queue at a stadium waiting for a pop concert).

Not only is the *type of document* important in considering whether the term has been brought to the party's reasonable notice but so is the *clarity* of the term.

In **Thornton v Shoe Lane Parking (1971)** Lord Denning suggested that the more far reaching the exclusion clause the more the care that must be taken to bring it to the attention of the other party. Factors such as

● the position of the term in the document
● the size of the typeface
● the colour of the typeface and whether it stood out from other terms

can all be important. Lord Denning suggested that in order to satisfy the requirement of notice some terms would have to be printed in red ink with a hand pointing towards them.

Both the factor of the timing of the notice and its being drawn to the attention of the other party may take on less significance where it can be shown that the parties have entered into previous contracts with each other. Although the notice may technically come too late for that particular contract or may not have been adequately brought to the party's attention on that particular occasion, it may still be part of the contract on the basis of the parties' previous dealings.

> In **Hardwick Game Farm v Suffolk Agricultural Poultry Producers Association (1968)** a customer received goods from a supplier together with a sale note with an exclusion clause on the back. When the note was received the contract had of course already been made. However, it was shown that in dealings in the past three years the customer had received over 100 similar sale notes with the same conditions on and thus had notice of them from the previous notes. The *course of dealings* which the parties had had previously, had the cumulative effect of giving the customer notice of the printed terms of the transaction.

6.2   Are exclusion clauses in contracts valid?

Assume that you have decided that the timing was right and that the steps to bring it to the other party's notice were reasonable. The exclusion clause is then one of the terms of the contract. The question to consider now is whether the party can rely on the term or whether it will be 'deleted' or modified by the Unfair Contract Terms Act.

The Unfair Contract Terms Act generally has two possible effects:

- it makes some contractual provisions void. That is, they have no effect whatsoever and may as well not have been written in the first place, or
- they may be valid if they are considered to be *reasonable* within the definition of 'reasonable' included in the Act.

6.2.1   Provisions which are void under the Unfair Contract Terms Act
Section 12 of the Sale of Goods Act and **section 2 of the Supply of Goods and Services Act** (the sections which imply that the seller has the right to sell the goods) *cannot be excluded* in any sale (s.6 UCTA).

Sections 13–15 of the Sale of Goods Act and **sections 3–5 of the Supply of Goods and Services Act** (relating to satisfactory quality, reasonable fitness for purpose etc) *cannot be excluded* in a 'consumer sale'. (A consumer sale is where one party is a consumer and the other party sells goods in the course of a business. A consumer is defined in s.12 UCTA.)

Liability for death or injury to a person which arises from the party's negligence cannot be excluded in a contract made 'in the course of a business' (s.2 UCTA). There are two factors to be remembered in this.

Firstly, it relates only to death or injury to people, not to other damage.

Secondly, it relates only to death or injury arising from negligence. The question of negligence is looked at in detail in Part 4 of this text but broadly the idea is that the injury need not have been caused deliberately but should be someone's 'fault'.

6.2.2 Provisions which are subject to the reasonableness test

Liability for loss or damage (of course apart from liability for death or injury mentioned above) *arising out of negligence* cannot be excluded unless the exclusion clause is reasonable.

Liability arising from the party's own breach of contract cannot be excluded unless the exclusion clause is reasonable. This provision applies to situations where the party is dealing with a *consumer* – which is defined in s.12 UCTA – or where the party has produced a set of their own standard contract terms and dealt on those terms only (s.3 UCTA).

Liability for non-performance of the contract cannot be excluded unless the exclusion clause is reasonable (s.3 UCTA).

Liability for performing the contract in a substantially different way cannot be excluded unless the clause is reasonable (s.3 UCTA).

Sections 13–15 of the Sale of Goods Act and **sections 3–5 of the Supply of Goods and Services Act** (relating to satisfactory quality, reasonable fitness for purpose etc) *cannot be excluded* in a 'consumer sale' and cannot be excluded in any other sale unless the clause is reasonable (s.6 UCTA).

6.2.3 The reasonableness test

Where a term is within section 6.2.2 above the courts must decide whether the term is reasonable within the definition in the Unfair Contract Terms Act (s.11 UCTA). The term will be reasonable if it is fair and reasonable bearing in mind all the circumstances which were or ought reasonably have been known to or in the contemplation of the parties at the time the contract was made.

It is important from this to note that it is not what a 'reasonable person' would have known. The question is what *those particular parties* knew or ought to have known.

It is also important to note that one must look at the parties' state of mind *at the time the contract was made* and not with the benefit of hindsight.

If the term is reasonable the parties will be bound by it. If it is not reasonable it will have no effect on the relationship between the parties.

In deciding whether or not the term is reasonable the courts are advised of a number of matters which they should take into account including:

- the relative strengths in the parties' bargaining positions
- whether the party objecting to the term was offered any incentive to agree to the term. (If he or she has already received some payment for agreeing to the term the courts may be likely to regard them as wanting to have their cake (the inducement) and eat it (if the clause is determined to be void).

- whether the customer knew or ought reasonably to have known of the existence and effect of the term.

The question of reasonableness is illustrated by the case of

Smith v Eric S Bush (1989). The situation was that a survey was undertaken on a house which a woman was proposing to buy. The survey was to be done on behalf of the building society (who were to give her a mortgage advance) but was paid for by her. The small print of the contract for the survey included a term that neither the building society nor the surveyor warranted that the report was accurate. The report was not accurate and the purchaser found herself with considerable damage to the property as a result of the chimneys collapsing. She then tried to sue the surveyor but was met with the response that they had excluded any liability for inaccuracies.

The House of Lords held that in these particular circumstances the surveyor knew that the purchaser would be provided with a copy of the report and would be likely to rely on it. The term purporting to exclude liability was therefore unreasonable and the surveyor could not rely on it.

It is important to note though that every case concerning reasonableness is likely to be different. The test requires the court to consider the circumstances which were or ought to have been known to *those particular parties*. The case of **Smith v Eric S Bush** might have been decided very differently if either the purchaser had been someone with particular knowledge of the property or the property was a particularly expensive one and the amount of the mortgage advance was a small part of the total purchase price.

✎   CASE STUDY 4

Last month you decided to visit a health club. You have visited the club twice a week since then. When you go you pay a fee of £5.00 which allows you to use all the facilities at the club.

At the reception there is a notice prominently displayed and entitled 'Terms of Use of this Club'. It includes the following terms:

1 The Company and its employees accept no liability for injury howsoever caused.
2 The Company and its employees accept no liability for loss or damage to clients' belongings howsoever caused unless stored in a locked locker.

Last week on a visit to the club you suffered a catalogue of disasters.

- You ripped your very expensive designer Pike shorts when one of the instructors let go of a weight which caught on your shorts as it fell.
- When you returned to your locker which had not been locked you discover that your bag containing £75 had been stolen.

> ● When you returned to get changed you slipped on the floor coming out of the changing rooms and broke your wrist.
>
> The club has pointed to the terms of use of the club and says that although they are very sorry they are not liable to you for anything.
>
> Undoubtedly you have suffered some injury and loss at the health club. Whatever basis you might believe that you have for suing the health club you are faced by the fact that the company says that the *exclusion clauses* displayed on the premises exempt them from any liability.
>
> We need, therefore, to consider two things.

1 Are the *exclusion clauses* terms of the contract at all?

2 If the exclusion clauses are terms of the contract, are they rendered ineffective by the provisions of the Unfair Contract Terms Act?

Regarding whether the terms are part of the contract between you and the club

If we assume that you did not sign anything agreeing to any of the terms then we need to consider whether the terms were incorporated into the contract by the appropriate notice.

We need to consider the question of timing and clarity.

Did the notification of them come before or after making the contract?
Consider:

The notice was 'displayed prominently in reception' – could it be clearly seen *before* the contract was made?

Would it make any difference if the only notice was on the back of the changing room door? Given that you have been there a number of times before, might it not be argued that the terms were incorporated into the contract by the *previous course of dealings?*

Would it make any difference if the only notice was on the back of the changing room door and this was your first visit to the club? The course of dealings argument could not be used, and if the contract were regarded as having been made in the reception area then the terms on the changing room door would have been notified to you too late to form part of the contract at all. They would therefore have no effect on your relationship.

Was the notification sufficiently clear?
How big were the terms? How many other terms were they hidden amongst?

This matter is really one of common sense. There may be all sorts of factors which added together mean that the notification is, on the particular facts, either clear or not.

If the term is part of the contract then the effect, if any, of the Unfair Contract Terms Act

Are any of the terms made void by the Act?
Do either of the terms or any part of them attempt to exclude liability for personal injury caused by the company or its employees' negligence? Answer: yes. Clause 1 attempts to limit liability for personal injury *howsoever caused*. To the extent that this clause purports to exclude liability for personal injury caused by *negligence* that part of the clause will be void and will have no effect on the relationship between the parties.

Are any of the terms subject to the reasonableness test?
Clause 1 purports to limit liability for personal injury caused by any means. Where the personal injury is not caused by negligence the clause will not be void but it will be subject to the reasonableness test.

Clause 2 does not relate to personal injury but to other loss or damage. The clause will be valid if reasonable and void if it is not.

The test for reasonableness involves considering what was, or ought to have been, in the reasonable contemplation of the parties at the time the contract was made.

Regarding the ripped shorts
The damage is not personal injury. The exclusion clause could be valid if it passes the reasonableness test. Would limiting liability for damage which is the 'fault' of the company's employee be likely to be regarded as reasonable?

Regarding the stolen bag
The exclusion clause again is one which is subject to the reasonableness test. One's gut reaction might say that the clause is reasonable and that if you had failed to lock your locker that was your fault. Consider, however, how your view of the situation might change if the lockers which were provided could not be locked because the company had lost the keys. Surely in that situation it would be unreasonable of the company to say that they are not liable unless belongings are put in a locked locker while denying that ability to lock the locker.

Regarding your broken wrist
The company cannot exclude liability for personal injury caused by their negligence. Attempts to exclude liability for injury caused otherwise than by their negligence will be subject to the reasonableness test.

The question is whether the injury was caused by the company's negligence. Was it their 'fault'? A factor which might be considered is whether the flooring surface was inherently slippery. Was it slippery because it was wet? If so were any warning notices put up?

Summary

You should now be able to:

- explain when a statement made during negotations for a contract will become a term of the contract
- explain the difference between statements made in negotiations for a contract which are
  an express term of the contract
  a misrepresentation
  any other statement
- explain the effect of the contractual terms implied by the Sale of Goods Act 1979 as amended
- explain what type of clause will be void under the Unfair Contract Terms Act 1977 and what type will be valid so long as they pass the test of reasonableness.

Now consider the following case study. This case study is intended to take you through most of the elements of this chapter by way of revision.

 CASE STUDY 5

Three months ago you ordered some new vinyl flooring for your bathroom. When you placed the order you specified the manufacturer's colour code. When the flooring was delivered the colour was not right. In addition there was not enough flooring to cover the whole area despite the fact that the company had taken the measurements. Within the following month a small hole wore through in the flooring next to the washbasin. Furthermore you suffered a sprained ankle when you tripped over a loose join in the flooring.

You have complained to the company and told them that you don't want anything more to do with them. You wrote to them and told them that they can take away the flooring and you will get some from elsewhere. You have also said that you want compensation for the injury to your ankle.

The response from the company was that they would be calling soon to fit an additional piece of flooring although it is not of quite the same thickness as the original one ordered. They also pointed out that the terms of the contract which you signed include the following:

'...

3 The company reserves the right to alter the specification of products provided from the original agreement.

4 The company accepts no liability for loss or damage howsoever caused.'

This flooring is a catalogue of small disasters. It is entirely understandable that you want to have nothing more to do with the company but we need to consider your position.

Regarding the flooring being the wrong colour

1 Was there an *express term* of the contract that the flooring should be a particular colour? If so, is the company in breach of this express term?

2 Does it make any difference if the term is a condition rather than a warranty? Consider in this respect whether or not you would be entitled to reject the flooring when it arrived.

3 What is the status of the exclusion clause which says that the company can change the specifications? Does the Unfair Contract Terms Act have any effect on it?

4 Given that you did not reject the flooring at the time how do you think your position might have changed?

Regarding only half being delivered

1 Again there was an *express term* for the purchase of sufficient flooring for the whole bathroom. Was the express term, in your opinion, a warranty or a condition?

2 What difference would it make to your rights if it were a warranty?

Regarding the fitting of a different thickness

1 Was the thickness actually discussed or did you simply order a particular type of flooring? Is there an *express term* in the form of an *exclusion clause* which purports to limit the company's liability for such a breach of contract?

2 Is this provision void under the Unfair Contract Terms Act? If not, will the provision be subject to the reasonableness test?

3 If it is subject to the reasonableness test how do you decide if it is in fact reasonable?

Regarding your sprained ankle

1 Is there an *express term* in the form of an *exclusion clause* which purports to limit the company's liability for personal injury however it is caused?

2 Is this provision void under the Unfair Contract Terms Act? Is it a provision which will be void in so far as it relates to certain types of injury but not to others?

3 To the extent that the clause is not void will the provision be subject to the reasonableness test? If it is subject to the reasonableness test how do you decide if it is in fact reasonable? How well should the flooring have been secured? How much care should you yourself have been expected to take?

Regarding the hole in the flooring

1 In the absence of any express discussions or guarantee there is no express term with regard to durability. Are you however entitled to expect some reasonable flooring for your money? Will a term as to satisfactory quality and reasonable fitness for purpose be implied under the Sale of Goods Act? If so, is one month a reasonable period for the flooring to last?

2 Would it make any difference how much you paid for it?

3 Would it make any difference if the use of the bathroom was heavier than usual because you had your sister and her family staying for three weeks?

4 Would it make any difference if instead you had recently taken as lodgers a group of eight workmen from the new road bypass scheme? The workmen all used the bathroom and often failed to remove their steel-toe-capped boots before doing so.

10 How are contracts completed?

Objectives

By the end of this chapter you should:

- understand the way in which contracts are terminated
- understand the doctrine of frustration and its consequences
- understand the application of the principal of *non est factum*
- appreciate the consequences arising where one or both of the parties is mistaken as to some aspect of the contract.

1 The termination of contracts

The majority of transactions do not result in either party's dissatisfaction. The majority of contracts are performed to both parties' satisfaction and that is where the matter ends.

The two satisfactory ways in which a contract can come to an end are by *performance* or *agreement*.

1.1 Termination of a contract by performance

This is the most obvious method of discharging a contract. Each party fulfils their obligations under the contract and there is an end of the matter. A problem can arise however if the performance does not comply exactly with the requirements of the contract. The general rule is that the parties must perform their obligations completely and exactly. The principle is illustrated by an early and somewhat draconian decision in

Cutter v Powell (1795). In this case a widow of a sailor claimed some of his pay for work done by him on a voyage. The voyage began on 2 August and ended on 9 October. The sailor had the misfortune not to have fully performed the contract! (He died on 20 September!) The court would not imply into the contract a term that proportional payment should be made in the case of partial performance.

The reasoning in this case is now, gladly, subject to a number of exceptions. The rule in principle, however, lives on; for example, section 13 of the Sale of Goods Act 1979 which we looked at in the last chapter says that in a contract for the sale of goods, the goods must correspond to their description. Any discrepancy between the description and the goods would therefore be likely to mean that the contract had not been performed completely and exactly and the party at fault would be regarded as not having performed his obligation under the contract.

Remember the case of **Re Moore and Landauer** which we looked at in the last chapter. The contract was to deliver a number of tins of fruit in cases of 30. The correct number of tins was delivered but some of the cases were of only 24 tins. The purchaser in that case was entitled to reject the whole consignment on a ground which might, to some people, appear trivial. However, as we saw in the last chapter, the Sale and Supply of Goods Act 1994 has introduced a new section 15A into the Sale of Goods Act. This in effect provides that if there is a breach of a term in section 13, 14 or 15 and the breach is of a slight nature such that to reject the goods for such a breach would be unreasonable, then the breach is not to be treated as a breach of 'condition' but may be treated as a breach of 'warranty'. (We saw the difference between these two types of term in the last chapter.)

This provision will apply unless a contrary intention appears from or can be implied into the contract and where the buyer is not a consumer. From the facts of **Re Moore and Landauer** the only breach was the failure to pack all the tins of fruit in cases of 30 tins. Arguably this breach could be regarded as so trivial that it would seem unreasonable for the buyer (who was not a consumer) to reject the goods. Consider though what difference it would have made if the supplier in **Re Moore and Landauer** knew that the buyer was reselling the fruit and required the delivery of cases of 30 tins for efficient packing into container transport.

2 What are the exceptions to the general rule requiring full and exact performance?

2.1 Is the contract 'divisible'?

A contract may be divisible depending on the intention of the parties. If it can reasonably be divided into a number of parts, then payments for those parts which have been completed can be claimed in spite of the fact that there is not completion of the entire contract.

For example, you contract to buy a quantity of frozen meals for your home freezer in fortnightly deliveries paying for each consignment on delivery. If after three deliveries the suppliers say that they are going into wholesale only and will not be making any more deliveries, the courts may consider that the three instalments could reasonably be separated from the rest of the contract.

2.2   Does the timing of performance have to be exact?

This is a most common irritant in everyday contracts. You agree that you will buy a product and it is to be delivered within 14 days. Let us say it is a three piece suite. You are particularly concerned that the suite is delivered within the time because your parents are coming to stay and at the moment you have nothing for them to sit on.

The failure to deliver the suite within the agreed period is a breach of contract. The question though is: does it entitle you to call the deal off and buy a suite elsewhere? If the time factor is so important that the suite can be rejected if it is delivered late then we say that *time is of the essence.* In a case known as

The Naxos (1990), rules stated that sellers of sugar had an obligation to '... have sugar ready to be delivered to the buyer at any time within the contract period'. Also, that the buyer '... having given reasonable notice shall be entitled to call for delivery of the sugar between the first and last working day inclusive of the period of delivery'. The sellers maintained that they had until the end of the delivery period to deliver the cargo and were not obliged to deliver on a date specified by the buyers. It was held by the House of Lords that '... Rule 14(1) was crucially important to the buyers since it removed the risk that the absence or insufficiency of cargo could be a cause of delay since it must be rare, if ever, for it to be in the sellers' interest to load a vessel very slowly. The rule ensures to a very large extent that loading will be promptly commenced and speedily carried out and thus enables the buyers punctually to perform their own obligations to their customers. The rule tends to provide certainty which is such an indispensable ingredient of mercantile contracts.'

Time is only of the essence in a limited number of circumstances:

* Where it is expressly stated in the contract to be so or can be inferred to be so. For example, if, when contracting to buy the suite, you had made it clear that the delivery date was of the utmost importance then the courts might say that you had made *time of the essence.*
* Time will be of the essence if the agreement is such that it is imperative that stipulations about time are adhered to. For example, the subject matter of the contract may be of a perishable nature. Or you might have booked a taxi for the airport for a certain time. If the taxi does not turn up at that time it would surely not be unreasonable for you to wait a short time and make alternative arrangements. If time was of the essence in the contract, then your making alternative arrangements still leaves you able, if you so wish, to sue them for failing to perform the contract. If time was not of the essence they could sue you for the lost fare, although of course you could counterclaim for damages in respect of their original breach of contract.
* If one party to the contract is guilty of undue delay then time can be made of the essence by the other party informing them that they have a specified (and reasonable) time in which to get the job done. For example, you leave your

car to be repaired and are told it will take two days. Four days later the car is still not ready. You cannot, at this stage, simply withdraw from the contract. You would have to give the garage a reasonable deadline to get the work done and make it clear that if it was not ready by then you would have it collected by another garage for them to carry out the work.

2.3 Has one of the parties prevented performance?

This is where performance of the contract is prevented by one of the parties, for example, where a contract is to provide carpeting for a whole house before the end of July. If the owner without warning goes on holiday for the second two weeks in July (thus preventing the supplier having access to the property) he cannot then resist a claim for payment by the supplier on the value of the work done so far. (It might even go further than that with a claim by the supplier for damages for breach of contract!)

> In **Planché v Colburn (1831)** Y agreed with X that Y would write a book to be published in serial form in X's magazine. After Y had undertaken research and started writing the book X decided to cease publication of the magazine thus preventing Y from completing his part of the contract. Y was able to claim an amount equivalent to the proportion of the work done (known as the *quantum meruit* basis).

2.4 Has one of the parties offered to perform the contract ('tendered performance') but the offer has been refused?

Closely allied to the idea of simple prevention of performance (which may or may not be deliberate) is the situation where one party offers to perform their obligations under the contract. If the party offers to perform the contract but needs the cooperation of the other party to do it, then if the other party refuses to cooperate surely it is reasonable for the innocent party to be regarded as having performed their part of the contract.

> In **Startup v MacDonald (1843)** X agreed to deliver oil to Y 'in the last 14 days of March'. Had X failed to deliver by the end of 31 March he would have been in breach of contract. X tried to deliver the oil to Y at 8.30 p.m. on 31 March. Y, somewhat displeased at the lateness of the hour, refused to accept delivery. Nevertheless it was held that X should be awarded damages for non-acceptance of the delivery. He had tried to perform his part of the contract and as such was discharged from further liability. In fact it went further than that, he could sue Y for breach of contract and his loss of profit!

This case should, however, be accompanied with a word of warning. It is an old case. It is likely that the courts might, in the present day, imply a term as to reasonable times for delivery. Most people would not like to think that they would be obliged to accept delivery of goods whatever the time of day or night.

2.5   Has there been acceptance by one party of the other party's part performance of the contract?

If one party only performs part of their obligations under the contract and the other party agrees to accept what has been done so far, then the party who has partly performed the contract can claim to be paid on the basis of the work done so far. For example, imagine that you have employed a window cleaner. The price is £30 for the outside and the inside of the house. When he has finished only the outside he receives a phone call on his mobile phone saying that his child is ill and needs to be collected from school. You then have two choices. Either you can say that you wanted the whole job doing and only part of it is no good and that he must come back later and finish it. Or, as is more likely under the circumstances, you could accept that he needs to leave the job half done. You may well say that you will finish it off yourself. You have accepted part performance of the contract and should accept that you will be expected to pay him for the cleaning of the outside of the windows on a *quantum meruit* basis.

It is important that the party who has not got all they contracted for is in a position either to reject or to accept the part performance. If the window cleaner simply attempts to stop, having cleaned only half of the windows, then there would be no obligation on you to pay for a half-done job unless you choose to.

2.6   Has the contract been performed 'substantially' if not absolutely?

In certain situations where a party to a contract has performed his obligations substantially, albeit defectively, then it seems that he can enforce the contract to the extent that he is entitled to the price less a reduction for making good the defects. For example in

Hoenig v Isaacs (1952) a supplier agreed to decorate and furnish X's flat for £750. There were various defects with the work which could be put right for £55. The Court of Appeal held that the supplier had substantially performed the contract and was entitled to the full contract price of £750 less the £55 required to remedy the defects.

The important factor obviously is whether the contract has been *substantially* performed. A different conclusion was reached in

Bolton v Mahadeva (1972). In this case a plumber had installed a combined heating and hot water system for £560. The work was defective in that the system failed to work adequately and gave off fumes. These defects could however be remedied for £174. The Court of Appeal felt that the contract had not been *substantially* performed. Lord Justice Cairns said: 'If a central heating system when installed is such that it does not heat the house adequately and is such, further, that fumes are given out ... and if the putting right of these defects is not something which can be done by some slight amendment of the system, then I think that the contract is not substantially performed ...'

Case Study 1

You enter into a contract with a firm of decorators that they will decorate your office in two weeks time. They were booked to start work last Monday. No one from the firm turned up on Monday. On Tuesday you telephoned to be told that someone had turned up on Tuesday to start work at 7 a.m. but had been unable to get into the office. The decorators eventually turned up on Wednesday. They purported to have finished by Friday morning but you think that the job has only been half done.

Consider the position.

With regard to the failure to turn up on time

This was obviously very irritating to you. You had clearly made an arrangement for them to start on the Monday. Would the fact that they did not turn up on the Monday as promised entitle you to call the whole deal off?

The answer is that although it is irritating it is unlikely that you could call the deal off. Only if time was regarded as being of the essence would it entitle you to withdraw from the contract. In the ordinary course of contracts with tradesmen time is unlikely to be regarded as being of the essence.

Would your reaction be any different if, when you negotiated the contract, you made it clear that their starting work on the Monday was vital as you had important clients visiting on the Thursday?

With regard to their inability to get into the office at 7 a.m.

The decorators have clearly tried to perform the contract but have been unable to. Does this mean that the fact that they could not start until Wednesday is their fault? If you follow **Startup v MacDonald** then it would seem that you might be liable for failing to allow them to get on with the job. Might it not be arguable though that, in an office situation, the work would be done within normal working hours unless alternative arrangements were made in advance?

With regard to the work not being finished

First of all we need to consider whether they have performed the terms of the contract. If they have then even if you had expected more, surely that is your problem. Has there been substantial performance? If there has, then you might simply be able to get someone else in to finish the job and deduct that amount from their bill. If it has not been substantially performed, then are you obliged to pay them anything under the contract or can you instead say that there was a failure of consideration? The question is surely one of degree and how far short of the contractual requirements their work falls.

3 Termination by agreement

The second method by which a contract can be discharged is by the parties agreeing to its discharge. In nearly all cases this involves the making of a second contract, under which fresh consideration is supplied. Remember when we looked at the formation of a contract in Chapter 8 we looked at whether the terms of the contract can subsequently be varied. The rule was that they could not be varied by one party where they provided no additional consideration. If extra consideration was provided then, in effect, the contract was varied (or terminated) by a superseding contract.

There are two possible situations where there can be termination by agreement.

3.1   Bilateral discharge

In this situation each party may have some remaining obligations under the contract. For example, an additional delivery may be due under the contract and an additional payment due to be made. If both parties *agree* to the discharge of the contract they are each providing fresh consideration. The fresh consideration consists in each party surrendering the right to insist on the other party's performance.

3.2   Unilateral discharge

In this case only one of the parties has the right to surrender. Where one party has completely performed his obligations under the contract and the other party has not, then any release of the other party must either be by formal documentation (a *deed*) or supported by fresh consideration. Effectively the terms of the original contract are being replaced by a new and superseding contract.

Performance and agreement are usually amicable forms of discharge of a contract. What we now need to consider are the circumstances in which things go wrong.

4   Non est factum

You will recall that the general rule in English law is that where a person signs a document without having read the contents they are nevertheless bound by it. We saw that the moral of the tale is *always read the small print*! One exception to the rule is the concept of *non est factum*. The basic meaning is 'this is not my deed'. It is used most commonly in a situation where a blind or illiterate person is persuaded to sign a document whilst they are unaware of the contents.

To succeed in a claim of *non est factum* the following have to be satisfied:

- the person who signs must not have been careless
- there must be a *fundamental* difference between the document that is signed and that which the person signing thinks they have signed
- the signature must have been induced by fraud.

The leading case is

Saunders v Anglia Building Society (1971). Briefly the facts are that an aunt, in order to help her nephew to raise money, agreed that her house should be mortgaged, although she was to continue to live in it until her death. The nephew arranged for his friend X to take the mortgage. In order for X to do this, the property had to be transferred to X. X drew up a deed transferring the house from the aunt to himself. When the aunt was asked to sign it, she could not read it as her glasses were broken. When she asked what the document was, she was told that it was a deed of gift of the house to her nephew. X later mortgaged the property but none of the money was paid to the nephew. The House of Lords held that the aunt could not succeed on a claim of *non est factum* as the mistake which induced her to sign the document was not sufficiently serious. She believed that the document she was signing was a means of raising money on her house – it was, although by different means and for a different purpose than she expected.

One or both of the parties may claim that the reason they should escape responsibility for the contract is not fraud but simply mistake.

5   Mistake

Normally the fact that one or both of the parties is mistaken as to some aspect of the contract will not mean that either one or both is necessarily discharged from the obligations which they have taken on. The fact that one party thought that circumstances were different from what they actually were should not affect the validity of any subsequent contract. For example, *mistake as to quality* or suitability. If, for example, you bought shrubs from a nursery, it might be that both parties were unsure whether or not those particular plants would tolerate frost. Even if it turns out that they will not, that is a mistake as to quality or suitability and will not entitle you to return the plants. In the case of

Smith v Hughes (1871) a buyer contracted to buy a quantity of oats. The buyer wanted old oats. The oats were in fact new oats and less valuable. When the mistake was discovered the buyer tried to reject the oats and to withdraw from the contract. It was held that this mistake was as to the quality of the goods and did not entitle the buyer to withdraw from the contract.

It should of course be remembered that if this case were being dealt with today the provisions of the **Sale of Goods Act 1979** (as amended by the **Sale and Supply of Goods Act 1994**) might be of some consolation to the disappointed party. If either the oats had been described as old oats and were not in fact old or if the buyer had made clear the purpose for which they were intended and that old oats were required, then the buyer would be entitled to reject the goods on the basis of sections 13 or 14 of the Sale of Goods Act.

There are however exceptional situations in which a mistake, an *operative mistake*, will render a contract *void*. That is, the contract is of no legal effect whatsoever and the ownership of property cannot be transferred under a void contract. Alternatively a contract may be rendered *voidable*. In this situation the contract remains valid until it is brought to an end and the ownership of property can pass under the contract whilst it is still valid.

Mistake can take a number of forms.

5.1 Common or bilateral mistake

In this situation the parties to the contract are in complete agreement but both are equally unaware of some fundamental aspect of the contract. For example in

> **Strickland v Turner (1852)** X bought an annuity from Y which was to continue for so long as Z was alive. Unbeknown to both X and Y, Z was already dead. The contract was held to be void on the basis of the common mistake of both parties and X was entitled to his money back.

The basis of a common mistake is often about the existence of the subject matter of the contract. In the case which we have just looked at the subject matter of the contract was Z who, being dead, did not exist. Similarly in

> **Couturier v Hastie (1856)** A sold a cargo of corn to B. Both parties believed the corn to be in transit from a Mediterranean port but unknown to them it had in fact been sold and removed because its condition was deteriorating. It was held that, since the subject matter of the contract no longer existed at the time the contract was made, there was a mistake which rendered the contract void. Neither party had to perform their obligations; indeed the seller could not as the corn did not exist.

Situations involving non-existent subject matter are known as *res extincta*. They are really situations where the contract is initially impossible. The contract is incapable of being performed from the outset. These situations should be distinguished from the situation where the subject matter did exist at the time of the contract but the contract has *subsequently* become impossible to perform. (This latter situation is where the concept of *frustration* may apply which is looked at in section 6 below.)

This area is dominated by well-established Victorian case law. However as recently as 1988 in

> **Associated Japanese Bank (International) Limited v Credit Du Nord SA (1988)** Mr Justice Steyn emphasised that in order to rely on *operative mistake* both parties to the contract must be mistaken as to the facts in existence at the time of contracting.

Again the subject matter in question must be radically different to what in fact both parties believed existed.

5.2   Mutual mistake

In the case of common mistake both parties are mistaken about the same thing. With *mutual mistake* the parties are at cross purposes. They each, no doubt, believe that they are in agreement but when the situation is looked at closely it is clear that each is labouring under a fundamental misunderstanding, the nature of which means that the ambiguity between them cannot be resolved.

> In **Raffles v Wichelhaus (1864)** X and Y contracted that Y should buy a cargo of cotton from a ship sailing from Bombay. The ship was named in the contract as the *Peerless*. Strangely enough there were two ships in Bombay, both laden with cotton and both called *Peerless*. One sailed in October, the other in December. X thought that he had contracted to sell the contents of the December sailing. Y thought that he had contracted to buy the contents of the October sailing. The case was never actually decided on the point but it was made clear that had it been necessary the contract would have been regarded as void as the parties were clearly at cross purposes and there was *mutual mistake*.

The matter must be one of mutual mistake and an irreconcilable ambiguity. It is not sufficient that one party made a mistake.

> In **Tamplin v James (1880)** a bidder at an auction offered (after the auction) to buy property which he believed included certain gardens. Had he examined the sale particulars displayed in the auction rooms he would have realised that they were not included. The buyer, on realising his mistake, refused to go ahead with the purchase. It was held that the buyer's mistake did not invalidate the contract. The point was also made that if a party were allowed to get out of a contract simply on the basis that he was mistaken when he made it, then almost no contract could be enforced against an unscrupulous person who later thought better of the deal.

5.3   Unilateral mistake

In the case of *unilateral mistake* only one of the parties to the contract is mistaken. As we have seen, usually this is just hard luck. However it may be viewed differently if the party who is not mistaken is aware of the other party's mistake. For example in

> **Hartog v Colin & Shields (1939)** X offered to sell to Y 30,000 Argentinian hare skins. The offer was in writing and the price was quoted in pence per pound. Prior to the offer negotiations had taken place on the basis of the price being per piece (i.e. each individual skin as opposed to pounds of skins). Y, realising that X had made a mistake, immediately accepted before X realised that they had erroneously expressed their offer. X, having discovered the mistake, refused to deliver claiming that no contract existed because of the mistake. This view was upheld by the High Court.

5.3.1   Mistake as to identity in face to face transactions

In the matter of unilateral mistake let's also consider a common occurrence. X is, let us say, the innocent seller of some goods. Y is a rogue pretending to be someone else and Z is an innocent purchaser from Y. So the goods pass from X to Y to Z.

The situation here may appear somewhat strange. If X and Y transact face to face (for example, across a shop counter) then usually the law will regard X as having intended to contract with Y. It is usually regarded as immaterial the fact that Y was pretending to be someone else in order to persuade X that he was creditworthy. The contract is still a valid one. It is simply that the contract can be *avoided* on the basis of misrepresentation when X discovers the deception. Up until the point when X discovers the deception and brings court action to get out of the contract it remains perfectly valid. Where does Z come into the picture? Imagine that Y sells the goods to Z under a perfectly straightforward contract. The contract between X and Y is valid until X does something about the misrepresentation. If, before X does anything, Y sells the goods to Z then Z will be regarded as the owner and X cannot get the goods back from Z.

This was the case in

> **Phillips v Brooks (1919)** when Y, a rogue customer, entered X's jewellers shop. The rogue pretended to be a well-known person and persuaded X to accept a 'dud' cheque for an expensive ring. He then pawned (equivalent to sold, for our purposes) the ring to Z. At the time of the transaction with Z, X had not taken any steps to get out of the contract on the basis of misrepresentation. The court said that the contract was a valid one and that as Z had acquired ownership of the ring before X did anything about the matter, so Z could keep the ring.

In **Ingram v Little (1961)** a different approach was taken. Three sisters advertised their car for sale. A rogue called at the house and they agreed a price for the car. The rogue then produced a cheque book. The sisters said that they were only prepared to take cash. The rogue then tried to persuade them to take a cheque by saying that he was a Mr P G M Hutchinson of Stanstead Road, Caterham, Surrey. The sisters took the precaution of checking the name and address in the telephone directory. They accepted the cheque and the rogue disappeared with the car. (The cheque inevitably bounced!) He then sold the car to Little who was entirely innocent and knew nothing of the deception by which the car had been obtained. If the rationale of *Phillips v Brooks* had been applied, then once the innocent Little had bought the car it would have been too late for the sisters to get out of the contract.

Somewhat strangely perhaps, the courts said that this situation was not the same as **Phillips v Brooks**. In that case they said the innocent seller, X, had been mistaken as to creditworthiness. They had intended to sell to the person in front of them but believed him to be good for a cheque. In **Ingram v Little** the court said it was different. The sisters intended to contract only with Mr P G M Hutchinson. They were not mistaken as to the creditworthiness of the person but rather as to who he was at all. On this basis the court said that the contract in **Ingram v Little** between the sisters and the rogue was *void*. This meant that the contract never existed in the first place. Ownership of the car could not therefore have been transferred to the rogue who, in turn, could not transfer the ownership to Little.

The distinction between these two cases is, on the facts, a subtle and confusing one. The outcome of the cases based on that subtle difference is devastating. In one case, X as the innocent seller to the rogue loses the goods and Z keeps them. In the other, Z as the innocent purchaser from the rogue loses the goods and the innocent seller, X, can have the goods returned. The distinction is not a happy one.

In **Lewis v Averay (1972)** the court applied the principle in **Phillips v Brooks** and cast considerable doubt on the reasoning in **Ingram v Little**.

As always in these situations the question concerns which of two innocent parties should get the goods and which should bear the loss created by the dishonesty of Y. The principle seems somewhat arbitrary because in the end the result is likely to depend on how quickly the rogue passes the goods on to an innocent buyer.

5.3.2 Mistake as to identity in transactions where the parties are not face to face
If the parties to the transaction are not face to face but are dealing with the transaction, for example through the post, then the situation may be somewhat easier to understand. One of the leading cases is

⚖

> **Cundy v Lindsay (1878)** in which Y wrote to X signing his correspondence so that Y appeared to be a real firm known to X. Y was in fact a rogue and not part of the real firm at all. X sent goods to Y believing that he was transacting with a reputable firm. Y then resold the goods to Z. It was held by the House of Lords that Z, although an innocent buyer, must return the goods to X. X had intended to deal only with the reputable firm and not with the rogue. The contract between X and Y was therefore *void* (or non-existent) and no ownership of the goods had passed to Y in the first place. Y could not therefore pass on any ownership to Z. The reasoning here is that X intended only to contract with the reputable firm, not with Y.
>
> In **King's Norton Metal Co v Edridge Merrett & Co (1897)**, the seller X received an order form by post from a firm. The firm was in fact an alias adopted by Y who was a rogue. The headed notepaper suggested that the firm was a substantial concern but X had never actually heard of the firm. Nevertheless X sent the goods to the firm. Y got possession of the goods and resold them to Z. The Court of Appeal held that X had intended to contract with the writer of the letter and so there was a contract between X and Y. The deception merely created a mistake as to Y's creditworthiness, not his identity.

The vital distinction between the cases is that in **Cundy v Lindsay** the intention of X was to contract with a firm which he knew and not the person who in fact wrote the letter. No such contract was ever actually made. In **King's Norton Metal** X intended to contract with the writer of the letter but the deception made X believe that the writer was a substantial concern. The contract was made with the writer of the letter but when X found out about the mistake he could get out of the contract since it was a *voidable* one.

5.4   Avoiding a voidable contract

We have looked so far at the difference between a *void* contract and a *voidable* one. So far all we have seen is:

- if the contract is void, then Y and so Z (the innocent purchaser) never get ownership of the goods at all
- if the contract is voidable, then Y gets ownership of the property but X can get it back again if he acts quickly enough.

If X does not act before Y passes the goods on to Z (the innocent purchaser), then Z will acquire the ownership and X has lost it forever. (X may be able to sue Y but that is often by the by; the problem with such rogues is that you can seldom, if ever, find them!)

If so much hinges on how quickly X acts, then we should also consider exactly what X must do in order to bring the contract to an end so that Y loses ownership, and so that although he may pass on the goods to Z he will be unable to pass on the rights of ownership.

Originally X had actually to confront Y and indicate to him that he no longer wished to contract with him. A moment's thought should suggest that this is not a likely scenario. Y is neither likely to hang around to be told, nor is he likely to be easily found. To overcome this problem the Court of Appeal said in

Car & Universal Finance Company v Caldwell (1965) that it is sufficient to display a manifest intention to the world in general of a desire not to continue with the contract. In this case the seller, having been induced by the fraud of a rogue to sell his car, immediately notified the police and the Automobile Association. It was held that the seller had successfully avoided the contract despite the fact that he was unable to confront the other party.

One or both of the parties may say that although they have the necessary capacity, and there was no fraud or mistake, nevertheless they should not be bound by the contract since the whole contract has been 'frustrated'.

6   Frustration

The doctrine of *frustration* applies where, due to some external event which is the fault of neither party, performance of the contract becomes either impossible or substantially different from what the parties must have had in mind when they made the contract. Note that this is not a situation of *mistake* because for common/bilateral mistake the question is whether or not the subject matter of the contract existed *at the time the contract was made*. The important difference between this concept and frustration is that with frustration the contract is quite capable of being performed at the time it is made, but subsequently becomes impossible.

A classic example of frustration is where, after the contract is made, the subject matter of the contract is destroyed or ceases to exist.

In **Taylor v Caldwell (1863)** X agreed to let a music hall to Y for four days. After the agreement but before the hall was due to be used the music hall was burned down. Neither party was to blame for it burning down. It was held that the contract was frustrated and so neither party was obliged to perform the contract.

Frustration can also occur where a party to a contract of personal service dies, becomes seriously ill or is called up for military service.

⚖️

> In **Morgan v Manser (1948)** a music hall performer made a ten year contract with his manager. The contract was made in 1938. In 1940 the performer was called up for military service. It was held that the contract was frustrated on the basis that the interruption was likely to be of some considerable duration and would certainly cover a large percentage of the contract period.

A contract may also be frustrated because, although the contract could technically be performed, nevertheless the whole point of the contract has been destroyed. For example, a number of cases concern the hiring of rooms from which to watch a coronation procession. One such case was

⚖️

> **Krell v Henry (1903)**. When the day arrived the rooms still existed and could have been used. However the procession was cancelled due to the King's illness. There would be no point in hiring the rooms. Given the specific reason for the hiring of the rooms and the subsequent events, the contract was frustrated.

It should be noted, however, that frustration is not something which the courts take lightly. Just because a contract becomes more difficult or expensive to perform will not mean that it is frustrated. If, for example, the cost to one party of performing the contract has risen steeply because of inflation this will not be sufficient grounds for frustration and getting out of the contract (**Davis Contractors v Fareham UDC (1956)**).

A party to a contract cannot rely on the doctrine of frustration to end the contract if he himself has caused the event which makes performance of the contract impossible. For example in **Taylor v Caldwell**, if one of the parties had deliberately burned down the music hall then that party could not have relied on the self-induced frustration.

6.1   Where frustration exists what is the effect on the parties?

The position between the parties is that the contract ceases to exist. Obviously one or both parties may have done some acts or paid some money towards the contract *before* it became impossible to perform. The situation between the parties is covered by the **Law Reform (Frustrated Contracts) Act 1943**.

Basically any money paid before the event which caused the frustration is recoverable and any amounts due are cancelled. However, if one of the parties has incurred expenses in pursuance of the contract then a court can exercise its power to order that that party be allowed to keep (or be paid) an amount up to but not exceeding their expenses. Similarly if one party has already performed part of the contract from which the other party has gained some valuable benefit, then the court may order the other party to pay a reasonable sum for it.

CASE STUDY 2

Imagine that you are a sales manager in a firm supplying extremely large houseplants suitable for businesses and offices. You are a wholesaler and you supply smaller firms who sell or lease the plants to individual businesses. In last week's post you received three letters.

The first was from a firm called Freshways, which was not known to you. The order was for three dozen large cheese plants. The firm appeared to be well established and the notepaper bore the phrase 'We've been making your lives Fresher for the last 20 years'. They also enclosed two financial references.

The second letter was from a firm called Greenscapes, whom you have dealt with before, saying that they had opened up a new branch and placing an order for two dozen extra large parlour palms.

The third letter was from a firm whom you believed you had dealt with before, who were placing an order for five dozen 100 leaf aspidistras.

You replied to all three letters confirming the orders.

Since then, delivery has been made of the cheese plants and the parlour palms but no payment has been received. You have heard that neither company is going to pay the bill and you want to get out of the contracts and collect the plants.

With regard to the aspidistras, although when the order was confirmed your computer showed a stock of 200 of this size, you now discover that you have only small plants. Your stock of larger plants was ruined by a student whom you employed who had watered the plants daily rather than weekly.

Consider the position.

With regard to the agreement with Freshways

You have now discovered that the firm is not in a good financial state. The financial references were in fact fabricated. Can you get out of the contract and retrieve the plants? The answer surely is no. You intended to make a contract with Freshways. The problem is simply that they are not as financially sound as you had presumed. The contract starts its 'life' as a valid one. You may be able to get out of it on the basis of misrepresentation by Freshways. However if, in the meantime, Freshways have sold the plants to their own customers, will you be able to retrieve them?

With regard to the agreement with Greenscapes

If you discover that Greenscapes has not opened a new branch but that the letter was sent by a disgruntled ex-employee of theirs who is setting up in competition, what would be the situation? The agreement which you thought you were making was with Greenscapes. It was in fact with the ex-employee. Arguably there is no contract at all between you and the ex-employee. If there was never any contract, what is to prevent you from collecting the plants? Even if the ex-employee of Greenscapes had sold the plants on, would you be entitled to retrieve them?

With regard to the perished aspidistras
Consider, if the plants had perished before the contract was made would it be a case of common mistake? If the plants were thriving at the time the contract was made, would the contract be frustrated? Does the fact that the perishing is the result of your own employee overwatering rather than, say, a freak frost make any difference?

Summary

[You should now be able to:

- explain how a contract is terminated by performance and the consequences of incomplete performance
- explain how a contract is terminated by agreement
- explain the doctrine of frustration
- explain the principle of *non est factum*
- understand and be able to identify contractual situations in which different types of mistake have occurred
- indicate the consequences which arise as a result of such mistakes.

   CASE STUDY 3
Your company provides prefabricated buildings such as portable site accommodation to building and construction companies. You have a contract to supply one such company with eight portable site cabins and ten portable toilet facilities by an agreed date and have been paid a deposit. You sub-contract the transport and installation of the buildings which are intended for the site of a new supermarket. The construction company tells you that the site will only be clear the day before the buildings are due, but the sub-contractor assures you that this will not present a problem.

However, on the day preceding the deadline one of the transporters, carrying four of the portable cabins, breaks down en route and only six arrive. The other four are delayed until the day after the deadline. When you discuss the matter with the site manager, he is clearly not very pleased but says that he can make do, since not all the workforce due on site have, in fact, turned up.

Secondly, the sub-contractor has told you that there will be no problem about installing the portable toilets but, in fact, because of a burst water main, they cannot be connected to the mains and the sub-contractor has not brought enough storage tanks for them to be used independently for more than a couple of days. Only half of them are available for use for the first three days, forcing the workforce to lose time leaving the site.

You are subsequently contacted by the head office of the construction company who placed the order with you and they tell you that they are very unhappy with your performance and consider you to be in breach of contract. They are threatening to deduct the time lost and to add a substantial penalty.

What is your position as far as the following issues are concerned?

1 The degree to which you have performed the original contract, including the delay in getting the buildings on site in time?

2 Does the site manager's response affect the situation?

3 Might the broken water main have any effect on your liability and, if so, how?

11 What happens when things go wrong?

Objectives

By the end of this chapter you should:

- understand what is meant by privity of contract
- understand the application of limitation statutes
- understand the circumstances in which a party acquires title to goods
- explain the remedies available to a party who is the victim of a breach of contract.

Introduction

This chapter perhaps requires some explanation about its order. In many texts a number of these matters will be found in chapters on formation of the contract or even in a chapter of their own. This chapter approaches contracts from a slightly different angle from other texts but from one which is, in practice, often the order in which the problems are encountered.

When two parties enter into a contract usually things will go smoothly and both parties will be happy at the outcome of the agreement. Neither party will usually stop to think about whether or how they could have enforced the contract had things gone wrong. The fact remains that they did not go wrong and so there is simply no need to consider these issues.

This chapter looks at the types of things which may crop up if things do go wrong and you need to consider bringing court proceedings against someone because the contract has not turned out how you expected it to.

Section 1 looks at if you can sue someone, then whom you can sue and within what time limits you must sue.

Section 2 looks at the situation where you decide that you want to get the goods back. You need to decide who owns them.

Section 3 takes the situation a step further. Assuming that you can sue someone, you do want the goods back, and the contract is one in which ownership *can* pass to the buyer, you then need to know *when* that will happen. If you are the seller and you want to recover the goods because the buyer has not paid you, you need to know whether they now belong to you (in which case you can retrieve them) or to the buyer (in which case you cannot retrieve them but can only sue for their money value).

Section 4 takes a more detailed look at remedies. Beyond simply whether or not you can get the goods back you also need to consider how much compensation you can get, and whether there might be any other court order which would be more appropriate to your particular needs.

1   Privity of contract and limitation of actions, or when things go wrong whom can you sue and when?

If something does go wrong with a contract, besides being forced to look at the validity of the contract more closely than you might otherwise have done, you need to consider who you can pursue and when. The question of who you can pursue involves the concept of *privity of contract*. When you can sue is a question of *limitation of actions*.

1.1   Privity of contract

The idea of privity of contract is that only a person who is a party to the contract can sue or be sued on the basis of that contract. The idea is closely allied to that of consideration. Consideration is one of the required elements for a contract. A party who has not given consideration should not, in all usual circumstances, be able to sue the other party to the transaction. So, too, the idea of privity of contract says that if someone is going to be sued successfully for breach of contract they must have been a party to that contract and provided some consideration.

> In **Tweddle v Atkinson (1861)** X and Y entered into a contract whereby each agreed to pay a sum of money to their respective offspring who were about to get married. Y failed to make the promised payment. It was held that the offspring could not sue Y for breach of contract as, quite simply, they were not parties to the contract.
>
> Similarly in **Beswick v Beswick (1968)** X contracted with his nephew that during X's lifetime the nephew could take over X's business in return for paying £6.50 per week. The arrangement went on to say that when X died the nephew should continue to pay £5 per week to X's widow. After X's death the nephew did not make the payments. It was held that X's widow could not sue the nephew as she was not a party to the contract. (The entitlement to sue on X's behalf passed to those administering his estate.)

To this general rule of privity there are some exceptions.

1.1.1   Agency

This topic is dealt with fully in Chapter 17, but briefly if A, acting on behalf of P, makes a contract with T then P can sue T even though he was not actually a party to the contract. This is the case even though A may not have disclosed the existence of P when he was making the contract.

1.1.2   Liability insurance

Section 149 of the **Road Traffic Act 1988** says that with regard to motor insurance and in relation to compulsory third party insurance an injured party can sue and recover direct from the insurance company. This is the case even though the contract of insurance was between the driver and the insurance company, not the injured person and the insurance company.

1.1.3   Leases

When a lease of land is created, rights and obligations attaching to the land are binding on the original landlord and the original tenant as they are parties to the contract. If the tenant then sells the lease, the obligations under the contract which relate to the leased property pass to the purchaser of the lease. In other words the original landlord and the purchaser can sue each other even though they have never entered a contract together. (The contract for sale, remember, was between the original tenant and the purchaser.)

1.1.4   Trusts

If X and Y make a contract creating a trust in which Z is the beneficiary, then if any of the contractual obligations are broken Z can sue in respect of the breach of trust.

1.1.5   Who can recover for the injured party who is not a party to the contract?

If one considers a case such as a holiday travel case, then the consequences of the rule on privity of contract can be seen. Imagine that you have booked a holiday for yourself and your parents. The contract is made by you with the travel agent and you pay the whole bill. The holiday turns out to be a disaster. Clearly you can sue the travel company for your lost holiday. But what about your parents? They were not parties to the contract. They cannot sue the travel company. The question then is, can you sue the travel company for the loss which your parents suffered?

> In **Jackson v Horizon Holidays (1975)** damages were awarded for the disappointment not only of the person who booked the holiday but also the other family members who went with him.

The reasoning in this case though has to be doubted (or perhaps limited to the specific case of holidays?) in the light of the House of Lords decision in

Woodar Investment Development Limited v Wimpey Construction UK Ltd (1980). In this case X agreed to sell land to Y provided that Y paid £750,000 to X and £150,000 to Z. It was claimed that Y did not fulfil his part of the bargain. Z could do nothing about it as he was not a party to the contract. X tried to solve the problem by suing Y for both his own (X's) loss and Z's loss also. In the event the court found that Y had fulfilled the bargain but commented that anyway X would not have been able to recover for any loss suffered by Z.

1.2 Limitation of actions

Someone who has a right to sue for breach of contract cannot afford to delay starting court proceedings indefinitely. After a certain period of time the *action will be barred*. In other words the courts will simply not allow the injured party to sue. Quite simply the **Limitation Act 1980** lays down specific periods of time within which court proceedings must be started.

Where it is a *simple* contract the period is six years from the date when the contract was first broken.

Where the contract was made in the form of a formal *deed* (the requirements for which are now contained in section 1 of the **Law of Property (Miscellaneous Provisions) Act 1989**), the period is 12 years from when the agreement was broken.

The period starts to run from the time that the breach of contract actually occurred. In contract law it is usually immaterial that the breach had not been discovered until later. So if the breach is discovered after the time period has elapsed the injured party may have no recourse to the courts at all. The rule is occasionally relaxed when, for example, the party who is at fault deliberately acts so as to conceal the breach.

If at the time of the breach of contract the injured person was either a minor or someone suffering from a mental disorder, then time will only start to run from the time the disability comes to an end. Imagine that a minor is a party to a contract and the adult breaches the contract. The breach occurs when the minor is 14 years old. The limitation period is six years but that time does not start to run until the minor reaches 18. In other words the minor can sue at any time up until he is 24 years old.

 CASE STUDY 1
Several years ago you instructed an architect to draw up plans for the complete modernisation of your house. On the basis of the architect's specifications you contracted with a major building firm and negotiated a lump sum price for all the work. That contract was made two years ago. The

building firm employed sub-contractors for the electrical work and the plumbing work. While work was in progress last year you found some faults with the electrics which have not yet been put right – you still get an electric shock if you use the shower! On completion of the work last month you discovered that the plumbing in the utility room is not to the architect's specifications.

Consider the position.

Who can you sue?

You may have got to know the plumber and the electrician quite well while they were on site. You may even have employed them separately to do additional work. But the basis of your complaint is that the contract which you made with *the builders* has not been performed satisfactorily. In the case of the electrical wiring the defect speaks (or sparks!) for itself. In the case of the plumber's work you can point to the original specifications to show that the work is inadequate. On the basis of privity of contract, can you sue the plumber and the electrician direct or must you sue the builder instead?

With regard to the timing

How long is the period during which you are safe to argue about the matter and still able to sue if you cannot reach a satisfactory conclusion by negotiation? Is the time limit different for the two breaches of contract?

Whether or not you can sue someone, if the 'contract' goes wrong one of the things which you may try to do is to get your goods back. You can only get the goods back if they belong to you. If the ownership of them has passed to someone else you may find yourself guilty of *theft* under the criminal law and sued for *conversion* under the civil law. You need therefore to consider whether and when title will have passed. (That is, sections 2 and 3 respectively.)

2   The passing of title/transfer of ownership – can it happen at all?

Very often if a party to a contract does not get what they anticipated from the contract they will want to do something about it. What we need to consider now is what they may be able to do.

It is very tempting to think of ownership of the goods being with whoever has possession of them at the time. This is not necessarily the case. In some situations the other party to the contract may have had the capacity to make the contract but did not actually own the goods that he contracted to sell. What then is the situation of the 'buyer' who buys goods from the seller and takes delivery of them?

2.1 Title to goods

The simple rule is that you cannot sell what you do not own. If the seller did not own the goods then he cannot sell you any rights of ownership. He may have physically delivered the goods to you but you may be at risk from having them taken away by the real owner if they track their goods down. This is why the thousands of people who innocently buy stolen cars lose out. If the police identify the car as stolen and can identify the original owner, the owner is entitled to the return of the car. The innocent buyer bought the car but acquired no rights of ownership. He couldn't acquire any such rights because the person he bought it from had none in the first place.

To this general rule that you can't sell what you don't own there are a number of exceptions, some examples of which are given below.

2.1.1 Estoppel

Section 21 of the Sale of Goods Act says that someone who does not own the property may be able to transfer the ownership rights of the true owner if the true owner is by his conduct precluded from denying the seller's right to sell. This means that where the true owner has allowed the buyer to believe that the seller has a right to sell the goods he will be prevented (*estopped*) from denying that the seller had that right.

In **Eastern Distributors Ltd v Goldring (1957)** X owned a van. He wanted to buy a car from Y, a car dealer, but had no money for the deposit. The dealer and X colluded together and decided to tell the finance company that X was buying both the van (which was already his) and the car. The finance company in fact advanced money on the van and not the car. The plan having gone wrong, X simply decided to sell the van and he sold it to Goldring who knew nothing about what had gone before. The finance company then tried to sue Goldring to get the van back. The argument of the finance company was that the company owned the van as they had bought it from Y. Goldring's argument was that the company could not own the van as it had never been the dealer's to sell in the first place, since the van had always belonged to X. The court held that the principle of you cannot sell what you do not own should not apply in this case as X had colluded with Y in representing to the finance company that Y had the right to sell it. The finance company therefore owned the van.

2.1.2 Sale by a factor

The general principle will not apply where the goods are in the possession of a mercantile agent who is known to sell goods on behalf of other people. If the goods were originally put in the possession of the agent with the consent of the owner, and then the agent sells the goods he can pass ownership as if he were expressly authorised to sell the goods. The purchaser from the agent will get good title to the goods and it is up to the original owner to sue the *factor* if the sale was contrary to instructions (**Factors Act 1889**).

2.1.3   Sale under common law or a statutory power of sale

If goods are sold under a court order then the buyer will acquire good title/ownership of the goods even if the original owner did not agree to the sale. Also there are some statutes which give someone who does not own the goods the right to sell them in certain circumstances. For example, if goods are left for repair and after a certain time they have not been collected and the repair has not been paid for, then the **Torts (Interference with Goods) Act 1977** permits the repairer to sell the goods.

3   Can you get the goods back? When does ownership pass from one party to another?

One thing which needs to be considered as a preliminary matter is, if the contract was for goods, who owns the goods now? If the seller still owns them then he cannot reclaim their value from the buyer but will be entitled to their return. If the seller or the buyer were to go bankrupt, it is vital to know whom the goods belonged to when the person went bankrupt in order to decide whether the other party can keep the goods or whether the trustee in bankruptcy is entitled to them.

As we have seen before, it is very tempting to think of ownership of the goods being with whoever has possession of them at the time. This is not necessarily the case. Think about the situations which we have looked at concerning mistake: it is clear that if the contract is void from the outset the ownership of the goods will not pass to the buyer, nor to anyone to whom they might then sell the goods. Also, with a voidable contract, the ownership/title will pass to the buyer initially but may return to the seller if the seller makes it clear he wants to avoid the contract and does so before an innocent third party has bought the goods.

In a straightforward contract which is neither void nor voidable we still need to consider who owns the goods at any particular time in order to decide whether or not they can be retrieved if that is what the injured party wants.

The point at which the ownership/title to the goods passes from the seller to the buyer depends on whether the goods are *specific, unascertained* or *ascertained.*

3.1   Specific, unascertained and ascertained goods

3.1.1   Specific goods

Specific goods are goods which are identified and agreed on at the time a contract of sale is made. In other words those particular goods and no others will suffice.

The title to specific goods passes whenever the parties intend it to pass and in deciding this the courts can look at 'the terms of the contract, the conduct of the parties and the circumstances of the case' (section 17, Sale of Goods Act 1979).

3.1.2 Unascertained goods

These are goods which are defined by description only, e.g. 'a jar of coffee' or 'five bags of flour'. The meaning of this is *any* jar of coffee and *any* five bags of flour. They are goods of which you have clearly identified the type (you might even be specific regarding the brand) but the actual jar itself and the precise five bags which are to become yours have not been picked out from the rest.

The title in unascertained goods passes either when there is an unconditional appropriation to the buyer or where the goods are despatched or delivered to the buyer. Whether there is an appropriation to the buyer or not will be a question of what has happened between the parties in that particular contract.

Appropriation may be where the goods are despatched or delivered to the buyer without any express retention of ownership (see section 18, rule 5, Sale of Goods Act 1979). There cannot, however, be an appropriation where the goods remain part of the seller's bulk stock. For example in

Healy v Howlett & Sons (1917) the buyers in London ordered 20 boxes of mackerel. The seller sent 122 boxes to their agent in Holyhead. Because of a delay in the transport (which was not the fault of either party) the fish was rotten when it arrived in Holyhead. It was held that there had been no appropriation of the fish in Ireland. The appropriation had taken place when the 20 boxes were separated by the Holyhead agent for onward transmission to the buyers. The risk and cost of the deterioration was with whoever owned/had title to the fish. In this case the seller in Ireland.

3.1.3 Ascertained goods

Once goods have been selected and identified (after the making of the contract) as the appropriate subject matter of the agreement, then the goods are said to be ascertained. For example, having contracted to buy 'a jar of jam', once that jar of jam is selected and set aside to fulfil the order it is classed as ascertained goods.

The title to ascertained goods, like specific goods, passes whenever the parties intend it to pass and in deciding this the courts can look at 'the terms of the contract, the conduct of the parties and the circumstances of the case' (section 17, Sale of Goods Act 1979).

3.2 Section 18 of the Sale of Goods Act 1979

In some cases it may be clear from the terms of the contract or the behaviour of the parties when the title to the goods should pass. The rules in section 18 apply only where no different intention appears. They are basically rules of thumb to be applied where there is no other evidence.

3.2.1 Rule 1

Rule 1 says that where there is an unconditional contract for the sale of specific goods in a deliverable state, the property in the goods passes to the buyer when the contract is made. The rule also says that, in such a case, it is immaterial that the time of payment or of delivery or of both is postponed.

⚖

> In **Tarling v Baxter (1827)** a buyer bought a haystack. Before he took it away with him it was burnt down. It was held (on the basis of a similar earlier common law rule) that the buyer must still pay the price as the ownership of the haystack had passed to the buyer when the contract was made.

3.2.2   Rule 2

Where there is a contract for the sale of specific goods but the seller needs to do something to put them in a deliverable state, the title does not pass until that thing has been done and the buyer has been told that it has been done. An obvious example would be the sale of a car where the seller has agreed to fit a new engine. The ownership of the car would not pass until the engine had been put in and the buyer notified.

3.2.3   Rules 3 and 4

Rule 3 states that 'where there is a contract for the sale of specific goods in a deliverable state but the seller is bound to weigh, measure, test or do some other act or thing with reference to the goods for the purpose of ascertaining the price, the property does not pass until the act or thing is done and the buyer has notice that it has been done.'

It should be noted that this rule only applies where it is the *seller* who is to 'weigh, measure, test' etc; if it is agreed that the buyer will do this then Rule 1 applies and the property in the goods passes when the contract is made.

⚖

> In **Nanka Bruce v Commonwealth Trust Ltd (1926)** N agreed to deliver cocoa to L at 59 shillings per 60 pounds. The parties agreed that L would resell to sub-purchasers and that when the latter took delivery, the cocoa would be weighed at their premises. By this method, the price due from L to N could be ascertained. It was held that such weighing did not make the contract conditional since property in the cocoa passed to L as soon as the contract was made by virtue of Rule 1.

Rule 4 states that 'when goods are delivered to the buyer on approval or on sale or return or other similar terms the property in the goods passes to the buyer

a) when he signifies his approval or acceptance to the seller or does any other act adopting the transaction;

b) if he does not signify his approval or acceptance to the seller but retains the goods without giving notice or rejection then, if a time has been fixed for the return of the goods, on the expiration of that time, and, if no time has been fixed, on the expiration of a reasonable time.'

The words 'any other act adopting the transaction' are illustrated by

Kirkham v Attenborough (1897) in which K sent jewellery to W on 'sale or return'. W pawned it with A. It was held that by pawning the jewellery, W had adopted the transaction and the property had therefore passed to him. K could not recover from A since the jewellery no longer belonged to K.

3.3   Romalpa clauses

Although usually the courts must look at the intention of the parties and, if that is not clear, at the rules contained in section 18, sometimes there will be an express provision in the contract as to when the ownership of the goods will pass. Often this clause accords with or is similar to what one would, on a commonsense basis, expect to be the moment when ownership in the goods passed. Sometimes, though, an express clause is used by the seller to try and retain ownership of the goods in case something goes wrong.

Imagine the situation where you sell a large quantity of greetings cards to a stationer. Common sense says that they become the property of the stationer at least when they are delivered to him. The invoice accompanying the cards may not be payable for 30 days. If the stationer goes bankrupt before the bill is paid wouldn't you prefer to take your cards back rather than try to fight for a share out of the bankrupt's assets? Without an express clause you would be unable to do so as ownership of the cards would already have passed to the stationer.

In **Aluminium Industrie Vaasen BV v Romalpa Aluminium (1976)** AIV sold some foil to Romalpa. It was stated in the contract that the ownership of the foil would only pass to Romalpa when the money owing to AIV had been paid. Further the contract said that if Romalpa used the foil to manufacture a new product then AIV would become the owners of the new product. Further still, if Romalpa then sold the new product then Romalpa's rights against the buyer would be transferred to AIV pending payment of their account. Romalpa later became insolvent and went into liquidation. It was held by the Court of Appeal that AIV could recover any unprocessed foil and the proceeds of the sale on any of the foil. The question of what should happen to goods with which the foil had been mixed was not decided.

Later cases suggest that such a clause might be successful but it is bound to be fraught with legal problems. For example, what if two products were mixed, both of which were subject to a Romalpa clause?

3.4   The transfer of risk

We all know that if you own goods and you don't insure them then if anything happens to them it's your loss. What though if something happens to goods which are the subject of a contract? Section 20 of the Sale of Goods Act 1979 says that unless otherwise agreed, the risk of what might happen to the goods is with the ownership and when ownership/title passes so does the risk.

It is important to note, however, that this section only applies if the parties have not reached agreement to the contrary.

Section 20(2) states that where delivery has been delayed through the fault of either the buyer or the seller, the goods are at the risk of the party at fault as regards any loss caused by the delay.

With regard to perishable goods section 6 of the Sale of Goods Act 1979 says that if the goods have, without the knowledge of the seller, perished at the time the contract is made then the contract is *void*. (This should not come as any surprise to you. It might just as easily be dealt with by the concept of bilateral mistake.) Section 7 says that where there is an agreement to sell specific goods and the goods, without any fault on the part of the seller or buyer, perish before risk has passed to the buyer then the agreement is avoided.

    CASE STUDY 2

This is a gruesome case study so please accept our apologies in advance!

Imagine that your aunt goes into a pet shop. She sees some puppies and some kittens and decides that she will have one of each. Most of the puppies are of a whippet type but one is a cute spaniel type. She chooses that one. The kittens are a mixture of colours and she chooses the only ginger one amongst them. Your aunt then pays for the animals and says that she will collect them when she has finished her other shopping. She also pays for a sack of puppy meal and a tray of kitten food.

While your aunt is doing her other shopping catastrophe strikes.

The sack of puppy meal which had been set aside for your aunt is eaten by a large alsatian which wandered into the shop.

The whole pallet of kitten food is dropped and the tins are badly damaged.

The police call and retrieve the spaniel puppy saying that it is one of a litter stolen yesterday from a nearby breeder.

The ginger kitten is attacked by a gerbil from the next cage and its face is badly scarred.

Consider the position.

With regard to the puppy meal

Who did the puppy meal belong to at the time when it was eaten? The shop owner may be prepared to replace the sack of meal but is he obliged to? Or is it your aunt's loss?

With regard to the kitten food

Who did the kitten food belong to? Does it make a difference that the tray which your aunt was to have was simply one of the trays which were all dropped from the pallet? Would it have made any difference if a single tray had been set aside and then damaged?

With regard to the puppy

Who does the puppy belong to? If it was stolen in the first place could the thief effectively transfer ownership of the dog to the shopkeeper? If the shopkeeper did own the dog in the first place could he sell it to your aunt? Can your aunt therefore get the puppy back from the breeder? Can your aunt get her money back from the shopkeeper? Can the shopkeeper get his money back from the thief – if he can find him?

With regard to the kitten

This poor little kitten is now no longer the attractive little soul which he was when your aunt bought him. In addition whoever owns him is going to have to pay a vet's bill for his face to be stitched.

Did the ownership of the kitten pass to your aunt when she selected and paid for the kitten? Is she obliged to take it? Or does it still belong to the shopkeeper? Did the risk of anything happening to the kitten pass at the same time as the ownership? Even if you decide that your aunt owns it, must she foot the vet's bill?

4   Remedies – what is the injured party entitled to?

4.1   The basic terminology

The matter of remedies really involves looking at who will be entitled to what if things go wrong. The first thing which we need to consider is what we mean by a *remedy*. Usually what is meant is an order which a court could make to make the other party do something which they should have done, refrain from doing something which they should not do, or pay compensation (*damages*) to the injured party. Occasionally the courts will simply be asked to adjudicate as to what the rights and obligations of the parties are and the court will make a *declaration* as to their relationship.

When we are looking at remedies the question of why there is a remedy at all must not be overlooked. What is it that has happened which gives the injured party a right to sue the other party? It is sometimes very easy to think in terms of 'I have been hurt, therefore someone must pay'. But we saw in Chapter 8 that this isn't actually the case. Someone who feels that they have suffered some injury because of the act or omission of another party must be able to establish a formal legal link by which that other party can be sued. This is what's known as a *cause of action*.

The next thing that we need to consider is the types of remedy available. The remedies available are often (and rather confusingly to the non-specialist lawyer) classified as *legal remedies* or *equitable remedies*. The distinction is really this:

- if the remedy is classified as legal remedy then the courts, if they believe your version of the contract and events, *must* give you the remedy you ask for
- if the remedy is an equitable remedy, then even if the courts believe what you say they are not obliged to make the order that you ask for. Equitable remedies are discretionary remedies and the courts can consider the matter as a whole when deciding whether or not they want to give you the order you ask for.

Put somewhat cynically, legal remedies can in effect be demanded, equitable remedies you ask very nicely for.

4.2   The likely causes of action

In the case of contract law there are likely to be two possible *causes of action.*

The most likely scenario is that the injured party can point to some term of the contract which has not been complied with. The term might be an express term or an implied term but either way they can actually point to some provision. If this is the case then the injured party would bring proceedings in court based on *breach of contract.* It must be remembered, however, that if your claim is that there has been a breach of contract then you must be able to identify the precise term which has not been complied with.

The other common cause of action in contractual situations is *misrepresentation.* This means showing that the other party made some misstatement of fact which then induced you to enter into the contract. In other words, and put at its simplest, you cannot point to a particular term of the contract but you do feel aggrieved that the situation is not as it was represented to you during negotiations. (We looked at this earlier, in Chapter 9, when we were looking at terms of the contract.)

4.3   Remedies for breach of contract

Assume that two parties, Alice and Brian, enter into a contract. Brian then fails to carry out his obligations under the contract as agreed. Alice will sue Brian for breach of contract. (That is the theory anyway. More likely than the matter actually reaching court is that Alice and Brian will reach some compromise agreement before they ever get to court. Going to court is, as we have seen in earlier chapters, a last resort.) In bringing an action for breach of contract Alice will be seeking a remedy. The main legal remedy is that Brain should be ordered to pay *damages.*

4.3.1   Damages
When looking at the question of damages there are two main things which need to be considered.

4.3.1.1   Remoteness of damage/which injuries should be compensated?
Firstly, can the injured party claim for *everything* which he or she has lost as a result of the breach of contract? If it is considered that the injured party should not be able to claim for some injuries these damages are said to be too *remote.*

Damage arising from a breach of contract can be compensated providing it is not too remote. In order to decide this we need to apply the rule in **Hadley v Baxendale**. The rule consists of two parts. The injured party can recover

- for loss arising naturally as a result of the breach of contract, or
- for loss which was in the contemplation of both parties at the time the contract was made.

> The case of **Victoria Laundry (Windsor) Ltd v Newman Industries Ltd (1949)** illustrates the point. The facts were that X agreed to sell a boiler to the laundry company. X knew that the boiler was required for immediate use. X breached the contract by delivering the boiler late. X was unaware that the laundry company had recently won a very lucrative contract which could only be carried out by using the boiler. The laundry company lost a considerable amount of money by not being able to use the boiler to fulfil the new contract. The laundry company was able to recover damages for general loss of profit but not for the extra-ordinary loss of profit on the new contract.

Had X been told about the new contract before the contract for the supply of the boiler was entered into the matter might have been different. The lost profit on the new contract might then have come within the second limb of the rule in **Hadley v Baxendale**.

>   **CASE STUDY 3**
>
> Consider, for example, the position if you contracted to buy a commercial premises for £200,000. At the time of the contract three months ago you intended to use the premises yourself, but after the contract was made you entered into another contract to sell the property on to a developer at a price of £300,000. Imagine that, when the time comes, the seller refuses to go through with the contract; how much will you be able to claim?
>
> Consider the following.

The loss arising directly from the seller's breach of contract

The seller's breach of contract consists in failing to sell you the premises as promised. You will now have to find similar suitable premises elsewhere. Under the first head you would be entitled to the cost of buying a similar property elsewhere. The cost of buying similar premises may now, at the time of the seller's breach of contract, be £250,000. You have surely lost £50,000 as a direct result of the breach.

The loss arising indirectly from the seller's breach of contract

The loss arising indirectly is that you have lost out on the profit on your new contract. You would have made £100,000 on the new deal. This extra profit is one stage removed from the original contract and will only be recoverable if it fits under the second limb of the rule in **Hadley v Baxendale**. We need to ask whether this lost profit is loss which was contemplated by both parties at the time of the contract. The answer must be no. The second contract was not even contemplated by you *at the time you entered into the contract* never mind by both of you.

Would the answer differ if you had always had it in mind to resell the property to developers?

The answer here is that it might. If either you had already entered into a contract with developers, or (more likely) were in negotiations with developers, then the question we would need to consider is whether the seller was aware of this situation. If the seller was aware of your intentions with regard to the property then you might be able to claim the lost profit on your second contract on the basis that it was loss which was within the *contemplation of both parties at the time the contract was made.*

4.3.1.2   Quantum of damages/how much compensation should be paid?

Secondly we need to consider how *much* monetary compensation should be awarded to the injured party. The rule is quite simply that the injured party should be paid enough to put them back in the same position as they would have been in if the contract had been carried out properly.

The injured party should not be able to make a profit out of their injury

Usually the loss will be easily quantified as it will be financial or relate to damage to property. Even if it relates to bodily injury this can usually be quantified reasonably easily on the basis of the type of injury and what other courts have awarded for that type.

The situation may be difficult to judge where you cannot say that the 'injured' party has actually suffered any damage. The Sale of Goods Act, sections 50 and 51 say that, in most usual situations, where there is a general market for goods and a party fails to deliver or accept goods, then the amount payable in damages is the difference between the contract price and the market price on the date when delivery should have taken place. This is only a general rule though. For example, if you enter a contract to buy a new Land Ranger four-wheel-drive vehicle which is due to come into the show rooms for the first time next month and you then back out of the contract, the dealer could argue that he has lost his profit on the deal. If it can be shown that demand for the new vehicles is such that the dealer can easily resell it for the same (or perhaps even a better) price, then to award damages where the dealer has suffered no loss may be considered inappropriate.

Returning to the basic rule, it is that a party should simply be compensated for the injury which they suffer. However, consider the situation where you enter into a contract where you agree to pay £100 for your garden to be tidied up. If the contractor fails to turn up you may be able to employ another contractor. If the other contractor cost you £130 then the damages due to you would be £30 (the difference between what the work should have cost you and what you in fact had to pay for it). You may also be able to claim the cost of the telephone call to engage the second contractor but that is where your loss ends. You may feel very aggrieved and feel that you ought to be able to make some money out of the situation because of all the aggravation you have suffered. Usually though you cannot.

The special case for holiday/pleasure contracts
One exceptional area is in the case of holidays.

In **Jarvis v Swan Tours (1973)** X booked a holiday costing £63.45. The holiday proved to be a disaster and the facilities were not what they were promised to be in the brochure. The Court of Appeal allowed X to recover not only the price of the holiday but also a similar amount to compensate him for his disappointment.

The exception in this case can be quite easily justified. The whole object of entering into a holiday is the pursuit of pleasure and enjoyment. There is no reason then why the holiday maker should not receive compensation if that part of the bargain is ruined by the other party. Compensation for feelings of frustration and anguish will not, however, normally be allowed (**Hayes v James & Charles Dodd (1990)**). The distinction between commercial and *pleasure contracts* is also illustrated by the case of

Addis v Gramophone Co (1909). In this case X was given six months notice of terminating his contract of employment. His employers told his successor to take over from him and told a local bank that X was no longer to act on its behalf. X left and sued his former employer for wrongful dismissal. The House of Lords held that X was entitled to:

- loss of salary
- loss of commission (which he would have earned had he been allowed to continue handling the bank's affairs)

but not compensation for his injured feelings.

Mitigating loss
A logical follow-on to the idea that the injured party should not make a profit from their damages is the idea that the injured person must keep their loss to a minimum. A failure to do so will mean that the damages awarded may be limited. For example, an employee who feels that they have been wrongly dismissed cannot simply sit back in the hope that their former employer will foot the bill in paying their lost salary. The former employee must take reasonable steps to try and find new work in order to limit the damages. A failure to accept new work or to look for new work may result in the complete loss of any damages.

Liquidated damages
Sometimes when the parties enter into a contract they may agree an amount which should be payable in the event of specified breaches of contract. Such

damages, the amount of which is decided in advance, are referred to as *liquidated damages*. In most situations the parties are free to negotiate whatever figure they wish for liquidated damages. The courts will usually only step in if they feel that the amount of the damages is not a genuine pre-estimate of the loss and is exorbitant in relation to the largest possible loss which could have occurred.

4.3.2   Rescission

Rescission is an equitable remedy which in essence means that the court releases the parties from the contract and its obligations. It is most usually awarded in the case of a mistake by one or both parties. We looked earlier at the question of mistake and we have also looked at the question of misrepresentation. In either of these cases the courts may be prepared to release the parties from the obligations of the contract. The possible options which are available to the court vary, depending on the cause of action. In any case the particular rules surrounding that cause of action should be checked. Generally, though, there are two possibilities with rescission: either the order may simply release the parties from their obligations under the contract or the situation may be restored to what it was before the contract (for example, papers and monies belonging to the other party must be returned). Alternatively (and particularly where the original situation of the parties cannot be restored), the court may include an award of damages with an order for rescission.

4.3.3   Rectification

This remedy applies where a mistake has occurred in reducing the terms of an oral contract to writing. A court may be prepared to order rectification so that the document expresses the true intention of the parties.

> In **Jocelyne v Nissen (1970)** a father lived in the same house as his daughter. The father and daughter orally contracted that if the father transferred his car hire business to the daughter she would, in turn, pay his household expenses. When this agreement was reduced to writing there was no mention of the daughter's liability to pay her father's household expenses. The court agreed to *rectify* the agreement to reflect the content of the oral agreement.

4.3.4   Specific performance

An order for specific performance is quite simply where a court orders a party to a contract to carry out his/her obligations as agreed. Failure to comply with the order will mean that the defaulting party is liable to imprisonment for contempt of court. This remedy is not commonly awarded. In most situations the law seems to recognise that the interests of the parties can be perfectly well served by the injured party being paid compensation and then allowing them to go their separate ways.

The remedy is an equitable one and so it is discretionary. It will never be awarded where the contract is for personal services. (For example, a court would not compel an employee to work for an employer.) It is most commonly encountered in contracts for the sale of land. In such contracts the attitude of the law is that each piece of land is unique and so damages are not an adequate remedy. Even in the case of contracts for land, the remedy will not be awarded if making the parties perform the contract would have an adverse effect on an innocent third party.

4.3.5   Injunction

This order is a *decree* by the court which either orders that a certain thing should be done (a *mandatory injunction*) or prohibits the doing of something (a *prohibitory injunction*). Usually the mandatory injunction is used to make a party do a particular thing which they are required to do under the contract. (An order for *specific performance* would relate to the whole contract and an injunction may relate simply to one aspect/obligation of the contract.) Prohibitory or ordinary injunctions are awarded in order to prevent a breach of contract.

So, for example, a mandatory injunction could be used to order a landlord to make repairs to premises under a lease. A prohibitory injunction could be used to prevent a landlord from trespassing on the premises which he has let to the tenant.

Summary

You should now be able to:

- explain how the doctrine of privity of contract is applied
- explain the main exceptions to the doctrine of privity
- explain the circumstances in which an action for breach of contract will be barred
- explain what is meant by having title to goods
- explain what is meant by estoppel
- identify specific, unascertained and ascertained goods
- indicate what is meant by a Romalpa clause
- explain how it is determined whether damage sustained as the result of a breach of contract is or is not too remote
- explain the circumstances in which a court will order specific performance
- explain the meaning of injunction.

 CASE STUDY 4

Your company buys second-hand TVs and reconditions them to sell to customers with a one year guarantee. You are approached by an agent on behalf of a large TV manufacturer which has a surplus stock of old models which it is prepared to sell. You agree to buy an initial consignment of 500, paying by instalments, and also take an option to buy a further 500 within six months.

Sales go well to start with, but five months later you begin to get a stream of complaints. Because the first consignments was not stored properly, some of the metal components have rusted. You approach the agent to ask for a refund on the damaged stock and some sort of compensation, and ask that the manufacturer honours the option on the second 500, providing they are in usable condition.

Consider your situation in the following circumstances:

1 The agent claims that your arrangement is with the manufacturer and not with him.

2 The manufacturer asserts that complaining after five months is too late.

3 Having not supplied them in the end, the manufacturer says that it is not under obligation to supply the second instalment of 500 TVs. To do so would mean supplying you with a different improved model since they no longer have any stock of the original model in satisfactory condition.

What remedies might be available to you?

12 What is tort?

Objectives

By the end of this chapter, you should:

- be able to understand the basis of a tort
- be able to give examples of a selection of different torts
- be able to distinguish between liability in tort and liability in criminal law
- be able to distinguish between liability in tort and liability in the law of contract.

1   What is tort?

Certainly tort is a strange word. Words like 'contract' not only have a specific meaning for a lawyer but are also part of everyday English. Tort on the other hand is not a word which you will find bandied around by non-lawyers; indeed most non-lawyers will never have heard of the word. Tort is really a large category of legal wrongs made up of individual torts, many of which you will already be familiar with even if you don't know exactly what they mean. The idea is not really so strange if we immediately look at some examples of torts.

In the case of a road accident you will quite often hear someone say that it was the other driver's fault: he or she was *negligent* in not looking when they pulled out at the junction. You may have heard in relation to a dispute between neighbours that the person from number 4 is often found *trespassing* in the garden of number 2. So the legal term for the category may be unfamiliar, but most of us will be familiar with many of the things included in that category. We just don't know it yet.

So far the situations that we have looked at in the chapters on contract all involve the parties entering into an agreement or bargain. But there will be situations where a person suffers damage or injury as a result of something done by someone whom they have never even met, let alone entered into a contractual relationship with. We need to go back to the idea that we first looked at in relation to the law of contracts.

'I have been hurt therefore someone must pay' – True or False?

Case Study 1

This case study is designed simply to test your gut reaction to different situations. Much of the law of tort is based on the idea of whether or not a person is *responsible* for damage/injury.

Imagine this situation. On your way into work you are walking along the pavement. My car mounts the pavement and runs into you breaking both your legs. It is true that you have been hurt. Initial reaction says that it must have been my fault and that I should be made to pay. But using your gut reaction just think about it again.

I   Would you still say that the accident was my *fault* and that I should be made to pay if the accident had happened because the brakes on my car had failed? Would it make any difference whether or not I had had the car regularly serviced?

2   Would you still say that the accident was my *fault* and that I should be made to pay if I had had a blackout and lost control of the car? Would it make any difference if this was not the first blackout that I had suffered recently?

Your reaction to each situation is likely to have varied, depending on the circumstances. The law often follows that reaction in terms of blame or fault. In some situations the law would say that the accident was my fault and that I should pay you compensation (*damages*). In others the law may say that the situation is simply an *accident* for which I should not be made to pay.

When we looked at the law of contract it was the terms of the contract itself which allowed the person who had suffered loss to sue the other. The contract was the formal legal link between the two people which allowed one to sue the other. In some cases where there is no contractual link, the law establishes a formal legal link by which a person who has suffered damage can sue the person who is responsible for that damage.

That formal legal link is often a *tort*.

Whether or not a formal legal link exists depends on history. There may be a tort established by case law. Alternatively, Parliament may have enacted a statute in situations where it was felt that there should be liability but either none existed in case law or it did exist but was considered to be unsatisfactory.

2   The different types of tort

The idea of torts is perhaps best illustrated by looking at specific examples of established torts. What follows is simply a selection of some of the more common or interesting torts with an everyday example of how they might arise.

2.1 Negligence

This is probably the most commonly encountered tort and the next chapter deals with it in more detail. It is certainly a vitally important tort in the business context. In essence, negligence is the idea that if I conduct myself in a careless manner in a situation where it is reasonably likely that my conduct will affect someone else, then if I cause that person injury I may be sued. In other words I have some sort of general responsibility to consider how my behaviour may affect other people.

A most common example is in driving a car. If I run into another car because I was busy changing a cassette in the car stereo and so had not bothered to look properly when joining a roundabout, then I may be sued for the damage that I cause as a result of my behaviour.

2.2 Private nuisance

If I behave in such a way as to interfere with a landowner's enjoyment of land, then that conduct may amount to a private nuisance. Obviously not all conduct of which you or I may disapprove will amount to a *nuisance* as a legal concept. Furthermore, whether something is simply an irritation or falls within the *legal definition* of a nuisance may be a matter of degree.

For example, you may not like the fact that my daughter has what you consider to be an irritating taste in music and that her CD player interferes with your enjoyment of sitting out in your garden in summer. If, however, the playing of the music is, on any reasonable view, acceptable and not repeated too often then it might not amount to a legal *nuisance*. The courts have actually acknowledged that where the interference with adjoining premises amounts simply to a complaint that the offended person has suffered discomfort or inconvenience, then the conflicting interests of both parties have to be considered and the courts must take into account 'the rule of give and take, live and let live' (**Bamford v Turnley (1862)**).

Another example of a potential nuisance might be a bonfire. Most people have a small bonfire in their gardens from time to time, either to burn autumn leaves or on bonfire night or even occasionally to get rid of a little domestic waste. If, however, your neighbour developed a habit of lighting a fire in the garden every other day to burn rubbish and, each time he lit it, it filled your house with offensive smoke, you might have a remedy for *private nuisance*. If all reasonable negotiations with your neighbour do not bear fruit then you might find that a more convenient method would be to report your neighbour to the environmental department of your local council and get them to tackle the problem. If however they were unwilling to do anything about it, then the remedy of private nuisance would be available for you to do something about it yourself.

Strictly speaking only the owner or occupier of land can bring an action for private nuisance. So in theory the family of a landowner living with him/her would be precluded from suing for private nuisance. If they could not persuade their relative who owned the property to start an action, then they might have none. This rule has been relaxed in more recent times.

⚖️

> In **Khorasandjian v Bush (1993)** the daughter of an occupier of land was granted an injunction to prevent nuisance phone calls from a former boyfriend. The decision in this case was apparently based on the need to adapt to 'changed special conditions'.

2.3   Public nuisance

A public nuisance is an act or omission 'which materially affects the reasonable comfort and convenience of life of a class of Her Majesty's subjects'.

The right to sue for public nuisance is not therefore limited to landowners or occupiers as in private nuisance. However other restrictions do apply. Because a public nuisance is something suffered by a considerable number of people it is not usually left to individuals to sue in respect of the nuisance. Usually the matter will be pursued by the Attorney General on behalf of the general public. An individual can only start proceedings for public nuisance if he or she can show that he or she has suffered *particular damage* (in other words damage over and above that suffered by the rest of the suffering group).

2.4   Trespass

Lay people often think of trespass as involving land. In fact there are three different types of trespass to be found in the law of tort. Firstly, let us consider trespass in relation to land.

2.4.1   Trespass to land

This involves direct unjustifiable interference with the possession of land.

The most usual form of trespass is to go on to land where you are not permitted to be. Alternatively you might be permitted on to land but refuse to leave when asked. (Imagine a door to door double-glazing salesman who, although initially asked into the house, refuses to leave when you have had enough!)

Alternatively the trespass might be placing objects on or above the land (for example, erecting a large 'for sale' sign which overhangs part of your neighbour's garden).

2.4.2   Trespass to the person

Forcible physical contact, or the threat of it, can amount to the tort of trespass to the person. If I were to push you through a door way (without your permission) that would, in all probability, be a trespass to the person in the form of *battery*. Even simply to threaten to do so (if the threat appeared serious) could amount to trespass to the person in the form of *assault*. Usually the two go hand in hand and are referred to together as *assault and battery*.

There are certain situations where even though no express consent has been given, the physical contact will not amount to trespass. Most of these situations are social situations where common sense tells us it would be unthinkable to allow one person to sue the other. Firmly taking someone by the arm at a party may, in certain special circumstances, be objectionable but generally speaking will not, even if it is subsequently found to be unwelcome, entitle the offended person to start proceedings for trespass.

2.4.3 Trespass to goods

Making off with someone else's belongings may amount to the crime of theft. The same actions will amount to trespass to goods and you can be sued for their return or for damages for their loss. Most forms of trespass to goods can now be found in statutory form in the **Torts (Interference with Goods) Act 1977** which assimilates the torts which affect goods under the global heading of *wrongful interference.*

Within the concept of wrongful interference the most common form of trespass to goods is *conversion.* Conversion is the intentional dealing with goods which is seriously inconsistent with the rights of another person in respect of those goods.

Conversion is commonly encountered in business transactions as it is the route by which the true owner of goods will attempt to ensure that they are returned to them, for example, where the goods are the subject of a *Romalpa clause* or where they have been parted with because of the fraud of another party. (See earlier in the chapters on contract and mistake.) Remember the case of **Cundy v Lindsay (1878)**. X sells a car to Y but Y is a rogue who has misled X as to his identity. Y never acquires title (or ownership) to the car. Therefore when Y sells the car to Z, even though Z is acting entirely honestly, Y cannot sell Z the ownership rights (or good title) as he never had them in the first place. The result of the scenario is that:

- X still owns the car
- Y, no doubt, is nowhere to be found
- Z, although blameless, has possession of a car which he does not own.

X cannot sue Z based on contract because there was none between X and Z. X cannot sue Y based on contract or other agreement because he cannot find him. X will have to sue Z for conversion.

2.5 Defamation

This is a tort with which most people will be familiar. It is the legal link by which film stars and media celebrities have sued the editors of many newspapers and magazines. *Private Eye* is particularly used to this type of court proceeding! The tort itself involves the publishing of statements about a person which tends to lower them in the estimation of right-thinking members of society generally. Defamation takes two forms: *slander* which usually involves the statement being spoken, and *libel* which usually involves a written statement. The actual categories are wider than this; slander can include simply defamatory gestures and libel extends to other forms of permanent record of the statement such as statements made not in writing but in films.

3   Tort compared with other areas of law

Often a factual scenario may give rise to various *causes of action* or formal legal links by which one person may sue or bring proceedings against another. It is not always easy to see which are the most likely proceedings to be brought. Indeed sometimes more than one set of proceedings may be brought based on the same incident.

3.1   Tort and criminal law

Very often the same facts may give rise to two sets of proceedings. For example, if I run you over with my car then:

- you may be able to sue me in negligence, and
- the state may be able to bring criminal proceedings for driving without due care and attention.

Similarly in the case of the neighbours' bonfire:

- the injured neighbour may be able to sue the other for private nuisance
- the state may be able to bring a prosecution based on environmental protection statutes.

One of the basic differences between the two types of law should be apparent from these examples. The law of torts is a law which protects the rights of individuals against one another. The criminal law protects the interests of society in general. Both areas of law involve the offender breaching a *duty* imposed by law. But in the case of tort it is a duty owed to another individual member of society, whereas in the case of the criminal law it is a duty owed to society at large.

3.2   Tort and the law of contract

There are some situations where a matter may give rise to liability both for breach of contract and for the commission of a tort. The main difference between the two types of provision is to be found in the existence of the contract itself:

- in the case of tort the two parties may never even have met, never mind entered into a contractual agreement
- in the case of tort the rules which govern the relationship between the parties arise out of statute or case law. In the case of contract the rules which govern the relationship between the parties are initially those contained *in the contract.* Statute and case law may apply but only if the terms of the contract itself are found to be lacking in substance or found to be unfair.

In addition to these differences there are numerous others based on the remedies available.

Summary

You should now be in a position to:

- explain what is meant by a tort
- give some everyday examples of different types of tort
- explain how other areas of law, apart from tort, may affect a given factual situation.

13 What is negligence?

Objectives

In the last chapter we looked at the nature of tort generally. In this chapter we take a detailed look at the tort of negligence.

By the end of the chapter, you should:

- be able to identify the essential elements of negligence
- understand the difference between negligence and a 'pure' accident
- be able to explain the factors which may be taken into account in establishing whether or not a duty of care is owed to another individual
- understand the importance to employers of vicarious liability
- be able to explain what is meant by 'the chain of causation'
- apply logical reasoning to decide what types of conduct might amount to a breach of the duty of care
- apply logical reasoning and legal principles to decide how much damage a negligent defendant may be liable for and to explain the concept of remoteness of damage.

1   The nature of negligence

Negligence is a form of legal action which is based on the idea of *fault* or *responsibility*. Before we start it is perhaps useful to look at a case study. Consider the following situation.

 CASE STUDY 1

Last month a lorry crashed into the walls of your business premises. The wall was destroyed and you suffered a broken arm.

An eyewitness at the time reported that the vehicle was travelling at approximately 60 miles per hour in a built-up area where the speed limit was 30 mph.

1 Was this an accident or is the lorry driver responsible and should be made to compensate you?

2 Would your opinion differ if you discovered that the driver had suffered a heart attack before the accident and lost control of the vehicle?

3 Would your opinion differ if you discovered that the driver had a history of heart problems and had been advised by his doctor to stop driving?

4 Would your opinion differ if you discovered not that the driver had suffered a heart attack but that the brakes on the vehicle had failed?

5 Would it make any difference if the driver admitted that his brakes were 'a bit dodgy' when he set off?

2   The essential elements of negligence

When we talk about negligence, what are the essential ingredients that we are looking for?

In short, someone will be liable for negligence if they can show

- that an individual or company owed them a *duty of care*
- that the individual or company *breached* that duty of care
- that the *damage* arose out of that breach of duty of care.

In other words we are looking for a series of events in which you can show interrelated

- duty of care
- breach of duty of care
- damage.

So far then, all we have looked at are the technical terms and we don't yet know exactly what they mean. We are going to have to examine those technical terms to decide:

- to whom we owe a responsibility to take care
- what type of behaviour will constitute behaviour falling short of the accepted requirements.

3   The duty of care

3.1   To whom do I owe a duty of care/'Who am I responsible to?'

3.1.1   Careless conduct
The tort of negligence is really concerned with careless conduct. But it is only concerned with:

'carelessness ... where there is a duty to take care and where failure in that duty has caused damage' (Lord MacMillan in **Donoghue v Stevenson (1932)**).

3.1.2   The 'snail in the ale'
Carelessness alone will not necessarily be sufficient to make a person liable to another in law. The modern tort of negligence begins with the landmark decision of

Donoghue v Stevenson (1932). The facts briefly are that X bought a bottle of ginger beer from the proprietor of a cafe. X then gave the bottle of ginger beer to her friend Mrs Donoghue who drank the ginger beer. Having drunk the beer, and having noticed a partly decomposed snail in the bottle, Mrs Donoghue became ill. Mrs Donoghue then sued the manufacturer of the ginger beer. Mrs Donoghue was not in a position to sue the cafe proprietor who supplied the ginger beer as she did not make the contract with the proprietor (her friend, X, had made the contract). There was certainly no contract between the manufacturer and Mrs Donoghue. The court had to consider whether or not Mrs Donoghue could sue the manufacturer of the ginger beer on the basis of their negligence. One of the first things that had to be considered was whether the manufacturer owed Mrs Donoghue a *duty of care.*

3.1.3   The test prior to Donoghue v Stevenson – the proximity test

In earlier cases the courts had used the idea of *proximity* to decide whether or not a duty of care was owed. The basis of this test was that

'whenever one person is by circumstance placed in such a position with regard to another that everyone of ordinary sense would at once recognise that if he did not use ordinary care and skill in his own conduct ... he would cause danger of injury to the person or property of the other, a duty arises to use ordinary care and skill to avoid such danger' (**Heaven v Pender (1883)** per Brett MR).

In **Donoghue v Stevenson** a slightly different test was introduced. This has become known as *the neighbour principle.* This test introduces the idea of *foreseeability of injury.*

You should note that the concept of foreseeability is also relevant to the question of damage looked at in section 7 later. The foreseeability of injury test is the preliminary test to decide whether a duty is owed at all. The later test of foreseeability is used not to establish liability but to decide how much, of a considerable amount of damage, the negligent person should be liable for.

3.1.4   The neighbour principle

In **Donoghue v Stevenson** Lord Atkin set out the *neighbour principle.* He said:

'The rule that you are to love your neighbour becomes, in law, you must not injure your neighbour ... you must take reasonable care to avoid acts or omissions which you can reasonably foresee would be likely to injure your neighbour.'

This then begs the question of what is meant in law by one's 'neighbour'? The answer given by Lord Atkin is:

> 'persons who are so closely and directly affected by my act that I ought reasonably to have them in contemplation as being so affected when I am directing my mind to the acts or omissions which are called in question.'

In applying the neighbour principle to the facts of **Donoghue v Stevenson** the manufacturer of the ginger beer (Stevenson) was liable in the tort of negligence to Mrs Donoghue as he could reasonably foresee that by failing to exercise reasonable care, an ultimate consumer of the product might be adversely affected. Mrs Donoghue came within the ambit of reasonable foreseeability, particularly because the bottle was made of dark glass and there was therefore no opportunity of reinspecting the contents of the bottle between its leaving the premises and being consumed.

3.1.5   How has the neighbour principle been applied?

When we are trying to decide whether someone is liable in negligence, the first thing we need to decide is whether or not the careless person owed the person who has suffered damage to themselves or their property a duty of care. The neighbour principle is applied and if the defendant could reasonably have foreseen that the injured party would be adversely affected by his acting or omitting to act then, on the face of it, the defendant will owe a duty of care.

The factual situations to which the neighbour principle can be applied 'may be as various … as human errancy', and 'the conception of legal responsibility may develop in adaptation to altering social conditions and standards … The categories of negligence are never closed' (per Lord MacMillan in **Donoghue v Stevenson**).

Essentially what Lord MacMillan was saying is that the types of behaviour which may amount to negligence are endless. Simply reading a newspaper tells us how diverse and bizarre people's behaviour can be. It would therefore be an impossible task to try and list the types of behaviour which amount to negligence. Perhaps the best that we can do is to have a look at some cases and see how the principles have been applied so far.

In **Carmarthenshire County Council v Lewis (1955)** a school gate gave access to a busy main road. The gate should have been kept locked but was in fact left open. A four-year-old child ran out through the gate and onto the road causing a lorry driver to swerve. As a result of having to swerve the lorry crashed and the driver was killed. The driver's widow sued the local authority. The neighbour test was applied and it was said that it was reasonably foreseeable that, as a result of leaving the gate unlocked, people using the highway might be injured. Notice that it was not simply the danger to the child which was regarded as foreseeable. Lord Reid said: '… if a child runs into the street the danger to others is almost as great as the danger to the child.'

In **Haley v London Electricity Board (1965)** the Electricity Board was excavating a pavement. They had dug a hole and, with the intention of warning and deterring pedestrians from falling into the hole, they leaned a long-handled hammer against the wall in front of the hole. This might have been an adequate precaution to protect fully sighted people; however, Haley was blind and obviously therefore could not see the hammer. Instead he tripped over it and fell into the hole. The Electricity Board was held to be liable as they should have been able to foresee the possible presence of blind people. In making this decision the court applied a dictum of Lord Sumner in an earlier case when he said: 'A measure of care appropriate to the inability or disability of those who are immature or feeble in mind or body is due from others, who know or ought to anticipate the presence of such persons within the scope and hazard of their own operations.'

In **Home Office v Dorset Yacht Company Limited (1970)** the House of Lords held that the Home Office owed a duty of care to yacht owners whose property was damaged by borstal boys who escaped from a Home Office institution. The Home Office owed a duty of care to people whose property it could reasonably foresee might suffer damage if an escape occurred.

In this case Lord Reid went on to re-emphasise the significance of the neighbour principle. He said:

> 'When a new point emerges, one should ask not whether it is covered by authority [in other words whether there is a directly similar case], but whether recognised principles apply to it. [**Donoghue v Stevenson**] may be regarded as a milestone, and the well known passage in Lord Atkin's speech should I think be regarded as a statement of principle. It is not to be treated as if it were a statutory definition. It will require qualification in new circumstances. But I think that the time has come when we can and should say that it ought to apply unless there is some justification or valid explanation for its exclusion.'

✎   CASE STUDY 2

Imagine that you are the manager of a firm of painters and decorators. You have recently received claims in respect of four incidents where people have suffered damage to their clothing as a result of touching wet paint. You are asked to consider whether the firm is likely to be liable in respect of each situation.

1   The first claim is from Mrs Selwyn who is a teacher at a comprehensive school. The firm had a contract to decorate the building during the school holidays. Mrs Selwyn damaged her coat when she brushed against a newly painted wall. They had not put up any 'Wet Paint' signs because, it being the school holidays, they did not expect anyone to be there.

> 2 The second claim is from Tony Johnson, a pupil at the school who had been 'larking around' during the holidays. He had climbed onto the roof and in getting down had damaged his leather jacket on the newly painted guttering.
>
> 3 The third claim is from Mr Taylor who sat on a park seat which had recently been painted by the firm. There was a 'Wet Paint' sign but Mr Taylor is very short sighted and did not see it.
>
> 4 The fourth claim is from Jenny Agnetha who is a student at the Ribberham College of Visual Arts. She too sat on a newly painted seat. The seat was in the grounds of the college and there was a 'Wet Paint' sign.

1 In respect of Mrs Selwyn, was it reasonably foreseeable that someone might be in the building notwithstanding that it was the school holidays? Would it make any difference if the firm had been assured that all the staff were on holiday?

2 In respect of Tony Johnson, was it reasonably foreseeable that someone would be on the roof of the building and that they might come into contact with the wet guttering?

3 In respect of Mr Taylor, was it reasonably foreseeable that there might be a short-sighted person in the park who would not see the notice?

4 In respect of Jenny Agnetha, was it reasonably foreseeable that anyone at the college might not see the notice?

5 Would your answer in respect of Mr Taylor differ if he had wandered into the grounds of the college? Does it make any difference whether or not the college grounds are restricted to students? Does it make any difference if there are security guards on the gates of the college?

3.2 In what exceptional cases will no duty be owed?

3.2.1 Should there be a duty of care?

There are certain exceptional situations where we might apply the 'neighbour test' from **Donoghue v Stevenson** and it may appear that a duty of care will be owed, but despite this the courts will say that, because of special circumstances, no duty will in fact be owed. The court is, if you like, using its own special reasons to depart from the original neighbour principle.

The judges will decide whether there *is* a duty of care, applying the **Donoghue v Stevenson** test. They may then go on to decide whether there *should* be a duty of care by using *judicial policy*.

3.2.2 What reasoning may be used in deciding that there is no duty of care?

If the courts are going to say that there are exceptional circumstances which exclude or suspend the duty of care, then how can we find out what they are and why they are taken into account? It is really a matter of what lawyers have been able to glean from the cases that have already been decided. In some cases the judges may decide that it is a special situation, that no duty of care is owed and they may discuss the reasons fully. In other cases they may be less candid. They may say there are exceptional circumstances and yet not give the full reasoning behind their decision. In essence, foreseeability is a necessary ingredient of a situation where there is a duty of care but it is not the only one. 'Otherwise there would be liability in negligence on the part of one who sees another about to walk over a cliff with his head in the air, and forbears to shout a warning.'

The following factors, among others, have been taken into account in cases in the past either expressly or by implication.

Who will lose out and who is in a position to bear best that loss?
This *policy* factor is one which is increasingly encountered in English law. The judges may take into account, among other factors, who has suffered loss and who is in the best position to bear that loss. At its most extreme this would mean that a very rich party to an action for negligence might expect that his ability to pay might count against him.

In practice this is not a factor which is usually employed between individuals. It is however of increasing importance where one of the parties is insured, particularly if they are required by law to have insurance. So, for example, in road traffic accident cases where all motor vehicles must be insured for liability to other road users (called third party insurance), the insured party may expect that the dice will be loaded against him if only on the basis that the court knows if it awards damages against him, he personally will not be paying. It will be the insurance company.

This policy factor is also now employed heavily in imposing liability on insured professionals such as solicitors and surveyors. The judges know that it is the insurance company which pays, not the individual professional, and in deciding whether or not there *should* be a duty of care they may take this into account.

The floodgates argument
This is the judges' old stand-by. In situations where they are asked to say that there is a duty of care where previous cases have been unclear, it is the reason that they often use to take a conservative line. The floodgates argument is, in essence, that you should not widen an area of negligence without good cause as it will lead to a 'flood' of claims through the courts.

The judicial role
Another factor which often plays a part in the decision-making as to whether there should or should not be a duty of care is the role of the judges in the legal process. Judges are particularly aware that their role is, predominantly, to interpret the law. The role of law making is only partly the judges'; in the main it is a role of Parliament. The judges therefore may be reluctant to say that there *should* be a duty of care where:

- they would be making a decision which is out of line with the general trend of statutory provisions. Statutes are, after all, made by Parliament
- they would be stepping into territory where they feel that, if Parliament had wanted to, they would already have made some provision.

Practical considerations
This factor allows the judges to look at a number of matters that affect the day to day provision of goods and services and how effectively that provision can be achieved. For example, it may allow them to take into account the fact that manufacturers can only function efficiently if they can be reasonably certain about the extent of their duty to consumers.

Doctors are perhaps one of the best examples of this. It can be appreciated that, in a situation where doctors are excessively worried by the possibility of being sued for negligence, they may function less efficiently. This obviously does not mean that doctors will not be held liable for negligence. It does however mean that the judges have shown some reluctance to go down the American route where doctors are sued so often for negligence that, at precisely the time when they may need all their skills to save a life, they are having to expend time and energy protecting their own backs against litigation.

3.2.3   Some exceptional situations where no duty is owed
The policy factors which we have just looked at in section 3.2.2 can be seen at work, together with statute, in certain specific situations where the law says that even though the neighbour test may establish a duty, nevertheless there *should not be one.*

Advocates
In **Rondel v Worsley (1969)** the courts decided that a barrister does not owe a duty of care in respect of proceedings in court. This principle is now extended to all advocates. The principle seems to be based on public policy. It clearly does not mean that lawyers cannot be sued – they can. What it does mean is that once in court they can concentrate on the matter in hand without having to guard every word so carefully that they effectively cannot get on with the job.

Where there could have been or is another opportunity to sue
Liability for negligence is liability which is initially regarded as filling the gap where no other proceedings are possible. There may be some well-established situations where a duty of care clearly exists and you can sue in negligence. You might also find that you can sue in respect of a contract. The option is yours. If, however, you are asking the court to say that a duty of care exists in a new type of situation, which the courts have not come across before, you must expect them to be less keen on extending the boundaries of negligence if they see that you could use another legal link, such as contract, to achieve the same end result.

This factor, in fact, goes wider than this. If the parties have had the opportunity to put their rights and obligations on a formal footing, but have failed to do so, the courts may not be keen to step in, after the event, and impose a duty of care on one of the parties. This was the situation in **Greater Nottingham Cooperative Society v Cementation Piling and Foundations (1988)**. In this case the parties had already been through the process of lengthy contractual negotiations to define their rights and obligations. The court was reluctant to go any further than the parties themselves had gone when they had quite clearly been considering all the possibilities for themselves.

Where there is another opportunity for compensation
In **Hill v Chief Constable of West Yorkshire (1988)** one of the relatives of a victim of the 'Yorkshire ripper' claimed compensation from the police for failing to catch the 'ripper' earlier. Among other factors which were considered was the availability of compensation under the Criminal Injuries Compensation system.

Public policy
This is the area where the judges have the most scope for saying that there is no duty of care owed to the injured person. They can apply the foreseeability test from **Donoghue v Stevenson**, but then decide to ignore it anyway on grounds of public policy.

This area is probably best illustrated by looking at some of the cases.

The police usually enjoy a special position in relation to a duty of care. For example in **Hill v Chief Constable of West Yorkshire** the decision saying that the police owed no duty of care to a relative of a victim of the Yorkshire ripper clearly included an issue of public policy. It was said that '... the imposition of liability may lead to the exercise of a function being carried on in a detrimentally defensive frame of mind ...'

> In **Hughes v National Union of Mineworkers (1991)** a serving police officer was injured when attempting to maintain peace on a picket line. He alleged that the officer in charge at the colliery had been negligent in his handling of the situation. It was held that no duty of care was owed to the injured policeman because fear of liability might prejudice senior police officers in making decisions when trying to control public order.

In other words it was not in the interests of public policy that senior police officers should be distracted from the task in hand by fear of being sued for negligence.

> In **Alexandrou v Oxford (1993)** the plaintiff's shop was burgled. The burglars activated the burglar alarm, including the telephone warning link to the local police station. The officers who attended the scene of the crime were allegedly negligent in failing to make an adequate inspection of the premises. It was held that the police could not be sued for negligence as they did not owe a duty of care. The plaintiff differed in no material way from any member of the public who informed the police about a crime or a potential crime.

Again it would not be in the public interest to impose such a duty of care on the police since, far from encouraging a higher standard of care, it would result in significantly diverting resources from the suppression of crime.

Other situations will arise from time to time in which the courts may use public policy as a ground for saying that no duty of care exists. For example in

McKay v Essex Area Health Authority (1982) a baby was born with serious disabilities because the mother had contracted German measles in the early part of her pregnancy. The mother sued the Health Authority for negligence, saying that they ought to have carried out tests to establish the problem and so the baby would never have been born. It was held that it would be against public policy for a duty of care to exist, in effect, to prevent a life coming into existence.

 CASE STUDY 3

Consider the situation where a woman has been subject to violence from her husband. She takes legal advice and obtains an order prohibiting the husband from going near her. Attached to that order is a power for the police to arrest the husband if he breaches the order. Imagine that the husband turns up at the woman's home and threatens her. The police are called and persuade him to leave peaceably. Two hours later he returns and threatens to 'punch her to a pulp'. The police are called again, and again they calm him down and persuade him to leave. An hour after that the husband returns again. The police are called but by the time they arrive he has 'beaten her to a pulp'.

I Can the woman sue the police for negligence in failing to protect her and for damages in respect of the injuries she suffered?

2 Is it foreseeable that, in their failure to take further action, she might be injured (the neighbour principle)? The answer surely is yes.

3 Do the interests of public policy say that the police should not be liable? Is it arguable that in domestic violence situations the police should have a mediation role to play and should not be forced into a confrontational role simply because of the risk of being sued?

4 Would it make any difference if the police had a hard and fast rule that they would mediate unless there had already been physical harm?

All these types of issues might be relevant. It is difficult to know how the English courts would react. Would they follow the public policy route and say that the police would be inhibited from doing a proper job by a fear of being sued for negligence? Or would they say that a duty of care was owed to protect someone who so clearly comes within the neighbour principle? Certainly the American courts have allowed a claim for compensation from the police in a similar situation.

3.3 Development beyond the neighbour test

In establishing whether a duty of care is owed we have seen in section 3.1 the requirement for the existence of a duty of care. In section 3.2 we looked at the factors which might restrict the neighbour principle and restrict the imposition of a duty of care. The approach suggested in the recent case of **Caparo v Dickman (1990)** was a three stage one.

1 You should apply the neighbour principle and see whether injury/damage was foreseeable
2 You should apply the proximity test (that is, the original test which was used prior to **Donoghue v Stevenson**)
3 You should then consider whether it is 'fair just and reasonable' in all the circumstances to impose a duty of care. (These are, in essence, the policy factors but put into a more general form.)

3.4 The exceptional situation of vicarious liability

So far we have looked at the general rules surrounding the imposition of a duty of care. We have also looked at situations where the courts may say that, despite *foreseeability* and *proximity*, they will refuse to impose a duty of care. Before examining it, it is perhaps worth mentioning one situation where liability is imposed indirectly and in circumstances where one might not expect it. The concept is called *vicarious liability*. (This is looked at in more detail in Chapter 14.)

Essentially this is where an employer may find him/herself liable for the negligent acts of an employee. The questions of

● whether a duty of care is owed
● whether there has been a breach of duty
● whether damage arises from that breach

are looked at in the light of the employee's conduct when determining the liability of the employer. In other words the employer is put into the shoes of his/her employee.

4 Breach of duty: what behaviour will amount to a breach of duty?

Earlier we looked at the essential ingredients of the tort of negligence. They are that *a duty of care* must be owed, there must have been a *breach* of that duty of care and *damage* must result from that breach.

In section 3 we looked at when and whether a duty of care will be owed. In this section we need to look at the situation where there is a duty of care and decide what level or standard of behaviour is required of someone who does owe a duty of care. What types of behaviour will amount to a breach of their duty of care?

4.1   The reasonable man test

In order to determine whether there has been a breach of the duty of care the courts will look at the situation and ask, 'How would a *reasonable man* have behaved in the same circumstances?' In other words the court creates an imaginary person, gives them all the characteristics of being a reasonable individual, and asks, 'How would they have reacted in this particular situation?'

Essentially, if the person who is accused of negligence has acted in the way that the court believes the hypothetical reasonable man would have done, then there may not be a breach of the duty of care and one of the essential elements of negligence will be missing. If, however, the person accused of negligence has acted differently to how the judge believes a reasonable man would have acted, then there will have been a breach of his/her duty of care.

> In **Glasgow Corporation v Muir (1943)** it was explained that 'the standard of foresight of the reasonable man … eliminates the personal equation and is independent of the idiosyncrasies of the particular person whose conduct is in question.'
>
> In **Hall v Brooklands Auto Racing Club (1933)** Greer LJ said: 'The person concerned is sometimes described as "the man in the street" or the "man on the Clapham omnibus" or … the "man who takes the magazines at home and in the evening pushes the lawnmower in his shirt sleeves".'

The fact remains that this 'reasonable man' test is not necessarily what you or I would think of as a reasonable man. A judge may say that he is measuring the matter by how a hypothetical reasonable man might behave. That will only rule out the particular idiosyncrasies of that particular judge. In reality it will not turn him/her overnight into the streetwise reasonable individual whom we believe ourselves to be!

In creating this hypothetical reasonable man we then need to decide what type of behaviour will be expected of him.

> In **Blyth v Birmingham Waterworks Co (1856)** it was said that: 'Negligence is the omission to do something which a reasonable man, guided upon the considerations which ordinarily regulate the conduct of human affairs, would do, or doing something which a prudent and reasonable man would not do.'

The reasonable man test may be subject to some modification for different cases. For example, if you are deciding whether or not a surgeon has been negligent, if the alleged negligence is in driving his car then the surgeon's status makes no difference since you ask what the ordinary reasonable man would have done. If, however, the alleged negligence is in performing an operation, you do not ask what the reasonable man would have done in the circumstances. Instead you ask what the reasonable, hypothetical surgeon would have done.

We need now to look at what factors the court will take into consideration in deciding whether or not the conduct complained of was such that a reasonable man would have behaved differently.

4.2   Reasonable probabilities not fantastic possibilities

It is clear that the courts do not expect the reasonable man to behave in an over-anxious way. The reasonable man is expected to look at the situation and decide whether precautions should be taken, bearing in mind both

- how likely the harm is, and
- the severity of the damage which might be caused.

The reasoning relating to 'How likely is the harm' is illustrated by the case of

Bolton v Stone (1951) where X was hit by a cricket ball which had been hit right out of the grounds of the cricket club. The ball travelled 100 yards between the batsman and X. It went above a 17 foot fence which was 78 yards away from the batsman. Evidence was brought at the hearing that this type of freak hit had happened only six times in the preceding 30 years. The House of Lords held that the defendant was not liable in negligence as it was improbable that the ball would leave the cricket ground or that, if it did, it would cause injury.

This decision should be contrasted with

Miller v Jackson (1977) where a housing estate and a cricket ground were next to each other. Y owned one of the houses on the housing estate. Between 1972 and 1974 cricket balls had been hit onto Y's property several times causing some damage. In 1975 the height of the cricket club fence was increased to 15 feet. (This was apparently the maximum possible height bearing in mind danger of wind speeds.) Despite the increase in the height of the fence balls still went over the fence, six times in the 1975 season and eight or nine times in the following season. The Court of Appeal held that the defendants were liable for negligence as the risk of injury was both foreseeable and foreseen.

The reasoning relating to 'How severe is the damage which would be caused' is illustrated by the case of

Paris v Stepney Borough Council (1951) where the defendants were held to have been negligent in failing to provide safety goggles for a one-eyed workman. The consequence of this failure was that, when injured in his one eye, the workman became totally blind. Lord Simmonds said in that case: '… I see no valid reason for excluding as irrelevant the gravity of the damage which the employee will suffer if an accident occurs … I cannot accept the view … that the greater risk of injury is, but the risk of greater injury is not, a relevant circumstance …'

This should be compared with the case of

Withers v Perry Chain Company Limited (1961) where an employee contracted dermatitis from contact with grease in the course of her work. When she returned to work her employers gave her the driest work they had available, but again she suffered attacks of dermatitis. The employers were held not to be liable in negligence as they had done everything that they could, short of not employing her at all!

Lord Justice Sellers said that the duty of the employer was '... to take all reasonable care for the plaintiff in the employment in which she was engaged, including, of course, a duty to have regard to the fact that she had had dermatitis previously ...' and Lord Justice Devlin said: '... It may be also ... that when the susceptibility of an employee to dermatitis is known there is a duty on the employer to take extra or special precautions to protect such an employee. But it is not suggested that there were any extra or special precautions here which could have been taken.'

4.3   The foreseeability of the risk (or the 'state of the art')

Rather confusingly in the law of negligence we keep returning to the concept of *foreseeability*. It is very easy to get confused as to how and why this concept is being used. There are a number of ways in which it is looked at. We have already looked at the foreseeability of harm – to establish whether or not a duty of care is owed. (This is what we looked at in the last section.)

Now we need foreseeability of the risk of injury – to establish whether there has been a breach of the duty of care in that the defendant should have done things differently or should have taken some special precautions.

In taking into account the *foreseeability of the risk of injury* we need to look at the state of mind of the reasonable man at the time of his actions. For example, it would not be fair to look at the behaviour of doctors treating AIDS eight years ago in the light of medical knowledge today. Similar reasoning was applied in the case of

Roe v Minister of Health (1954) where an anaesthetist administered a spinal anaesthetic. Unknown to the anaesthetist the anaesthetic had, because of hairline cracks in the ampoules, been contaminated by the disinfectant chemical in which the ampoules themselves were stored. The contamination of the anaesthetic caused paralysis in the patient. It was accepted by the judges in that case that there was no evidence of previous contamination in this way and that it was not a risk that could reasonably be foreseen and therefore guarded against.

> Lord Justice Denning said: '... It is so easy to be wise after the event and to condemn as negligence that which was only a misadventure ... Every advance in technique is also attended by risks. Doctors, like the rest of us, have to learn by experience; and experience often teaches in a hard way. Something goes wrong and shows up a weakness, and then it is put right ... We must not look at the 1947 accident with 1954 spectacles.'

4.4 The social desirability of the conduct

In taking into account this particular factor the judges allow themselves to consider, when deciding how a reasonable man would behave, the importance to society of the act which is being done. It allows the judges to create different standards for emergencies and non-emergencies and perhaps for charities as opposed to commercial ventures.

The factor is illustrated by the case of

> **Watt v Hertfordshire County Council (1954)** where a fireman was injured while on duty. He had attended a car accident in which a woman was trapped under a car. A jack was needed but the fire brigade did not have the necessary type. Arrangements were made to bring one to the scene. The jack was put into the back of a lorry. It was not adequately secured and it fell onto the fireman causing him injury. The failure to secure the jack was held not to be negligence. Furthermore a distinction was drawn between this emergency situation, and the social desirability of getting the jack there quickly in order to save a life, and the commercial situation where there was no such hurry and better precautions would have been required.

4.5 The expense of avoiding the risk

We all exercise this type of decision in everyday matters. A family with three children might decide that they would like a car with three inertia-reel seat belts in the back. (This would be a sound safety-conscious decision, given the known benefits of the superior types of seat belt.) On checking out new cars, however, they may find that only the most expensive cars have this added safety feature. If the family decides to forego the extra protection and buy a cheaper car, are the parents negligent towards the child if it subsequently suffers injury because of the inferior seat belt? Initial reaction says no – surely not.

Everyone may be expected to take reasonable precautions for the safety of their family and others – but the issue of relative cost compared with the level of the risk must come into it somewhere. Only the lucky few have sufficient money that they can afford all the latest state of the art safety features without considering the advantage against the cost.

The courts do the same thing. If the risk is a small one, and the cost of precautions against the risk is very great, they will not necessarily say that those precautions should have been taken. They may say that a reasonable man would compare the risk with the cost and make a reasonable decision in the light of those factors.

> In **Latimer v AEC (1953)** the defendants owned a factory which had flooded. The flooding had made the floor very slippery. The defendants took the precaution of covering the floor with sawdust in order to make it safer; nevertheless one of their employees slipped and injured himself. The court looked at the situation and held that the defendants were not liable. They had taken all reasonable precautions. There were further precautions which could have been taken, i.e. closing the factory, but the expense of this compared with the likelihood of harm did not require them to do so.

4.6   The skill of the person involved

We have already seen that the level of skill possessed by the defendant may affect how the court looks at the behaviour of a reasonable man. The behaviour of a surgeon in an allegation of medical negligence will be looked at not in the light of how an 'average punter' would have behaved but how a reasonable surgeon would have behaved. Experts are expected to behave as a reasonable expert would, not as a reasonable man would.

If, generally, greater skills require greater care then lesser skills require lesser care. For example, a jeweller who pierced a person's ears would not be expected to deal with the 'operation' in the same way as a surgeon would have done (**Phillips v William Whitely Ltd (1938)**).

So the general rule is that you apply the reasonable man test. But you can qualify that to take into account the particular skills of the individual involved. There are, however, some particular instances where the rules may vary.

4.6.1   The varying views of experts

Many cases will be entirely straightforward. For example, if the facts can be agreed, surely all surgeons would say that to leave a needle inside the stomach when performing a gall bladder operation is negligent. There may be more difficult cases however where the matter becomes one of medical opinion. An expert who finds himself with a choice between two differing but widely accepted views as to the appropriate course of action may be able to defend a claim of negligence on those grounds.

> In **Bolam v Friern Hospital Management Committee (1957)** it was said that a doctor '... is not guilty of negligence if he has acted in accordance with a practice accepted as proper by a responsible body of medical men skilled in that particular art ... Putting it the other way round, a man is not negligent, if he is acting in accordance with such a practice, merely because there is a body of opinion who would take a contrary view.'

4.6.2   Children

Children are not expected to behave in the same way as adults. The test to apply is not the reasonable man test but the reasonable child. What is more, we all know that a reasonable six-year-old is a very different creature to a reasonable ten-year-old. The test then is how would a reasonable child of the same age have behaved (**McHale v Watson (1966)**).

4.6.3   The ill or disabled

If allowances are made for the fact that children do not behave in the same way as adults, then it would seem logical to take into account someone's illness or disability and consider how someone with a similar illness or disability would have behaved.

4.6.4   Drivers

Drivers are an exceptional situation which is probably explained, at least in part, by the requirement for compulsory third party insurance.

⚖️

> In **Nettleship v Weston (1971)** a learner driver crashed causing injury. She was held to have been negligent. The court said that although she was only learning to drive she was expected to exercise the same skill as a reasonably competent experienced driver.

(Perhaps one who had passed her test?) Interestingly the court recognised that to impose this high level of responsibility was moving away from the original idea of fault. The defendant was told, in effect, that she should use the same skill and care as an experienced driver, but if an accident did happen she should not consider herself to be morally blameworthy in the same way.

> ✎   **CASE STUDY 4**
>
> The Swiftclean Railway Company operates electric trains out of a number of stations in the area. It has arrangements for the overnight 'garaging' of its trains at several stations. The stations are all locked between the hours of 1 a.m. and 5 a.m.
>
> Last week two 'accidents' occurred.
>
> a) In the first accident a station cleaner was injured when he received an electric shock. He had opened a locked door believing it to be a store cupboard. He received an electric shock which had apparently come from some live wires in the cupboard. The cupboard was in fact not a storeroom at all but a mains fuse circuit cupboard.
>
> b) In the second accident a youth had climbed on top of one of the stationary trains and had touched the overhead cables and electrocuted himself. Reports from his friends show that he had climbed over the 10 foot high fence at 2 a.m. and done it for a dare.

a) In respect of the injury to the cleaner

1 Was the cleaner owed a duty of care? (Apply the **Donoghue v Stevenson** test and the **Caparo v Dickman** test and consider whether there is any policy reason why a duty should not be imposed.)

2 Would a reasonable person have guarded against this risk? Is it right to assume that it was a known risk to be guarded against generally since it was housed in a locked cupboard? Is it a reasonable probability or a fantastic possibility that someone might have access to the cupboard and suffer an injury as a result?

3 Would the expense of avoiding the risk have been too great? (Consider here the very serious nature of the accident compared with the precautions which might have been taken. For example, could the wires in the cupboard not have been made safe? Could the fact that the room was a high voltage area not have been made clear by a notice?)

b) In respect of the injury to the youth

1 Was the youth owed a duty of care? (Apply the **Donoghue v Stevenson** test and the **Caparo v Dickman** test and consider whether there is any policy reason why a duty should not be imposed. This discussion may be more complicated than in the case of the cleaner. The youth may fall within the neighbour principle. He may fall within the proximity test. Might there be a policy reason for denying a duty – by a public service company to a trespasser?)

2 If the youth was owed a duty of care, has the company done or omitted to do anything which amounts to a breach of that duty of care?

3 How likely was the harm? One answer is that such behaviour is extreme but on the other hand experience shows that trains and railways are often an unnaturally strong temptation for youngsters.

4 Does the severity of the damage count at all? Even if the harm is not particularly likely, the consequences surely are likely to be catastrophic.

5 Does the social desirability of the conduct have any bearing on the matter? The evidence may show that the risks inherent with electric trains are much greater than they were with diesel trains but that the social and environmental benefits are of considerable importance.

6 Would the cost of guarding against this type of a risk be so great that the court would say that, even if the risk was foreseeable, the company was not expected to guard against it? For example, evidence might show that the overhead cables could have been made safe by a coating which meant that they would only contact with a particular type of metal on the train's connections. Would it make any difference if the cost of doing this was £100,000 or £100,000,000? Would it make any difference if all other electric train companies had taken this precaution?

7 Would it make any difference if it was shown that the accident could have been avoided by simply turning the current off during the hours when the station was locked and unattended?

5   Who must prove that there has been a breach of duty?

5.1   The general rule

The usual rule is that it is the plaintiff (the person complaining of injury or damage) who has the responsibility of *proving* that the other party has been negligent. This is known as *the burden of proof.* It means that the plaintiff must do two things:

- gather together the evidence of what happened. (This may be in the form of witness statements, documentary evidence etc.)
- make sure that there is enough evidence before the court to 'tip the scales' in his/her favour. If you imagine that the scales start off tipped slightly in the defendant's favour, then it is up to the plaintiff to bring sufficient evidence to tip the scales slightly back again in the plaintiff's favour. Lawyers call this *the balance of probabilities*. In other words the plaintiff must show that the defendant owed him/her a duty of care and that, on the balance of probabilities, it is more likely than not that the defendant breached that duty of care and caused the damage which is complained of.

5.2   Res ipsa loquitur/the obvious cases

There are some situations where it is so obvious that the damage could only have happened as a result of the defendant's negligence that the courts will, unusually, start from the other way round. They will look at the circumstances and say that 'the circumstances speak for themselves' (or *res ipsa loquitur*). They will say that the apparent negligence is, from the facts, so obvious, that it is up to the defendant to prove that he was not negligent.

What types of situation may give rise to *res ipsa loquitur*? Examples are where a barrel fell from the defendant's upper floor window of a warehouse (**Byrne v Boadle (1863)**). Another example was where a stone was found in a bun. The conclusion of the court was that it could only have got there by negligence during the course of its manufacture (**Chaproniere v Mason (1905)**).

When *res ipsa loquitur* will apply is largely a matter of common sense but the courts have provided certain criteria by which we can attempt to decide in advance whether *res ipsa loquitur* will be accepted. (If it is, remember it makes the plaintiff's job a lot easier and means that the defendant must do some work to bring evidence to show that what looks like his fault, was not.)

- The accident must be one which cannot easily be explained (unless it was the defendant's fault)
- The accident would not have happened if proper care had been taken
- The defendant must have been in control of the situation.

CASE STUDY 5

This case study is really an exercise in trying to think about the situations in which *res ipsa loquitur* could apply and its effects.

Imagine that a chain of supermarkets has a 'pick and mix' display of fresh bread rolls. The rolls are unwrapped and tongs are provided for customers to put the bread rolls into a plastic bag. On getting the rolls home, Mrs Warner eats one and feels ill. She is discovered to have consumed rat poison. Examination of the remaining bread rolls shows that a number of them contain small pellets of the poison.

1 Is this a situation where *res ipsa loquitur* would apply? Is there any other apparent explanation for the presence of the rat poison? Could rat poison have got into the bread rolls otherwise than by a failure to exercise proper care? Was the supermarket in control of the situation?

2 If the answer to these is yes and it looks as if *res ipsa loquitur* will apply, what should the supermarket do now? Has negligence against them been proved? Or is it simply that they must now do some hard work to show that it wasn't their fault?

3 Supposing you are in charge, what would you do?
   - How about checking the rolls which are still in store?
   - How about checking whether the store's records show any other reports of illness?
   - How about checking whether any of the processes used in the store could bring the raw materials into contact with such a poison?

If the chances of the poison getting into the product in your store seem unlikely, you must do some further hard work to prove that there could be another cause. Expert examination of one of the remaining rolls might show that the pellet had been inserted in the roll after manufacture.

If someone else is responsible it would help if you could show who! Was it a malicious blackmailer or animal rights activists? Or was it Mr Warner trying to get rid of his wife!

6   Causation – did the breach cause the damage?

6.1   Establishing causation – did the careless conduct cause the damage?

The third essential element is that the breach of duty complained of must have caused the damage or injury. In other words you must show a clear link between what the defendant did (which he shouldn't have done) or did not do (which he should have done) and the damage. The task of establishing a direct link between the breach of duty and the damage may be made more difficult than you imagine. The facts of situations are rarely simple and straightforward. Sorting out what action led to what damage or injury can be eased by a number of factors which are looked at below.

6.1.1   Would the harm have happened anyway?

If it can be shown that the damage or injury would have happened anyway, then the fact that there was a breach of duty by the defendant is really irrelevant. The situation is perhaps best illustrated by a simple case study.

   CASE STUDY 6

Imagine the situation where a solicitor is acting for a client in buying a house. One of the usual things which should be done is to send out a form which comprises questions about the property. These are called pre-contract enquiries. Imagine that the solicitor forgot to send the enquiries out. After the client buys the property he discovers that the premises have no hot water. If you look at the essential elements of negligence you would ask:

- Did the solicitor owe the client a duty of care – answer yes
- By not sending out the pre-contract enquiries did the solicitor breach that duty of care – answer yes
- Did the damage arise out of the breach of the duty of care – answer no – it is not one of the matters dealt with in the questions anyway.

You can see from this that the last element of negligence is missing. The damage would have occurred anyway even if the solicitor had not breached his duty of care.

The cases may also help in considering this problem. They look at whether the damage or injury would have happened anyway.

In **Robinson v Post Office (1974)** a patient required an urgent anti-tetanus vaccination. The patient was not first tested to see whether he would have an allergic reaction. The patient did have an allergic reaction. The court however looked at the situation and said that, even if the test had been done, it would not have produced a result in time and the anti-tetanus was urgent. The anti-tetanus would have had to have been administered and the reaction would have occurred even if the doctor had undertaken the test. In other words the failure to carry out the test was coincidental – it did not cause the damage.

The essence of other cases has been to look at whether the injury or damage complained of would have happened anyway despite the careless conduct of the defendant. So, for example, in

Barnett v Chelsea and Kensington Hospital Management Committee (1969), another case of alleged medical negligence, which here concerned the treatment of, or rather failure to treat, arsenic poisoning, the case seemed to turn on whether the individual would have died anyway even if the antidote had been administered at the earliest opportunity.

If the death would have occurred whatever the doctor had done, then the fact that he did not do all he could is really irrelevant. However, if it can be shown that the deceased would have had a chance of survival but for the doctor's careless treatment then the carelessness may amount to actionable negligence. The careless treatment and the death are directly linked.

6.2 Novus actus interveniens – is there an intervening act which bears responsibility for the ultimate damage?

6.2.1 Is the chain of causation broken?

In many ways this is a similar idea to the one which we have just looked at. In section 6.1.1 we were looking at whether the injury would have happened anyway. Now we need to look at the problem from another angle. Is it likely that the original negligence would lead to that damage or has there been some new and unexpected act which caused the ultimate damage?

We all know the type of reasoning that we are talking about. That awful day when everything seems to have gone wrong. By the end of the day you have received a warning about the inadequacy of your work. In a filthy temper your reasoning might well go like this:

- If Mrs So and So hadn't kept me talking on the phone before I left for work then I would have left home earlier.
- If I had left home earlier I wouldn't have been at the traffic lights at the same time as that blue van ran into the side of my car.
- If that blue van hadn't run into my car I would not have been in a bad mood.
- If I had not been in a bad mood I would have done that work properly.

Your bad tempered conclusion is probably that all the mishaps of the day were Mrs So and So's fault!

We all do it, but it simply isn't logical. The car accident was most unlikely to be Mrs So and So's fault. It was either yours or the other driver's. Your poor work was certainly not her fault, it was yours!

What *novus actus interveniens* (or new intervening act) is looking at is whether there is another act, done by someone else, which has *broken the chain of causation* and relieved the original person who was negligent from liability.

 CASE STUDY 7

Try thinking through this exercise just to see whether you are following the type of thing that we are looking at here. Imagine that I am involved in a car accident which is my fault. The other driver suffered a cut finger and was taken into a nearby house to have it bandaged. If on the way into the house the other driver, in her shocked state, trips over a raised paving stone and breaks her arm, am I liable for that too? Or is her tripping a new intervening act? Isn't it likely that, as a result of my negligence, she may need treatment, may be dazed and may in the course of recovery suffer a further accident? If so, the chain of causation may go:

- I caused the accident – which caused the cut finger – which caused the tripping – which caused the broken arm.

Imagine the same situation with different facts – the other driver did not trip, but is assaulted on her way to the nearby house and the attacker breaks her arm in the attack. This is likely to be a *novus actus interveniens*. The chain of causation goes:

- I caused the accident – which caused the cut finger – *the act of the attacker intervened* to cause the broken arm.

6.2.2 Was the new intervening act foreseeable?

If the new intervening act is one which could have been anticipated or expected (it was *foreseeable*) then the person who was originally in breach of their duty of care will remain liable for the ultimate damage. It is not simply a new act which is being looked for, but one which is so far from what could be foreseen that it intervenes to break the chain of causation.

In **Scott v Shephard (1773)** a man threw a lighted squib into a covered market. The person whose stall it landed on picked it up and threw it away from his stall. It landed on another stall and the owner of that stall did the same thing. At the last place it landed it exploded and the plaintiff lost an eye. The person who originally threw the squib was held to be liable. The action taken by the other stallholders was foreseeable and did not break the chain of causation between the original thrower of the squib and the injured person.

In **Kirkham v The Chief Constable of Greater Manchester Police (1990)** the police were sued for negligence in respect of the death of a young prisoner on remand. The basis of the claim was that the police knew that the prisoner was a suicide risk but failed to pass on the information to the remand centre. The prisoner then took his own life. The taking of his own life was not regarded by the court as a new intervening act as the balance of his mind was disturbed. The police knew this and could have foreseen what would happen.

This idea of whether the intervening act was foreseeable can be argued when the plaintiff has, to some extent, brought about their own injury. So for example in

Sayers v Harlow Urban District Council (1958) a woman became locked in a public toilet because of a faulty door. The council was responsible for the door being faulty. The woman however decided to try and climb out rather than perhaps risk having to spend the night in there. She climbed up using the toilet roll holder as a step. It spun round and she fell injuring herself. The council argued that the woman herself had committed a new intervening act which caused her injury and broke the chain of causation. The court said that it was not a new intervening act which completely broke the chain of causation and so the council were still liable (although they reduced the amount of damages because they thought the injury was *partly* the woman's fault).

Consider whether the decision in this case might have been different if

- the woman was a diabetic and knew that she needed sugar within the next 20 minutes or so or she might go into a hypoglycaemic coma, or
- an attendant had been alerted and had told the woman to wait 15 minutes while she fetched a carpenter, but the woman attempted to climb out after only 10 minutes.

6.3   What do you do when there are several causes?

The idea of a new intervening act is a fairly simple one. You look at the situation and see whether there is a new intervening act which is so strong and unforeseen that it cuts clean through the chain of causation. If a new intervening act is established you can say that all damage up to the new act is the responsibility of X and after that of Y. In practice the division is often not so easy to make. So for example in

Performance Cars v Abraham (1962) a Rolls Royce was damaged in an accident which was caused by X. The same car was then involved in another accident caused by Y. The car required respraying. The question was: should X or Y or both be liable? It was held that Y was not liable for the respray since it was already necessary as a result of the accident with X. X was liable for the respray.

What would have been the situation if the collision with Y had done additional damage and the vehicle required two new wheels and wheel axles?

This type of situation was looked at in

Baker v Willoughby (1969) where a man had injured his ankle in an accident. He was therefore only able to undertake light work. He was employed as a night watchman. While at work he was shot in the leg by a robber and had to have the leg amputated. X was responsible for the first injury. Y (the robber) was responsible for the second injury. The not unnatural reaction of the man (particularly seeing that the robber could not be found in order to be sued!) was that if it had not been for the negligence of X he would not have had to have had his leg amputated, since he would not have been at the scene of the robbery at all. The court said no: X was only liable for the injury to the ankle. Y, the robber, could be sued for turning an imperfect leg into a non-existent one – if he could be found.

6.4   Contributory negligence – what if the plaintiff is partly to blame for his/her own injury?

If the intervening act is done by someone who has nothing to do with the original accident, then we only have to decide two things:

- Was the new intervening act sufficiently unlikely that it actually breaks the chain of causation?
- Which of the two 'injurers' is liable for which injury?

We have already seen from **Sayers v Harlow Urban District Council** that the intervening act may be an act done by the injured person themselves. This means that we need to consider:

- Was the new act done by the injured person one which broke the chain of causation? This may often be looked at in terms of whether the injured person was taking unreasonable risks.
- If it was not an act sufficient to completely break the chain of causation, it may nevertheless be enough to make the courts say that the injured person themselves is 'partly to blame'.

If the courts decide that they are partly to blame they will say that the injured person was *contributorily negligent*.

The form that contributory negligence usually takes is that the court will assess the extent of the damage arising out of the course of events. Let us say the court assesses the monetary compensation at £100,000. The court then looks at the course of events again and decides how much of the damage arose as a result of the injured person's own carelessness. Let us say they decide that it was 75 per cent the fault of the defendant and 25 per cent the fault of the injured person. The defendant is liable for his/her negligence but the actual amount they are required to pay is only 75 per cent of the total awarded, i.e. £75,000. (This concept is looked at in more detail in section 8.2 of this chapter.)

7   Remoteness of damage – for how much damage is the defendant liable?

7.1   The relationship between causation and remoteness of damage

The chain of causation which we have just looked at in section 6 deals with showing that there is a direct and unbroken relationship between what the defendant did and the damage that was caused to the plaintiff. In other words, proving that it was the defendant's careless act which caused the damage.

The rules of remoteness of damage overlap with this area a little. Once you have established

- that it was the defendant's action which caused the original damage, and
- that the chain of causation has not been broken by a new intervening act

you then need to establish how far the liability of the defendant should stretch.

7.2   The remoteness of damage rules – where do you draw the line?

Does the defendant have to pay for everything which then results from his original negligence or is there a point at which the court will say that although there has been no *new intervening act*, the damage suffered is becoming so remote from the original act that the defendant should no longer have to pay for it?

Before 1961 the rule was that the defendant was liable for everything which was a direct consequence of his negligent act. It did not matter that those consequences were not foreseeable and may in fact have been a catalogue of improbable (but direct) consequences. A prime example of the operation of this principle was the case of

Re Polemis and Furness, Withy & Co Ltd (1921). The facts were that a stevedore was unloading a ship and negligently dropped a plank into the hold of the ship. The plank caused a spark which ignited chemical vapour that had leaked from containers in the hold. The fire eventually destroyed the whole ship. It was established that the stevedore

- owed a duty of care to the shipowner
- breached that duty of care when he dropped the plank into the hold
- caused damage as a result of the fall.

The fact that it was most unlikely and perhaps unimaginable and certainly not *foreseeable* that the end result would be the total destruction of the ship was not relevant. The causal link existed and the original negligence led to liability for the whole cost of the ship.

This somewhat unreasonable approach is now no longer good law. In **The Wagon Mound (1961)** the court introduced the idea of *reasonable foreseeability of damage*. What this means is that you look at all the damage which arises directly from the negligent behaviour and ask whether the damage that occurred was a foreseeable result of the original negligence. The defendant will be liable for all the types of damage which were foreseeable but not for types of damage which would only have been thought a fantastic possibility.

It is important to remember when applying the foreseeability of damage test that you should be considering not whether that particular damage was foreseeable but whether damage of that general type was foreseeable. This was illustrated in

Hughes v Lord Advocate (1963) where some Post Office workers had left a street manhole cover open. The precautions taken consisted of covering the hole with a tent and surrounding it with paraffin lamps. Some boys decided to go down the manhole and take a lamp with them. They dropped the lamp and the result was an explosion which injured the boys. The court seems to have taken the view that

- a fire was foreseeable
- but an explosion was not
- but fire and explosion were the same general types of damage.

The exact method by which the damage occurs does not, it seems, need to be foreseen; simply damage of that general type. If the decision in a case is that the type of injury was not foreseeable in the first place, then the result can be very different.

⚖ In **Doughty v Turner Manufacturing Company Limited (1964)** some men were injured in a work accident. Due to the defendants' negligence a lid fell into a tank of sulphuric acid. The result was an explosion in which the men were burned. The first decision which the court had to come to was whether or not the *type* of injury was foreseeable. The court decided (on the basis of scientific evidence at the time) that a splash injury was foreseeable but not an explosion. The type of injury, they said, was not foreseeable and therefore the men could claim nothing.

7.3   The egg shell skull principle – how much damage within a general class of foreseeable types of injury is the defendant liable for?

We have just seen that first you have to establish that the type of injury is generally foreseeable and therefore the damage is not too remote for the defendant to be liable. Thereafter the rules revert to a stricter approach. When you look at the damage *within a foreseeable type* you then need to decide how much damage within that type the defendant will be liable for. The answer is likely to be: all of it. The principle behind this is that you must 'take your victim as you find him'.

The general idea is that if you were negligently to cause injury by dropping a book on someone's head, then injury to the head is of a *type* which is foreseeable. If the person on whose head you dropped the book has a particularly thin (egg shell) skull, then that is your misfortune. The fact that some damage of that type is foreseeable means that you will be liable for all the damage, even if the person's condition and susceptibility was not something which was foreseeable. The principle is illustrated by the following case.

⚖ In **Smith v Leech Brain & Co (1962)** the result of the defendant's negligence was that a man, while at work, was splashed on the lip with molten metal. The splash itself was not a particularly serious one but the particular susceptibility of the man meant that he developed cancer where the splash had occurred. He died from the cancer. The fact that the type of injury was foreseeable, combined with the egg shell skull principle, meant that the defendant was liable not only for the minor burn but also for the man's death.

In this case, because the type of damage was foreseeable and the actual damage followed directly on from that, the defendant was liable.

7.4 The special situation for nervous shock/mental trauma

Lawyers have developed special rules for what they call 'nervous shock' or psychiatric injury. In the early days the courts were extremely sceptical about claims for mental injury and tended only to allow them when linked to some physical injury as well. This is not now the case, but a person claiming damages in negligence for nervous shock will have to show a serious mental condition, not simply grief or fright. This distinction is fraught with difficulties.

For example, whether post-traumatic stress disorder counts as nervous shock is one thing. What the difference is between that and mere fright is quite another. (Lawyers will be found turning to weighty and recognised tomes on psychiatric disorders for the 'answers'.) What is clear is that damages cannot be claimed in negligence simply for 'upset', 'distress' or 'grief'.

The number of successful cases in the area of nervous shock has also been limited by the courts refusing to allow claims from those who were not directly involved in the incident. Originally this meant that the person who suffered shock had to have been concerned for their own safety. This was gradually extended to allow for claims where the person who suffered the shock was sufficiently close to the accident that they feared for the safety of relatives or close friends.

There have been some recent disasters, for example, the Zeebrugge ferry disaster, the Kings Cross Underground fire, Hillsborough Football Stadium. Most notable from the point of view of providing clarification of the law on nervous shock is the Hillsborough football disaster from which emerged the case of

Alcock v Chief Constable of South Yorkshire (1991). The police were negligent in allowing a large number of spectators to have access to a football stadium which was already full. In the inevitable crush which took place 95 spectators died and over 400 were injured. The disaster was broadcast live on television. The plaintiffs claimed that, as a result of witnessing the disaster in various ways, they had suffered psychiatric damage. Plaintiffs X were actually present in the stadium (but not in the area where the disaster occurred), plaintiffs Y saw the events on television, while plaintiffs Z heard about what was happening on the radio. Some of the plaintiffs were related to victims while others were simply friends. The House of Lords held that the police were not liable to any of the plaintiffs.

A person who suffers nervous shock as a result of fear for the safety of another person threatened by serious injury caused by a negligent defendant must satisfy the following:

● close ties of love and affection with the victim. In the absence of other evidence the court will presume the existence of these 'close ties' where the relationship is parent and child or husband and wife. More remote relations would have to prove the strength or closeness of the ties between them
● the proximity of the plaintiff suffering nervous shock to the accident must be close in both time and space.

None of the television broadcasts depicted pictures of suffering by recognisable individuals as a result of the code of ethics adhered to by the television authorities. Lord Ackner said:

> '... although the television pictures certainly gave rise to feelings of the deepest anxiety and distress, in the circumstances of this case the simultaneous television broadcasts of what occurred cannot be equated with the "sight or hearing of the event or its immediate aftermath"; accordingly shocks sustained by reason of these broadcasts cannot found a claim ...'

So it is clear that, even if someone claiming damages for nervous shock manages to satisfy the requirement for medically recognised damage rather than just upset, they still have substantial hurdles to overcome. Hurdles which may actually be there for policy reasons rather than as a real reflection of the likely damage. How many people watched with horror the events at Hillsborough. If you knew someone who died there could you fail to suffer some sort of nervous disorder as a result?

8 Defences

We have seen that if a person who suffers injury or damage wants compensation they must prove negligence on the part of the defendant. That is they must prove

- that the defendant owed them a duty of care
- that the defendant's conduct breached that duty of care, and
- that the damage/injury suffered was caused by the defendant's conduct, and
- that the damage/injury was of a type that was foreseeable.

Even after all that has been proved, the defendant may still be able to escape liability if he or she can prove that they have a recognised *defence* to the negligence. What we are going to do now is to look at some of the defences to the tort of negligence and how they operate.

8.1 Volenti – did the plaintiff consent to the risk involved?

The idea of *volenti* or consent to the risk is well illustrated by sporting events.

In **Wooldridge v Sumner (1962)**, during a horse show a photographer was knocked down and injured by the defendant's horse after the rider attempted to take a corner too fast. The court said that the rider was guilty of an error of judgement and not of negligence. Lord Justice Diplock said: 'A person attending a game or competition takes the risk of any damage caused to him by any act of a participant done in the course of and for the purposes of the game or competition, notwithstanding that such act may involve an error of judgement or a lapse of skill, unless the participant's conduct is such as to evince a reckless disregard of the spectators' safety.'

In early cases the concept of *volenti* was also applied in the situation where someone was employed in a dangerous job. The application of the principle must surely though be complicated by the fact that most people do a job because they have to. In times of high unemployment people cannot be too choosy about what job they do and under what circumstances. To say that they have consented to the risks involved may not, in these circumstances, be entirely fair.

The defence of *volenti* will not apply where someone takes a lift in a car with a drunk driver. The reason for this is not that the principle of *volenti* is not appropriate but rather because the **Road Traffic Act 1988** says so. In principle there might be a defence of *volenti* if someone is stupid enough to get themselves into a risky situation with someone who they know to be incapable or at least the worse for wear through drink or drugs. In one case a joyrider in an aeroplane failed in his claim for negligence because he got into the stolen plane knowing that the other person was in no fit state to fly it properly.

8.2 Contributory negligence

We have already looked briefly at the defence of contributory negligence. It is usually not a complete defence but will simply allow the court to apportion the 'blame' for the injury/damage between the plaintiff and the defendant. As we have seen, this will usually take the form of a percentage reduction in the damages.

The defence of contributory negligence is covered by the **Law Reform (Contributory Negligence) Act 1945**. The Act says that:

> 'Where any person suffers damage as the result partly of his own fault, and partly of the fault of any other person ..., a claim in respect of that damage shall not be defeated by reason of the fault of the person suffering the damage, but the damages (compensation) recoverable ... shall be reduced to such extent as the court thinks just ... having regard to the claimant's share in the responsibility for the damage ...'

If a defendant wants to prove contributory negligence, it is slightly simpler than the task which faced the injured person in proving negligence in the first place. For example, there is no need to deal with whether a duty of care was owed. The defendant simply needs to show that the injured person failed to take sufficient care for their own safety. In deciding whether the injured person has taken sufficient care for their own safety the courts may impose some standards of responsibility on individuals.

This was illustrated by the early cases concerning road accidents and seat belts. Even before the wearing of seat belts became compulsory, the courts made it clear that those who chose not to wear a seat belt and suffered greater injury as a result might expect their claim for damages to be reduced on the grounds of contributory negligence.

8.3 Rescuers

When looking at either *volenti* or *contributory negligence* the courts tend to take a different view where the person has suffered injury while acting as a rescuer. The reasoning seems to be a combination of the fact that if someone creates a dangerous situation they should be able to foresee that someone might come to the rescue and that on the grounds of policy those who act as rescuers should be encouraged (or at least not discouraged). Those who can claim, when they have gone into a situation in order to help, have not been limited to members of the public but can also include members of the rescue services, for example firemen.

In **Salmon v Seafarers Restaurant (1983)** a fireman was injured in attempting to put out a fire in a fish and chip shop which was caused by the owner's negligence. There is some debate, however, as to how widely this should be applied given the argument that the rescue services are paid precisely for the purpose of rescue and that their pay may reflect the risks involved.

What is clear from the cases however is that the rescue must be 'necessary'.

In **Cutler v United Dairies (1933)** a man was injured when he entered a field in order to calm a horse. The court decided that he had consented to the risk as he had intervened in a situation where there was no risk to property or to people.

8.4 Limitation of actions

Limitation of actions is a defence which can be used where the defendant can point to a particular legal rule and say that the plaintiff is 'out of time' for bringing an action for negligence. The basis of the rules is that it would be unfair to leave a possible claim hanging over a defendant. There should be a time period within which he can be sued but after which, if the injured person has not started proceedings, it is then too late. Much of the current law relating to limitation of actions can be found in the **Limitation Act 1980**.

Section 2 of the Limitation Act says that proceedings in tort (including negligence) must be brought within six years of the incident. Where the damage suffered is personal injury the limitation period is three years. Special rules apply to situations where the fact that damage has occurred may not be discovered until some time later.

If the person who suffers the injury or damage is a minor or of unsound mind then the time period for limitation only starts to run when their disability passes. For example, a 13-year-old who is injured in a car accident can sue within three years after attaining the age of 18.

Summary

You should now be in a position to:

- explain the essential elements of negligence
  the existence of a duty of care
  the breach of the duty of care
  damage resulting from that breach
- identify factual situations in which a duty of care is likely to be owed and identify the types of situation where the court may say that there are special reasons why no duty of care should be imposed
- explain how the reasonable man test is used in practical situations and the factors which may be taken into account. You should also know how the situation may alter where the defendant is an expert
- know what level of proof will be required to prove negligence. You should also know what is meant by *res ipsa loquitur*
- explain what is meant by 'the breach must cause the damage'. You should understand what is meant by 'a new intervening act'
- present a reasoned argument as to how much damage/injury the defendant, if found to have been negligent, will be liable for. You should be able to explain the difference between a 'foreseeable type of damage' and 'foreseeable damage'. You should be able to explain the relevance of the egg shell skull principle to this situation
- explain the difference between *volenti* and contributory negligence. You should be able to explain the special treatment of rescuers
- understand the effect of the **Limitation Act 1980**.

Now look at the following case study and see if you can tease out some of the important threads. You should, having made a particular point, then try to find one of the cases in this chapter which you could apply to this situation to support any point of view that you might adopt.

 CASE STUDY 8

Joan worked as a machinist in a shortbread factory. She worked on the cutting machine which makes shortbread fingers. Last year the machine malfunctioned and the owner of the company undertook a temporary repair. When he finished, he left off the guard of the cutting machine saying that it would be easier to get at when the repair man came. Joan had complained that she did not like using the machine but had been told that there were plenty of other people who would like the job. She therefore said nothing more.

Six months ago while using the machine her bracelet caught in the cutter dragging her hand into it. She lost her right index finger. A ring from her finger also struck the blade and caused a small fire which injured her workmate Alison. In a state of shock Joan rushed out of the factory door and was run over by Fred who was making a delivery of butter. That accident broke her left leg. Her leg is now mended but she finds that she suffers from arthritic pain and limited mobility.

In respect of the lost finger

I Did the factory owner owe Joan a duty of care?

2 Did leaving the guard off constitute a breach of duty? Was the accident a reasonable probability or a fantastic possibility? Was the risk foreseeable? How great was the risk compared with the cost of putting the guard back? Would it be relevant whether guards are normally fitted to machines like this or whether this owner usually takes exceptional safety precautions?

3 If leaving the guard off did constitute a breach of duty, did the breach cause the damage? Would the accident have happened even if the guard had been fitted?

4 If the factory owner did breach his duty of care, is the damage of a type foreseeable as a result of the breach of duty? (This is likely to be common sense anyway but what is the purpose of the guard if not that some physical injury had been foreseen?)

5 Could it be said that Joan consented to the risk? Does her objection make any difference?

6 Could Joan have been said to be contributorily negligent? Was she concentrating or chattering? Was she fooling around at the time?

7 How long can Joan afford to wait before taking legal action?

In respect of Alison's fire injuries

I Did the factory owner owe Alison a duty of care?

2 Did leaving the guard off constitute a breach of duty? Was the accident a reasonable probability or a fantastic possibility? Was the risk foreseeable? How great was the risk compared with the cost of putting the guard back? Would it be relevant whether guards are normally fitted to machines like this or whether this owner usually takes exceptional safety precautions?

3 If leaving the guard off did constitute a breach of duty, did the breach cause the damage? Would the accident have happened even if the guard had been fitted?

4 If the factory owner did breach his duty of care, is the damage of a type foreseeable as a result of the breach of duty? Is it arguable that the foreseeable result of leaving off the guard of a cutting machine is mechanical injury not burns? Is the classification of the 'type' of injury so precise? If it is, can Alison claim damages from the factory owner?

5 Could it be said that Joan's wearing of a ring was a new intervening act? Is it foreseeable that Joan might wear a ring? Would it make any difference if jewellery was banned at the factory? Is it possible that Joan might be liable to Alison for negligence in wearing the ring?

In respect of the broken leg

Apply all the same questions which we have looked at in respect of *Joan's finger* and ask:

I Could Fred's act be a new intervening act which breaks the chain of causation? Was it foreseeable that Fred might be driving there? Is it relevant whether or not Fred was driving at excessive speed? If so, was it foreseeable that Fred would be driving at excessive speed?

2 If Fred's act is not a new intervening act, is the factory owner liable for the broken leg as well? Is the damage too remote? Is the type of injury foreseeable even if the actual events were not?

3 If Fred's act is a new intervening act, what would Joan have to establish in order to sue Fred for negligence?

14 What other torts are relevant in business?

In Chapter 12 we looked at the nature of tort in general. In the last chapter we took a more detailed look at the tort of negligence. In this chapter we shall be looking in more detail at a selection of torts which may be of particular relevance to businesses.

Objectives

By the end of this chapter, you should:

- have an understanding of an employer's duty to his/her employees
- be able to explain the nature and effect of vicarious liability
- have an understanding of when breach of statutory duty may be regarded as a tort
- have an understanding of some product liability provisions
- be able to explain the nature and effect of occupier's liability
- recognise the rules relating to 'passing off' a product as something else
- understand what is meant by 'economic loss'
- be able to explain the basis of liability for negligent misstatement.

I Liability to employees

Anyone who employs individuals will owe certain duties to them. Some of these duties will be contained in the express contract of employment. Those which are contained in the contract will be dealt with in accordance with the law of contract. The employer may also be liable for negligence on the basis of the ordinary rules which we have looked at in the last chapter. The employer may also be liable as a result of obligations imposed on him/her by statute. In addition there are certain well-established common law duties owed by an employer to an employee. Breach of one of these duties may render the employer liable to pay compensation to his/her employee.

The duties of the employer largely relate to the safety of the employee while at work and include a duty to provide a safe work place and safe work systems.

1.1   Duty to provide a safe working environment

An employer is under a duty to ensure that reasonable steps are taken to ensure that the employee's work place is safe. In respect of the actual work place this duty is relatively easy to deal with where the employee works in one place only. The responsibility of the employer is more difficult to deal with where the employee visits clients or customers at their own homes. It seems to be generally established that in such situations it would be taking the duty too far to expect the employer to visit and check each property before his/her employee visits.

If the employer is aware of any danger, the employee should be warned about it. For example, it may not be sufficient simply to provide an employee with ear protectors unless the employer also warns the employee that it is not just a question of comfort but is also to guard against the risk of deafness.

⚖

> In **Pape v Cumbria County Council (1992)** a cleaner developed dermatitis through contact with an irritant cleaning product. The council had provided her with rubber gloves but it was held that they also had a responsibility to explain the risk to her if she did not wear the gloves.

Where the work that is being done could involve risk to employees unless a particular system or routine is followed, then there is a responsibility on employers not only to devise a safe system but also to ensure that the employees use those systems. The responsibility may extend to an obligation to provide training sessions and perhaps even, in some cases, to appointing supervisors to ensure that the system is followed. There is of course an inherent problem in deciding whether or not a 'system' of work is required. It must surely depend on the level of danger in the work and on the number of employees.

1.2   Duty to take care of the health of the employee

There is some overlap here with the obligation to provide safe working conditions. But the duty here seems to be a wider one. It seems that there is a general duty to ensure that the work requirements do not unreasonably damage an employee's health. Too much compulsory overtime might be an example of a breach of this duty. What is more, if the employer does breach this duty he or she is unlikely to be able to rely on an express contractual term to avoid liability. (Remember the **Unfair Contract Terms Act 1977** and the rules about exclusion clauses.)

1.3   Other duties

Other duties imposed on the employer relate to the provision of proper equipment to do the job and of competent staff to operate it. An employer is not necessarily expected to buy 'state of the art' equipment for the use of employees, but whatever is provided must be safe to use and the equipment should be inspected regularly. (That is why many companies have labels on electrical equipment showing the date it was checked and indicating the date for the next check.) Furthermore the employee is entitled to receive training in how to use any equipment which is provided.

The employee is also entitled to expect that other staff employed will be competent to do the job for which they are employed. If the employee is injured as a result of the incompetency of a fellow employee, the employer may be liable for damages.

2 Vicarious liability/liability for employees' conduct

We have already looked briefly at the idea of vicarious liability in the last chapter. We have seen that if an individual behaves carelessly and causes damage or injury they may be liable to compensate the injured person. If the individual who causes the damage is an employee then the injured person may sue the employer for the negligence of his/her employee. This is known as *vicarious liability*. For the injured person it may be a very useful remedy indeed. There may be little point in suing the employee. If he/she lives in rented accommodation, owns few luxury possessions and has a low wage, then even if you are awarded a substantial amount of money it may take forever to get the money. (You cannot, after all, get blood out of a stone!)

2.2 Was the person an employee?

Vicarious liability will only be imposed on an *employer* in respect of acts done by the employee *during the course of his/her employment*. There are therefore two distinctions which we need to consider:

- the distinction between an employee and some other person, e.g. an independent contractor
- the distinction between acts done in the course of employment and acts which are outside the scope of the employer's liability.

2.2.1 Is the person an employee?
A number of tests have been developed which can be used as guides to try and establish whether or not someone is an employee.

Is the individual an employee for income tax purposes?
One factor to look at is the tax and national insurance status of the individual. Generally an employee pays Schedule E income tax and someone who is self-employed pays Schedule D income tax. This test always had its faults. Often the way in which an individual is treated does not really have a bearing on the true relationship.

The nature of the employment
The essence of the test is to look at the nature of the contract between the 'employer' and the 'employee'. Amongst other matters which can be considered

are if the contract appears to be a contract 'of service', in other words for the individual to provide his/her time, or whether it is a contract 'for services', in other words to provide certain services or perform certain tasks.

The control test

The essence of this test is that you look at the relationship between the two parties and see how much control the 'employer' has over the way in which the individual carries out the work. This test is inevitably of limited use in some situations such as in the case of medical staff employed by a Health Authority. The employer in this situation cannot exercise real control over the way in which a skilled professional works and yet the member of staff is extremely likely to be an employee.

Is the work an integral part of the business?

In **Stevenson Jordan and Harrison Ltd v Macdonald and Evans (1952)** Lord Denning said: 'Under a contract of service, a man is employed as part of the business; whereas under a contract for services, his work, although done for the business, is not integrated into it but is only accessory to it.'

None of these tests can be regarded as foolproof or conclusive. Other factors may also be taken into account, such as whether the work is paid for in a lump sum or in regular payments, or who owns the tools or equipment used by the individual. In reality the test of whether someone is or is not an employee is likely to be combination of all these factors combined with common sense.

2.2.2 Was the act done in the course of employment?

An employer will not be liable for acts done by the employee except where they are done *in the course of employment*. To a certain extent each case will have to be different as each case will depend on its own special facts. However there are a number of cases which do give an indication of the types of approach that the courts have taken to this question.

If an act is authorised by the employer then the employer can expect to be vicariously liable if the employee does the act negligently. The distinction is however then made between:

- authorised acts which are being done in a manner which was not authorised and
- unauthorised acts.

The cases provide some useful illustrations.

In **Limpus v London General Omnibus Company (1862)** a person was injured when two bus drivers raced their buses against each other. The company was held to be liable for the conduct of the employees despite the fact that racing was prohibited by the company. The reasoning was that the drivers were doing what they were authorised to do, but they were doing it in an unauthorised way.

Contrast this with

> **Beard v London General Omnibus Company (1900)** in which a bus conductor drove a bus and in doing so injured someone. The bus company was held not to be vicariously liable for the conductor's negligence since he was not acting in the course of his employment. Driving the bus was outside the scope of what he was employed to do.

The concept has been further refined by looking at whether the act which was done contributed to or provided some benefit for the employer's business. If it did, then, if there is doubt about whether the act was an unauthorised act or an authorised act done in an unauthorised way, the decision is likely to go against the employer.

Consider here what precautions you would take if you were an employer in the light of the concept of vicarious liability. For example, occasionally you may pass a van which says on it, 'If this van is being driven discourteously please telephone 0113 989979'. The reason for this may not be simple politeness. The employer may be trying to make sure that the driver's behaviour is controlled so that the driver does not take risks which might lead to the employer being vicariously liable for damages for the driver's negligence.

3   Breach of statutory duty

Many Acts of Parliament protect victims of crimes or torts and expressly provide that the wrongdoer can be sued in the civil courts for compensation. Two examples of such Acts are considered in this chapter: the **Consumer Protection Act 1987** and the **Occupiers' Liability Act 1984**. There are numerous other statutes which may impose liability on individual members of the public, employers etc.

Some other statutes, however, provide that a victim will not be able to claim damages under the Act. Such an Act is simply intended to provide a criminal punishment or public reprimand of the offender. The victim will only be able to recover compensation if he or she can prove that the offender was *negligent*. An example of this type of statute is the **Health and Safety at Work Act 1974**. An employer could be prosecuted under this Act but proceedings by an employee for damages would have to be based on either negligence or breach of a common law duty of the employer. The victim could not simply rely on the breach of the statute.

Some Acts of Parliament may remain silent as to whether or not a victim can obtain damages through the civil courts based on the breach of duty under the statute. Assuming that a statute clarifies and imposes certain duties and declares that breach of those duties will be a criminal offence with criminal penalties, can an injured victim obtain damages by suing the defendant in the tort of breach of statutory duty? The answer depends on how the courts interpret the wording of the statute in question.

Consider the following:

1 It may be that the injured person has suffered damage but that the damage is different from what the statute in question was passed to prevent.

In **Gorris v Scott (1874)** the Contagious Diseases (Animals) Act 1869 imposed a statutory duty to keep animals in pens when on board ship. In a storm a number of sheep were swept overboard. The shipowner could not recover compensation under the Act as its objective was to prevent the spread of disease and not to prevent sheep from being drowned.

2 Industrial safety legislation generally imposes criminal penalties on an employer for being in breach of safety provisions (for example, the duty to fence dangerous machinery) but remains silent as to the ability of an injured employee to sue for the tort of breach of statutory duty in order to obtain a remedy.

In **Groves v Lord Wimbourne (1898)** an employee was badly injured when his arm was trapped in unfenced machinery. The employer was under a statutory duty to fence all dangerous machinery. The employee was able to recover damages for the tort of breach of statutory duty since the duty was clearly intended to benefit employees such as himself. The Court of Appeal were prepared to infer a right to sue for the tort of breach of statutory duty even though nothing was actually said in the statute itself.

(Consider now whether, in the light of this, your answer to the case study concerning the shortbread cutting machine and liability in negligence might differ!)

3 If a statute has imposed a duty but Parliament has failed to provide a criminal sanction or other method of enforcing the duty, then, in that situation, the courts may assume the intention of civil liability.

In **Reffell v Surrey County Council (1964)** a 12-year-old girl was injured when she put her hand through a glass panel in a swing door at her school. The panel had not been toughened and it was obvious to the Council (who controlled the school) that there was a risk in using that type of glass. The **Education Act 1944** imposed a duty 'that the ... safety of the occupants ... shall be reasonably assured' but the Act did not impose any penalty or sanction. It was held that the girl was entitled to damages for the tort of breach of statutory duty.

4 It may be that the statute in question does impose a penalty on the defendant. It may be that, on the facts, such penalty is intended to be the only penalty and an injured person has to rely on a tort other than breach of statutory duty, e.g. negligence.

⚖

> In **Atkinson v The Newcastle and Gateshead Waterworks Co Ltd (1877)**
> the Waterworks Clauses Act 1874 demanded that the Water Company
> maintain a certain pressure in their pipes and if they failed to do so they
> would be subject to a fine. The defendants allowed the pressure to fall below
> the specified minimum. The plaintiff's timber yard burned down because
> there was insufficient pressure of water to put it out. It was held that the
> statute did not entitle the plaintiff to sue for breach of statutory duty. The
> statutory obligation was owed to the public generally.

Deciding whether or not an injured person can sue for the tort of breach of
statutory duty is obviously a complex issue which will mean looking at each
statute carefully and applying the principles which we have looked at above. It
would seem that the problem of whether a right to sue in tort is to be inferred or
not could easily be resolved by a statute containing express wording. As Lord
Du Parcq said in

⚖

> **Cutler v Wandsworth Stadium Ltd (1949)**: '… to a person unversed in the
> science or art of legislation it may well seem strange that Parliament has not
> by now made it a rule to state explicitly what its intention is in a matter
> which is often of no little importance, instead of leaving it to the courts to
> discover, … what that intention may be supposed probably to be …'

4   Product liability/the Consumer Protection Act 1987

4.1   Why was the Consumer Protection Act needed?

Before the Consumer Protection Act 1987 it was often difficult for a consumer to
sue the producer of a defective product. The outcome of proceedings was often
uncertain. If the consumer was also the one who purchased the goods he/she
might have a successful action against the supplier based on the contract
between them. This is not always a successful route if the supplier has used
exclusion clauses in the contract.

The only other possible avenue for the consumer to sue the manufacturer was
in the tort of negligence. This was also the only avenue available to the
consumer who was not a party to the original contract with the supplier.
(Remember in **Donoghue v Stevenson**, it was the friend and not Mrs
Donoghue who had actually bought the ginger beer.) An action in negligence
requires the injured person to prove that there has been a *breach of the duty of
care*; in essence the plaintiff is required to show fault on the part of the
manufacturer.

English law was, to say the least, somewhat unsatisfactory in this area. As a result of European Community legislation English law has improved in that Part 1 of the **Consumer Protection Act 1987** (referred to from now on as 'the CPA') has added to *but not replaced* potential actions in tort and/or contract.

The CPA is divided into three parts. Part 1 deals with product liability. Part 2 deals with consumer safety and Part 3 deals with misleading price indications. We shall be dealing here only with Part 1 of the Act.

4.2   Particular points to note about the CPA

Part 1 in effect creates a scheme of strict liability in that the plaintiff does not have to overcome the hurdle of proving negligence. Three points should be noted at the outset:

- Part 1 will only apply if the product is of a type '... ordinarily intended for *private* use, occupation or consumption'. This means of course that a business consumer will have to rely on one of the traditional claims in contract or tort.
- Part 1 does not apply to any '... loss of or any damage to the product itself ...'. In other words the defective product must cause damage to something else.
- Part 1 does not apply to '... any loss of or damage to any property if the amount ... does not exceed £275'. Hence for a small claim the plaintiff will still have to rely on the rules of contract or tort.

4.3   What defects are covered by the CPA?

Liability will arise under the CPA where a defective product causes damage. The notion of 'defect' is governed by section 3 which basically says that 'there is a defect in a product ... if the safety of the product is not such as persons generally are entitled to expect'.

Section 3 specifies criteria for deciding 'defectiveness'. All the circumstances must be taken into account including:

- the way in which and the purposes for which the product has been marketed
- the use of any mark, instructions or warnings
- the use to which the product might reasonably be put
- the time at which the producer supplied the product.

4.4   Who may be liable under the provisions of the CPA?

By virtue of section 2(1), where damage is caused by a product the people who are liable for the damage include:

a) the producer of the product (in other words the manufacturer)

b) any person who, by putting his name on the product or using a trade mark or other distinguishing mark in relation to the product, has held himself out to be the producer of the product. (This will cover the 'own branders', e.g. large supermarkets who purchase goods from a manufacturer and market these goods under their own label.)

c) any person who has imported the product into a member state of the European Union from a place outside the European Union in order, in the course of any business of his, to supply it to another.

Under section 2(3) suppliers may also be liable if they cannot identify the producer or importer.

4.5   What defences are available under the CPA?

It appears at first sight that the defendant will be liable under the CPA irrespective of any fault. (It is not sufficient, as it would be in a claim for negligence, to show that the defendant exercised reasonable care.) However there are a number of defences available to the defendant. These are contained in section 4 and include:

● that the product complied with a legal requirement
● that the product was not supplied in the course of business and that the supply was not with a view to profit
● that there was no defect in the product at the time of supply (in other words the defect is the result of the use or handling of the product after it left the defendant's control)
● where the product in question eventually became part of another product and the defect is actually in the ultimate product not the original one
● that, given the state of technical knowledge at the time, the producer could not have been expected to have discovered the defect while the product was in his control.

This last defence is the well-known 'state of the art' defence. It is probably the most important. You may also find it referred to as the 'development risks' defence. The defence is controversial in that it undermines the concept of strict liability. It has its greatest impact in the field of drugs where new developments are frequently being made which are inevitably at the periphery of scientific and medical knowledge. If such drugs contain a defect, then producers could argue that they could not have been expected to discover the defect at the time of putting the product into circulation. The result of the defence is that numerous victims may go uncompensated.

In addition to these defences the defendant can also plead contributory negligence with the object of reducing the amount of damages he or she will have to pay to the person who has suffered injury or damage.

We saw with negligence that proceedings must be started within a particular time period or they will be *statute barred*. An action under the CPA will be 'out of time' if over 10 years have elapsed since the producer, own brander, or importer supplied the product.

CASE STUDY 1

Last year you bought a new Missazda estate car. Last month you were taking some friends for a trip out when the car caught fire. The accident report blames the blaze on an inadequate carburettor housing. The explanation for the problem not having arisen before seems to be that the car was heavily laden at the time and the engine was likely to have been under more pressure than previously. In the accident the following damage occurred:

- You suffered minor, but painful, burns to your hands and lost belongings valued at £700.
- Your friend Brian is in a serious condition in hospital and is likely to suffer some permanent scarring from the burns which he has suffered.
- Your friend Alice lost her expensive duckdown anorak in the fire. It cost £200.

Consider what remedies might be available to each of you.

In respect of your injuries

1 Could you sue the supplier under the contract? Would there be any implied term as to fitness for purpose?

2 Could you sue the manufacturer in negligence? If you did, what would you have to prove?

3 Do you have a claim under the CPA? If so:
   a) what do you have to prove?
   b) whom could you sue – the manufacturer, the supplier?

4 If you have a claim under the CPA, is it likely that the manufacturer could claim the state of the art defence?

5 Would it make any difference to the manufacturer's liability if there were warning signs about overloading the vehicle and in fact it was overloaded?

6 Might the manufacturer be able to suggest that, at the very least, you were contributorily negligent in overloading the car?

In respect of Brian's injuries

1 Would he have any grounds for suing anyone based on contract? Was he a party to any contract at all?

2 Could he sue the manufacturer in negligence? If so, what would he have to prove?

3 Could he have any claim under the CPA?

In respect of Alice's anorak

1 Would she have any grounds for suing anyone based on contract? Was she a party to any contract at all?

2 Could she sue the manufacturer in negligence? If so, what would she have to prove?

3 Could she have any claim under the CPA? What is the amount of the damage which she has suffered?

5   Passing off

The tort of passing off involves one party trying to 'pass off' his goods as someone else's with the result that the other person suffers loss. Assume that I market a soft drink which is very popular. It goes under the name of 'Ginja' and is packaged in a distinctive bright pink can. If you were to make a product which you called 'Jinga' and which was packaged in a very similarly presented and coloured can, it would be fair to assume that the resemblance was so close that you would get the custom of some buyers who had intended to buy my product. In this case you might well be sued for passing off.

In **Warnink (Erwen) BV v J Townsend (Hull) Ltd (1979)**, a case which involved the marketing of an advocaat type drink made to look like Warninks advocaat, the court identified the elements which must be proved before damages can be claimed on the basis of this tort.

The court said you must show

- a misrepresentation
- made by a trader in the course of business
- to prospective customers
- which it is reasonably foreseeable will injure the business or goodwill of another trader
- and which causes actual damage to the trader or will probably do so in the future.

6   Occupiers liability

An occupier of premises may find themselves liable for the tort of breach of statutory duty if he or she fails to comply with the **Occupiers Liability Acts 1957 and 1984**.

The 1957 Act sets out the duty (called in the 1957 Act a *common duty of care* which an *occupier* of *premises* owes to a *visitor* to the premises. The italics here show the terms which we will need to look at in closer detail in order to understand the effect of the 1957 Act.

6.1 Who is an 'occupier'?

The duty of care which is imposed by the Acts is owed by an occupier of premises to a visitor. In order to understand who the duty is imposed on by the Acts we need to consider what is meant by occupier. The Acts do not actually define the term. What is clear is that the term is not necessarily the same thing as the 'owner' of the premises. Originally the test which was used was whether or not the person was in *control* of the premises. This test is still appropriate but the cases have added some extra dimensions to it.

> In **Wheat v E Lacon Ltd (1966)** it was held that the manager and the owner of the pub could both be occupiers of the same premises. (There was a complicated arrangement between the owner and the manager as to who should use which part of the premises and on what terms.)

It is also clear from the cases that someone can be an occupier of premises even though they are not actually in possession of the premises in the sense of being in them in order to exercise control.

6.2 What is meant by 'premises'?

If the duty of care is owed to a visitor to premises, then we need to understand what is meant by the term. Again there is no definition in the Act. Usually there will be no problem. The term *will* include: houses, buildings, land, factories, workshops, tradesmen's yards, etc. In the disastrous fire at Bradford City Football Stadium the stadium was regarded as 'premises' under the Occupiers Liability Acts.

It will *probably also* include such things as boats at moorings and scaffolding structures.

6.3 What is meant by 'visitor'?

The 1957 Act deals with visitors to the premises. These are lawful visitors, in other words people who have either been invited or permitted to be there. The 1984 Act (see section 6.6 below) also deals with the duty owed to *trespassers*.

6.4 What is the common duty of care?

The duty imposed by the 1957 Act is the common duty of care which is defined in the Act as '... a duty to take such care as in all the circumstances of the case is reasonable to see that the visitor will be reasonably safe in using the premises for the purposes for which he is invited or permitted by the occupier to be there'.

It is possible to comply with this duty of care simply by making sure that the visitor stays away from any dangerous part of the premises (e.g. by fencing it off). A warning notice might also discharge the occupier's duty but only if the effect of that notice is in fact to make the occupier safe. So if, for example, the notice says not to enter a particular area, that may be sufficient. If the notice allows the visitor to proceed and also tells them what safety precautions they must take, this too may be sufficient. The test is whether the notice makes the visitor safe in visiting the premises. If the notice simply states the danger and disclaims liability for damage, that does not of itself make the visitor safe – it is simply an attempt by the occupier to avoid liability.

The occupier is allowed to presume that someone who is visiting the premises for a particular purpose will take care of themselves to some extent. So, for example, if the visitor is a roofer who has come to repair the roof and ceiling joists, he will be expected to take into account that the reason he is there is because the roof and joists are not safe. An ordinary visitor to the attic on whom one of the joists collapsed might be able to sue under the Occupiers Liability Act; the roofer will not.

6.5   Can the occupier avoid liability?

The situation is now covered by the **Unfair Contract Terms Act 1977**. Section 2(1) of UCTA says that any attempt to exclude liability for death or personal injury caused by negligence shall be void. It also renders void any attempt to exclude liability for death or personal injury where the occupier has breached the duty of care under the Occupiers Liability Act.

The Unfair Contract Terms Act only applies in respect of business premises. If the premises are private premises, then liability may be effectively excluded by notices or agreement. A specific exception has also been made for liability towards visitors to business premises who visit not for the main purpose of the business but rather for recreation or educational purposes. This allows, for example, farmers to make their land available to visitors for recreation and, despite the fact that the farm itself is a business, not to be covered by the Unfair Contract Terms Act.

6.6   What duty is owed to trespassers?

The 1957 Act imposed a duty of care only in relation to visitors. The 1984 Act imposes a duty of care on occupiers in respect of trespassers. The duty will be owed if:

- the occupier is aware of the danger or has reasonable grounds to believe it exists
- the occupier knows or has reasonable grounds to believe that the trespasser may be on the premises
- the risk is one against which, in all the circumstances of the case, he may reasonably be expected to offer some protection.

It is not entirely clear whether the first two requirements will be interpreted on a *subjective* basis (in other words what *that* occupier knew) or an *objective* basis (in other words what a *reasonable* occupier knew).

> In **White v St Albans City Council (1990)** a person took a short cut across land which belonged to the Council. In taking the short cut the person suffered injury. The court held that the Council was not liable as they had no reason to expect a trespasser to take a short cut. The fact that the Council had fenced the land was not regarded as evidence that the Council believed people would take a short cut.

If a duty of care is owed to a trespasser, then the duty is 'to take such care as is reasonable in all the circumstances of the case to see that [the trespasser] does not suffer injury on the premises' as a result of the particular danger.

The Act requires reasonable protection in all the circumstances. Factors which may be relevant include:

- how old the trespasser is. (A 10-year-old is not expected to behave in the same way as a 30-year-old)
- how the trespasser got onto the premises. (If they have scaled an 8 foot wall and shinned up 20 feet of drainpipe it might be fair to say that they are reasonably capable of looking after themselves in respect of minor dangers!)

Warnings may be used, in appropriate circumstances, to discharge the duty of care to a trespasser. It will depend on the facts. For example, a warning notice, however big and convincing it is, in the case of 5-year-old trespassers is unlikely to be adequate.

6.7 Are any defences available to the occupier?

If the trespasser was on the premises for illegal purposes, such as burglary, he will be most unlikely to succeed in a claim under the Occupiers Liability Acts. In other cases the occupier may be able to claim, in appropriate cases, either consent (*volenti*) or contributory negligence.

> **CASE STUDY 2**
>
> Putemup Builders recently purchased and is developing a building site for 20 new luxury houses. The site includes a show house which is open to public view. The site is fenced with an 8 foot high wire fence. During the last month there have been the following incidents at the site:
>
> - Adam came to view the show house and suffered injury when one of the floorboards in the house gave way.
> - Mary came to visit the show house. She said that she wanted to look at the rest of the site. It was agreed that she could. While walking around the site she came across a trench. In order to get across the trench she attempted to jump it, missed her footing and broke her ankle.
> - Simon, a surveyor, visited the site and ignored a sign which said: 'Danger. Only Employees Allowed Beyond This Point'. He went past the sign and suffered injury when a pile of bricks tumbled onto him.

- Jennifer visited the show house and said that she wanted to look at the rest of the site. One of the partners in Putemup agreed that she could but said that 'she must take care and that the firm would accept no liability'. Jennifer was injured when she walked across a plank boarding over a trench which gave way.
- Nigel and Naomi are aged 11. They climbed into the site at night (through the strands of the wire fence) and were injured when they climbed on a ladder which was leaning up against a wall. A rung on the ladder had given way.

a) Are Putemup Builders 'occupiers' of 'premises'?

b) Which of the six individuals mentioned above are 'visitors' and which are 'trespassers'?

In respect of Adam

1 What is the duty of care which was owed to Adam?

2 Was the duty of care breached?

3 Did Adam suffer injury as a result of the breach of the duty?

4 Is it likely that Adam either consented to the risk or was contributorily negligent?

In respect of Mary

1 What is the duty of care which was owed to Mary?

2 Was the duty of care breached? Was she made reasonably safe in visiting the premises?

3 Did Mary suffer injury as a result of the breach of the duty?

4 Would it make any difference if Mary had chosen to jump the trench rather than walk round to the bridge 15 yards further up the trench?

5 If you consider that the occupier is liable, is it likely that Mary either consented to the risk or was contributorily negligent?

In respect of Simon

1 Was the sign sufficient warning to make Simon safe?

2 Would it make any difference if Simon had visited the site in order to inspect one of the houses which lay beyond the sign?

In respect of Jennifer

1 What is the status of the exclusion clause? Would it be valid if she suffered injury otherwise than through negligence? Is the fact that the boarding gave way likely to amount to negligence? (Consider here the basic principles which we looked at in the last chapter.)

In respect of Nigel and Naomi

1 Are the two children visitors or trespassers?

2 Is the occupier aware of the danger? Consider whether ladders themselves may be an inherent danger. Was the occupier aware of their being in a worn condition?

3 Did Putemup know or have reasonable grounds to believe the children would be there? Does the fact that the fence is only strands rather than mesh make any difference? Would it make any difference if the site were several miles from the nearest house or if it was in the middle of a residential area? Would it make any difference if children had been discovered on the site before?

4 Was the risk one against which Putemup could reasonably be expected to take precautions? What precautions could have been taken? Could the risk have been avoided by making sure that ladders were secured before the site was locked at night?

7 Economic loss

There are special rules which relate to financial loss, particularly where that loss is not connected with any physical damage. In this section we take a look at those special rules in a general context. The most important exception to these rules, however, is the rules relating to negligent misstatement. Negligent misstatement is dealt with in section 8.

7.1 What is economic loss?

If the injured person is able to sue the defendant on the basis of his/her breach of a contract between them, then purely financial loss is recoverable. In the tort of negligence, however, a plaintiff may experience some difficulty in recovering for plain financial loss.

In an action for negligence you can be compensated for physical damage. You can also be compensated for financial loss arising directly from some physical damage, but you cannot, generally, be paid compensation for pure economic loss.

> In **Weller v Foot & Mouth Disease Research Institute (1966)** the defendants negligently allowed the foot and mouth disease virus to escape from its premises. The result was an outbreak of foot and mouth disease. Many farmers had to slaughter their cattle. A firm of local cattle auctioneers claimed compensation for their lost trade and profit. The court refused to allow their claim for purely economic loss. The court said that the claim for the lost profit was too remote.

If you simply applied the rules of remoteness of damage which we have looked at in the last chapter the decision seems to be a strange one.

There seems to be no real basis for the distinction between economic and other loss. The rules on remoteness of damage would not necessarily preclude it. The special rule for economic loss seems to be based on a policy decision. Probably the fear of a flood of claims (the 'floodgates' argument) is the main reason.

One basis for this might be the question of insurance. For an individual to insure against the loss of profit if an accident happened is relatively easy. That individual can easily provide the insurance company with an estimate of what his/her losses would be if such an accident occurred. On the other hand, if a firm tried to obtain insurance for third party liability it would be difficult enough to quantify the possible liability for physical damage, never mind working out how much profit all the possible claimants might lose.

Another basis is probably the impossibility of quantifying such claims. In a case like **Spartan Steel** (which is looked at in section 7.2) it was probably comparatively straightforward; they knew how many batches they would process in a day and probably what price they would get. Imagine though the case of a shop. It would take a considerable amount of time in each case to work out, based on the facts, how much profit is likely to have been lost.

7.2   The distinction between economic loss arising from physical damage and other economic loss

Perhaps the best way of understanding the distinction between financial loss which arises directly from some physical damage, and pure financial/economic loss is to look at some cases. In the case of

Spartan Steel & Alloys v Martin (1973) the defendants were digging up the road near to the Spartan Steel works. During the digging they negligently cut through the cable supplying electricity to the steelworks. The effect was that work at the factory had to stop. Spartan Steel claimed compensation for the following:

1 damage to the batch of steel which was spoiled since it was already in process when the cable was cut and the loss of profit on that batch
2 damage to the machinery which occurred as a result of the process being stopped at mid point
3 lost profit on four further batches which they were unable to process that day.

The Court of Appeal allowed the first claim (including the lost profit on that particular batch). Also, as you would expect, they allowed the second claim – for the damage to the machinery. They did not, however, allow the claim for lost profit on the batches which had not yet been put into process. This latter claim was said to be a claim for pure economic loss.

7.3   The special situation with sub-contractors

The courts have created one major exception to the rules on economic loss. They added another twist to the situation, in the case of

Junior Books v Veitchi Company Ltd (1983). The facts were that the plaintiff had contracted with X for some work to its factory. They had entered into the contract with X but had requested that X should employ Veitchi Ltd to lay the flooring. This was done and the defendants laid the flooring, but did it badly. The plaintiff's claim amounted to one of pure financial loss rather than physical damage. The court, however, departed from its usual rule and said that the economic loss could be recovered.

The reasoning seems to have gone like this:

- Junior Books (JB) entered into a contract with X
- If X themselves had done the work JB could have sued X for the economic loss on the basis of the contract
- JB specified Veitchi Ltd (V Ltd) to be the sub-contractors and X entered into a contract with V Ltd
- If JB had contracted directly with V Ltd they could have sued V Ltd on the basis of the contract
- As it was, the only link between JB and V Ltd was the tort of negligence which did not allow the recovery of the economic loss
- The relationship between JB and V Ltd was so close to a contract that special rules should apply. JB could only sue V Ltd in negligence – but the rules would, exceptionally, be widened so as to allow a claim for economic loss.
- This decision effectively brought JB's right to compensation in respect of negligence into line with their rights in respect of a contract, had there been one.

8   Negligent misstatements

8.1   What is a negligent misstatement?

Within the business context a common area of liability in negligence is that of negligent misstatement. Where a business person is asked to give professional advice, the communication of that advice is going to be in the form of *statements* whether they are made in writing or orally. The nature of professional advice is that often there will be no physical damage involved. If the advice is wrong, then the damage that the plaintiff suffers is likely to be financial damage. If there is a *contract* between the two parties there is no problem in a claim for economic loss. However, if the claim is not or cannot be made in contract (perhaps because the transaction never got that far), then, as we have just seen in the last section, usually *economic loss* cannot be claimed for. The courts have accepted that, in the case of negligent misstatements, the rules must be different.

8.2 Hedley Byrne v Heller & Partners

The starting point for an examination of this area of negligence is the House of Lords decision in

Hedley Byrne v Heller & Partners (1963). The facts, briefly, were that X who were advertising agents had a client to whom they were thinking of giving credit and whose creditworthiness they were anxious to establish. The client was a customer of Y Bank. X therefore asked Y for a financial reference for the client. Y replied giving the client a satisfactory reference. This reply was a negligent one. The reply added that the reference was given 'in confidence and without responsibility on our part'. X relied on the negligently given reference and, on the strength of it, personally committed themselves to payment to newspaper and TV companies on the client's behalf. The client went into liquidation with the result that X lost over £17,000. X sued Y for negligence claiming the loss of the £17,000.

Let's just recap a little. Up to the time of **Hedley Byrne v Heller** there had been no successful claim in negligence where the loss suffered was purely financial and incurred as the result of the defendant's negligent statement.

This scenario needs to be distinguished from two others:

- If X makes a negligent statement to Y, and Y, relying on the statement, suffers physical injury to himself or his property as a result of such reliance, then, provided that the injury incurred by Y was *reasonably foreseeable* by X at the time of making the statement, Y can successfully sue X in negligence under the principle of **Donoghue v Stevenson**.

For example, if I negligently tell you that it is perfectly safe to ascend a flight of wooden stairs despite the fact that the stairs are dangerous since they are riddled with woodworm, then, if you are injured as a result of taking my advice, you can sue me in negligence provided that the consequences of giving such advice were reasonably foreseeable.

- If X through his negligent act or statement causes Y to suffer physical damage to property, which in turn leads to Y suffering financial loss in the form of, for example, lost profits which are a direct consequence of the damage sustained, then Y may be able to be compensated for such financial loss under the principle explained in **Spartan Steel v Martin**.

These two scenarios are simply the result of general principles involving the application of the principle of reasonable foreseeability and are not the result of the development of the principle in **Hedley Byrne v Heller**.

Returning to **Hedley Byrne v Heller**. The House of Lords said that X would have been successful in an action in negligence to recover damages had it not been for the disclaimer clause. In 1963 this disclaimer clause proved 'watertight' against X's claim. As you will recall from our discussion of exclusion clauses, since the **Unfair Contract Terms Act 1977** it is now much more difficult to rely successfully on clauses which limit liability or remedies. (Test yourself on this by imagining that UCTA applied in 1963: would the bankers have been able to rely on their clause?)

For the bankers the insertion of the exclusion clause was certainly of importance, because it meant that they won the case and did not have to pay damages to the advertising agents. The case is however still of importance in the development of the law of negligence. From this case the idea of liability for financial loss became accepted (it was simply the exclusion clause which had saved this particular defendant).

8.3 The development of liability for negligent misstatements – was there a special relationship?

The law after **Hedley Byrne v Heller & Partners** developed in order to impose liability for financial loss arising out of negligent misstatements. It did not, however, develop on the basis that the financial loss was reasonably foreseeable. (If it had, it would have opened the floodgates on all claims for economic loss.) Rather the law developed liability in this area on the basis that there was a 'special relationship' between the maker of the statement and the person suffering financial loss as a result of reliance on the statement. As this concept of the 'special relationship' is the whole basis of exceptional rules relating to economic/financial loss for this special area, it is essential that we understand what the 'special relationship' is.

8.3.1 What the 'special relationship' is not

It does not mean that there is a contract between the maker of the statement and the recipient. There may ultimately be a contract but it is not an essential requirement. In the House of Lords Lord Devlin said that such special relationships are where '... there is an assumption of responsibility in circumstances in which, but for the absence of consideration, there would be a contract'.

Neither does it mean that between the maker of the statement and the recipient there is a *fiduciary relationship.*

A fiduciary relationship arises where the law imposes a duty on one person to behave towards another in a scrupulously honest fashion and take care for their financial welfare. This type of relationship arises, for example, where an individual is a trustee of a trust. It also arises, as a common example, in the relationship between business partners and is the origin of requirements such as the disclosing of information and accounting for profits and the avoiding of situations where their interests are in conflict.

Where a fiduciary relationship exists, the injured party can sue on the basis of the law of equity; they do not need to use the law of tort.

8.3.2 What the 'special relationship' is

The special relationship envisaged in **Hedley Byrne v Heller & Partners** as one which can impose liability in negligence on the maker of a negligent statement causing financial loss to the recipient is as follows:

- X makes a negligent statement to Y, knowing that Y will rely on it
- the statement is made in circumstances in which it is reasonable for Y to rely on the statement
- Y does rely on the statement and as a consequence of such reliance suffers financial loss.

The result is that Y can sue X in negligence to recover damages to cover the loss that he has sustained. The so-called 'special relationship' is therefore one based on reliance.

It is important to remember the second requirement that the statement must be made in circumstances in which it is reasonable for Y to rely on the statement. This is explained by Lord Reid in **Hedley Byrne v Heller** who said:

> '... Quite careful people often express definite opinions on social or informal occasions even when they see that others are likely to be influenced by them; and they often do that without taking that care which they would take if asked for their opinion professionally or in a business connection ... there can be no duty of care on such occasions ...'

So, for example, if during a party I, being slightly tipsy, indicate to you that you should invest in certain shares, then despite the fact that I may be an accountant, a solicitor or even a stockbroker, I cannot be held liable to you if my statements at the party prove to be negligent and the shares which you bought by relying on my advice turn out to be worthless.

This brings us on to another point. The social occasion may mean that the accountant should not be liable for financial advice. Whatever the occasion, in order for liability to follow the person is likely to have to be in the type of business where such advice might be given, or, at the very least, the person asking for the information must have made it clear that they are seeking considered advice and had the intention of acting on it in a specific way.

It is clear that there is not likely to be any liability when statements are made on purely social occasions. This idea is of course analogous to the idea of there being no intention to create legal relations in contract when agreements are entered into within a social context. Having said this, each case will need to be looked at on its facts.

In **Chaudhry v Prabhaker (1988)**, X, totally lacking any knowledge of cars, asked her friend Y to find a second-hand car for her. She stipulated that the car must not have been in an accident. Y was not a car mechanic but had some knowledge of cars. He located a car and recommended it to X who bought the car. X subsequently discovered it to have been in a serious accident and to be unroadworthy. X sued Y. In this particular case Y was held liable (on the basis that he was acting as agent for X and therefore owed her a duty of care). Stocker LJ said, however, that '... in the absence of other factors giving rise to such a duty, the giving of advice sought in the context of family, domestic or social relationships will not in itself give rise to any liability in respect of such advice.'

Consider the following case study.

 CASE STUDY 3
You receive the following information:

- Your dentist tells you that British Ceramics plc are a 'really good investment' for the future.
- Your solicitor tells you that Gunge Fertilisers plc are so sound that he has put most of his savings into the company.

In respect of the statement made by your dentist

1 Should you be relying on that statement? Would the dentist expect you to rely on it? Would it be reasonable for you to rely on it?

2 Would it make any difference if the statement was made during the course of a dental appointment when you were chatting generally about the state of the economy?

3 Would it make any difference if it was made at a meeting of the local 'Professional Advisers Bureau'?

In respect of the statement made by your solicitor

1 Should you be relying on that statement? Would the solicitor expect you to rely on it? Would it be reasonable for you to rely on it?

2 Would it make any difference if the statement was made during the course of an appointment when you were discussing your will and tax planning?

3 Would it make any difference if the statement was made by the solicitor over dinner? Would it make any difference whether it was dinner in a restaurant attended by the three dentists in the partnership and the solicitor? Would it make any difference if it was a dinner party held at the solicitor's home? Would the composition of the guests and the purpose of the dinner party have any bearing on the situation?

8.4   Could silence amount to a negligent misstatement?

When we looked at misrepresentation in the law of contract we saw that, generally, silence would not amount to the misstatement of fact which is necessary for misrepresentation. We also saw, however, that there are a very few situations where silence could amount to misrepresentation (e.g. where the remaining silent about a particular matter meant that what was said amounted to a misleading 'half truth'). In the case of negligent misstatements there seems to be no reason why, if a defendant has assumed responsibility and a plaintiff has relied on such an assumption, silence on the part of the defendant could not, in certain circumstances, give rise to a liability. This idea was accepted by the Court of Appeal in **La Banque Financière de la Cité SA v Westgate Insurance Company (1988)**. The particular scenarios which might give rise to liability must inevitably be limited and be examined very carefully on the facts.

In **Banque Keyser Ullman SA v Skandia (UK) Insurance (1989)** Lord Justice Slade asked: '... Can a mere failure to speak ever give rise to liability in negligence under **Hedley Byrne** principles?' He believed it could, '... subject to the all important proviso that there has been on the facts a voluntary assumption of responsibility in the relevant sense and reliance on that assumption ...'.

✎   CASE STUDY 4

Consider the following situations and decide whether, based on the principles we have looked at, the defendant might be liable for negligent misstatement:

1 X, who is a financial adviser, tells you that Anchovie plc is a good investment. This advice is negligent. You lose money as a result of a substantial investment in the company after receiving the advice.
2 Y, who is a financial adviser, tells you that Borage plc is in a strong market position. He omits to tell you that a takeover bid is planned by an asset stripping company. You invest heavily in Borage as a result of this advice and lose a considerable amount on the takeover.
3 Z, who is a tax adviser, tells you that if you give assets valued at £100,000 to your brother now, you will save a substantial amount of inheritance tax. Relying on this you make the gift. Z failed to mention that the gift would lead to a substantial liability to capital gains tax.

8.5   Some specific categories of advisers

Some professions, by their very nature, inevitably proffer advice or information in some way. Consider the following categories.

8.5.1   Accountants and auditors

When a company's accounts are audited, the company's accounts and the auditors' report will be made available to various parties. Assuming that the audit has been carried out negligently, are those who carried out the audit likely to be liable to parties who relied on the figures produced and as a result suffered financial loss?

In **Caparo Industries plc v Dickman and Others (1990)** auditors audited the accounts of a public company, X plc. The accounts were allegedly inaccurate but this was not picked up, due the appellants' negligence. Caparo, relying on these accounts, bought further shares in X plc in addition to those they already held and eventually they acquired a controlling interest in the company. Due to the misleading figures they suffered financial loss.

Caparo indicated that if they had been aware of the true nature of the accounts they might not have attempted to acquire a further interest in the company at all and certainly not at the price they did.

The question which ultimately came before the House of Lords was: did the auditors owe a duty of care to Caparo in their auditing of the company's accounts? The House of Lords held that a duty of care was certainly owed to shareholders as a body in order that proper control could be exercised over the company. The auditors did not, however, owe a duty of care to individual shareholders contemplating the purchase of additional shares.

Lord Oliver focused on the statutory requirements in the **Companies Act 1985**, namely that a company's accounts shall be audited annually. He went on:

'... it is the Auditor's function to ensure so far as possible, that the financial information as to the Company's affairs ... accurately reflects the company's position in order, first, to protect the company itself from consequences of undetected errors, or possibly from wrongdoing, ... and, second, to provide shareholders with reliable intelligence for the purpose of enabling them to scrutinise the conduct of the company's affairs and to exercise their collective powers to reward or control or remove ... the directors.'

He went on:

'... I find it difficult to believe however that the legislature ... can have been inspired also by consideration for the public at large and investors in the market in particular.'

This decision seems to confirm that liability for negligent misstatement requires specific knowledge of who is actually relying on the statement and also the purpose for which they will be relying on the statement. In line with this the courts reached a different but consistent decision in

Morgan Crucible Co plc v Hill Samuel Bank Ltd (1991) where Morgan Crucible ('MC') made a bid to acquire the entire shareholding of another company. General statements as to the financial state and profit forecasts of the company turned out to have been negligent. Could MC sue the makers of the statements? The answer was yes. This situation was different to **Caparo v Dickman** in that the negligent statements were made after the bidder had emerged and it was intended that they should be relied upon by such a bidder.

It seems that the question of whether reliance was to be expected can vary depending on the particular facts of each case.

⚖️

In **McNaughton Paper Group v Hicks Anderson (1991)** negotiations were in progress for the takeover of a company ('MK') by the plaintiffs. The defendants who were accountants drew up, at short notice, draft accounts and gave them to the chairman of MK. These accounts, which were negligently drawn up, were subsequently used in negotiations and relied on by the plaintiffs, who bought the company. The Court of Appeal said that the defendants (the accountants) did not owe a duty of care to the plaintiffs as the accounts had been provided for MK and the accountants were entitled to assume that the plaintiffs would seek independent financial advice and not rely solely on the draft accounts.

In **Al-Nakib Investments v Longcroft (1990)** the defendant company issued a prospectus inviting shareholders to subscribe for additional shares in the company by way of a rights issue. The plaintiff, relying on the statements made in the prospectus, bought rights issue shares in the company and extra ones on the stock market. It was held that the defendants owed the plaintiff a duty of care in relation to the shares purchased by way of the rights issue but no duty of care was owed in relation to the shares bought by the plaintiff on the stock market, on the basis that the statements contained in the prospectus were intended to be relied upon only by the shareholders taking up the rights issue.

To summarise the position of accountants and auditors:

- Auditors do not owe a duty of care to potential investors in a company even where those investors already own shares in the company.
- Auditors do owe a duty of care to people who rely on their accounts when the identities of those people are known and
  the auditors know the use to which the figures will be put.
- Auditors may be able to escape liability if they can show that it was reasonable to assume that the people who in fact relied on the figures would have taken their own independent advice.

8.5.2   Surveyors and valuers

If a building society is taking a mortgage over a property which a buyer is buying, it is likely to request a surveyor to undertake a valuation of the property. The valuation is likely to be shown to the potential buyer who will probably rely on it in deciding whether or not to buy the property. The question is: if the valuation is negligent and the buyer pays more than the house is actually worth, can the buyer sue the surveyor?

The buyer is unlikely to be able to sue in contract as it is the building society who entered into the contract with the surveyor and not the buyer. The buyer may, however, be able to sue the surveyor for negligent misstatement on the basis that he has breached his duty of care to the buyer. Again we need to show that there is a special relationship between the surveyor and the buyer.

In **Yianni v Edwin Evans & Sons (1981)** the buyer decided to purchase a house and obtain a mortgage advance from a building society. The building society arranged for the house to be valued and told the surveyor the name of the prospective buyers and the proposed purchase price. The valuation inspection was carried out negligently. The buyer, relying on the valuation report, bought the property. When the foundations of the property were discovered to be defective, the buyer attempted to sue the surveyor for negligent misstatement. It was held that the surveyor owed the buyer a duty of care and was in breach of that duty. It had been reasonable for the buyer to rely on the surveyor's valuation despite being advised to instruct an independent surveyor. The great majority of purchasers rely on the building society's valuation and so such reliance was reasonable.

The backlash from this case was that surveyors immediately inserted clauses into their valuations saying that buyers could not rely on the report. In **Smith v Eric S Bush (1989)** the court looked again at this type of situation. They still said that the surveyor owed a duty of care and that the buyer could rely on the survey. They said that most exclusion clauses would have no effect as they would be unfair under the provisions of the **Unfair Contract Terms Act 1977**. They did, however, also say that it would not be acceptable for a buyer to rely on a survey in all circumstances; for example, if the house was of enormous value or if the buyer had some special knowledge or skill.

To summarise the position of surveyors and valuers:

- A purchaser of a modest house can safely rely on a valuation prepared by a surveyor acting on behalf of a building society.
- Attempted exclusion clauses in such valuations are likely to be void under UCTA.
- The courts will still decide the reasonableness of reliance on the statement on the particular facts of each case.

8.6   Negligent misstatement which affects a third party

So far we have looked at negligent misstatements from the example of: X makes a negligent misstatement to Y, Y suffers damage as a result, therefore can Y sue X?

What we need to look at now is the situation where X makes a negligent misstatement to Y, but Z suffers damage as a result, therefore can Z sue X?

In **Ross v Caunters (1980)** a firm of solicitors prepared a will for a client. They were negligent in failing to warn the client as to who should and who should not act as witnesses to the will. The result was that someone who should not have witnessed the will did so. The effect of that was that the intended beneficiary was not able to receive the gift which the client had left to her in his will. The intended beneficiary sued the solicitors on the basis of their negligent misstatement. The court held that the solicitors were liable.

In **White v Jones (1994)** solicitors were liable in negligence for the financial damage suffered by an intended beneficiary when they delayed in drawing up the client's will. The result was that the client died before the will was properly drawn up and the intended beneficiary did not get her legacy.

Obviously the rationale of these decisions could not be based on the principle of **Hedley Byrne v Heller & Partners** as the intended beneficiaries had not relied on anything that the solicitors had or had not said. Realistically this area of law is an extension of liability on the basis of **Donoghue v Stevenson** and reasonable foreseeability. It is a clear departure from the usual rule about economic loss, but is probably justified simply on the policy ground that without this liability *no one* is in a position to sue the solicitor for his/her negligence. (The client cannot sue because (a) he is dead and (b) he has lost nothing!) Sir Donald Nicholls V-C said that '… if the court holds a solicitor liable to an intended beneficiary, what the court is doing is fashioning an effective remedy for the solicitor's breach of his professional duty to his client …'.

Summary

You should now be able to:

- understand the main features of the common law duty of an employer to his/her employees
- understand the consequences for an employer of vicarious liability
- understand the inherent problems in deciding whether or not someone is an employee
- understand what is meant by 'in the course of employment'
- understand the difference between an unauthorised act and an authorised act being done in an unauthorised way
- examine a statute and decide whether or not an injured person might be able to sue for breach of statutory duty based on that particular statute
- understand how the Consumer Protection Act has widened the liability of manufacturers and suppliers beyond their liability in negligence
- understand what is meant by 'passing off'
- understand the provisions of the Occupiers Liability Acts
- know the difference in the duty of care owed to visitors as opposed to trespassers, and understand the effect of warnings and disclaimers in relation to these Acts
- explain the extent to which a defendant may be liable for economic loss

- distinguish between financial loss arising directly from physical damage and other financial loss
- explain the special situation of sub-contractors
- understand the exceptional situation of recovery of financial loss arising from negligent misstatement
- explain the nature of the 'special relationship'
- explain the basis on which an advisor may be liable to a third party.

15 How does the law protect consumers?

Objectives

By the end of this chapter, you should:

- understand why consumers are considered to need special protection
- understand some of the ways in which the civil and the criminal law may be used to protect consumers.

1   What type of law is consumer law?

Consumer law is essentially designed to redress the inequality of knowledge and bargaining power which exists between consumers and suppliers.

The law approaches the protection of consumers from two angles. Firstly it creates a number of criminal offences which are often enforced by the Office of Fair Trading or Local Authorities.

Secondly it imposes on the relationship between suppliers and consumers a number of provisions which are designed to help the consumer and in respect of which the consumer may be able to sue the supplier. We have seen some of these in operation in the areas of contract and tort, for example the **Unfair Contract Terms Act 1977** in relation to contracts.

2   What types of matters are covered by criminal provisions?

Many of the consumer protection provisions which are enforced by the criminal law are *delegated legislation*. It is necessary therefore not only to check the original statute but also any further rules (*Statutory Instruments*) which derive from the statute.

For example, the types of matters which are protected in this way are as follows.

2.1   Mismeasured/weighed goods

These are covered by the **Weights and Measures Act 1985**. If you buy 800 grams of sweets you are entitled to 800 grams and not 797 grams. If there is any inaccuracy in measurement it must be in the consumer's favour.

2.2   Prices

There are numerous provisions which affect how goods are priced in a shop. Most of us will have come across this type of provision in the small print on Sale labels. For example, you might see a sale label which says '£10 off previous price (previously offered for sale at one of our branches at the higher price for a period of 6 months)'. In order for the consumer to know whether this is a real reduction or just a con trick you need to know that the product had in fact previously been offered at a higher price. What's more, in order to judge whether or not this is a genuine bargain, you need to know whether it was offered at that higher price for months or only minutes! The statutory protection imposes restrictions on this type of price statement. All sorts of pricing and special offers are covered by the provisions.

2.3   Unsolicited goods and services

The **Unsolicited Goods and Services Acts 1971 and 1975** are designed to deal with those producers who send you things which you have not asked for, such as books, on a month's approval. If you ask for the book to be sent, then the contract which you have entered into will govern the relationship between you and the supplier. If you are sent them without asking, the statutes say that not only need you do nothing but also, after a specified period of time, the goods may become yours anyway. The effect is clear discouragement of this type of behaviour by business suppliers.

2.4   Hardsell techniques

Nearly everyone will have received, at some stage, an invitation to attend a timeshare sale (probably with substantial incentives offered for those who attend). We have all certainly heard horror stories of how people have been pressurised into buying a timeshare about which they were not entirely sure. Most of us will also have had the door to door salesperson who offers special terms for double glazing which you don't really want. This type of pressurised selling can be very difficult to resist. The salespeople are practical experts in psychology and usually extremely good at their jobs.

These types of situations are covered by a number of statutes including the **Timeshare Act 1992** and the **Consumer Protection (Cancellation of Contracts Concluded away from Business Premises) Regulations 1987**. Often the remedy which is offered by the statutes is to require the contract to include what is known as a *cooling off* period during which time the consumer can withdraw from the contract without any penalty.

2.5 Financial services

Consumers are protected against shark or incompetent financial advisers by the **Financial Services Act 1986**. This statute makes it a criminal offence to carry on investment business unless authorised under the Act. Even someone who is authorised must follow rigorous procedures aimed at ensuring that the consumer is advised fully as to the investment products which are available.

Summary

You should now:

- understand why consumers are considered to need special protection
- be able to distinguish between consumer protection by means of the civil law and by means of the criminal law
- be able to explain the different types of method which may be used to discourage or prevent unfair advantage being taken of consumers.

16 How is credit regulated?

Objectives

By the end of this chapter, you should:

- understand what is meant by a credit agreement
- understand what agreements will be regulated under the **Consumer Credit Act 1974** and what the effect of regulation will be
- understand the role of the courts in an extortionate credit bargain.

1   What is credit?

Credit is probably one of the most important areas of consumer protection. Most of us make use of credit in some shape or form. Most of us have a credit card or have bought something on instalment payments. Some of us have enormous credit bills in the form of mortgages. Running up an overdraft at the bank or borrowing money from a friend are also forms of credit.

Credit involves either borrowing money with a promise to pay it back later *or* acquiring property or goods and agreeing to pay for them at some future date. Credit agreements are extremely commonplace. Most people cannot go through a week's mail without receiving some sort of offer of a loan at 'special rates' and you certainly would be lucky to watch an evening of commercial channel television without seeing an advert 'for buy now pay later' furnishings and electrical goods.

The person who provides the credit is called the *creditor.* The person who makes use of the credit is the *debtor.* Since the creditor is providing a service, there is often a price to be paid for it by the debtor in the form of a rate of interest.

It should be clear that in our consumer orientated society where credit is easily available both the debtor and the creditor are to a certain extent vulnerable. The debtor may be offered credit without any real consideration of his/her ability to repay the debt. He/she may find it impossible to repay the debt. The creditor having advanced a loan finds that there is little chance of him being repaid, or, having released goods on promise of later payment, finds that no payment is received and the goods, even if they can be retrieved, are now worth very little.

2   What types of credit are there?

There may be straightforward credit in the form of a loan in return for repayments plus interest. In the case of credit which is directly related to the purchase of goods it is useful to distinguish between different terms. We need to distinguish between *conditional sale, credit sale* and *hire purchase.*

2.1   Conditional sale

This is a contract for the sale of goods under which the buyer obtains immediate possession of the goods. However, although the buyer obtains possession, he/she does not obtain ownership until he/she satisfies a specific condition. The usual condition is that the purchase price must have been paid by instalments. Until the time that the condition is satisfied the goods remain the property of the supplier. The goods do not therefore belong to the buyer and cannot be sold on by him/her until all the payments have been made.

2.2   Credit sale

This is a contract for the sale of goods under which the buyer obtains immediate possession *and ownership* of the goods. The purchase price is payable later, usually by five or more instalments, but the goods become the property immediately and in advance of the final payment. In this situation the buyer can resell the goods to someone else before the final payment is made.

2.3   Hire purchase

This is a method of buying on credit under which the buyer initially hires the goods and later is given the opportunity to exercise an option to buy the goods and to acquire ownership of them. It is clear, therefore, that like conditional sale, ownership of the goods is delayed until after the initial contract is made: prior to exercising the option to purchase, the hirer is not the owner of the goods and so cannot sell the goods on.

It is true but rather simplistic to say that, in a hire purchase agreement, the ownership of the goods does not pass to the buyer until all the payments are made and the hirer elects to buy the goods. In fact the supplier of the goods will transfer ownership of the goods to a finance company who will be the creditor. Ownership of the goods then stays with the creditor until all the payments are made and the hirer elects to buy the goods.

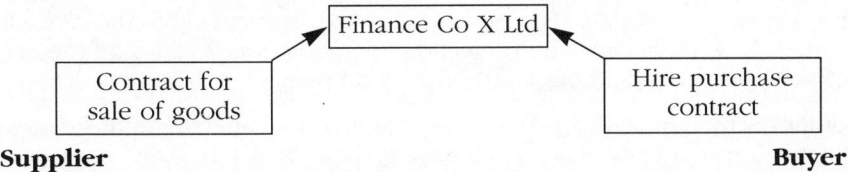

Assume that you agree to buy a car on hire purchase. Terms are agreed between the supplier (which is a firm in the business of selling cars) and a buyer. You may think that the supplier has sold you the car. In fact the supplier will 'sell'

the car to a finance company (X Ltd) who will pay the supplier the full purchase price of the car. This transaction is a contract for the sale of goods governed by the **Sale of Goods Act 1979** (as amended). The supplier will now drop out of the scenario (except that in the context of the Consumer Credit Act ('CCA') 1974 he/she is deemed to be an agent of the finance company – see the next chapter on agency law). The finance company will then enter into a hire purchase contract with the buyer, who will acquire possession, but not ownership, of the car. The car will be paid for by instalments and the buyer will eventually acquire ownership by making all the payments and exercising an option to purchase.

2.4   Possibilities for abuse

In a transaction where simple credit is being obtained the potential for abuse by the creditor is in terms of persuading clients/customers to take loans which they do not really want. Also there is potential for abuse in the terms of the credit. For example, how many people really understand the difference between different types of interest rate? Some interest rates may be represented as low interest rates but periods over which the rate is payable may mean it is not the best deal for the consumer. The Annual Percentage Rate (APR) is the way in which consumers can actually compare like with like to see which is truly offering the best deal.

Conditional Sale Agreements and Hire Purchase Agreements have the additional potential for abuse by the creditor in that, as the goods remain the property of the creditor, if payments are not kept up the goods may be retrieved. Many of the provisions in this respect are aimed at ensuring that this is not done in an unduly punitive way.

3   Agreements covered by the Consumer Credit Act

Two types of agreement are regulated under the Act: 'consumer credit agreements' and 'consumer hire agreements'. (Conditional sale agreements are regulated in a similar way to consumer hire agreements.)

3.1   Consumer hire agreements

Hirers under hire purchase agreements are given statutory protection under the Consumer Credit Act 1974. The protection relates particularly to the cancellation of certain agreements and the protection of goods from seizure by the creditor once the debtor has paid one third of the total price.

In order for the terms of the CCA 1974 to apply, the agreement must fall within the definition of a *consumer hire agreement* and three provisions must be met:

- the amount of the credit must not exceed £15,000
- the buyer/debtor must not be a company
- the goods must be loaned for a period in excess of three months.

3.2 Consumer credit agreements

A consumer credit agreement is a credit agreement whereby a creditor provides a debtor with credit not exceeding £15,000. The debtor must be an individual, a partnership, or an unincorporated association. A consumer credit agreement can take numerous forms.

Section 10 of the CCA provides that credit can be either *fixed sum credit* where credit is for a specific amount (e.g. a £5,000 bank loan) or *running account credit* where the debtor is allowed credit up to a certain limit. Examples of running account credit are credit cards or bank overdrafts.

Section 11 classifies credit agreements with regard to their objective. They can be either *restricted credit agreements* where credit relates to a particular purpose only (e.g. a hire purchase agreement) or *unrestricted credit agreements* where the debtor is free to use the credit as he or she wishes (e.g. a bank overdraft).

The Consumer Credit Act also clarifies the types of relationship which it regulates. Section 12 deals with the regulation of *debtor–creditor–supplier* agreements. These are where credit is supplied to finance an arrangement between a debtor and a supplier. Two possibilities arise here. It may be the type of arrangement which we have just looked at in relation to hire purchase, where the supplier and the creditor are separate people. Alternatively the supplier may combine the two roles of creditor and supplier and not involve a third party finance company. Section 13 refers to *debtor–creditor* agreements where there is no connection between the party providing credit and a supplier. (For example, with a bank overdraft there is no connection between the creditor (the bank) and the supplier(s) of all the goods which the debtor may buy with the overdraft.)

3.3 Exempt agreements

Some agreements which might appear to fall within the definitions above are in fact exempt from regulation under the Consumer Credit Act (although the courts will retain the power to examine and decide upon an exempt agreement which it considers to be an *extortionate credit bargain* – see section 6 of this chapter). Those agreements which are exempt include the following.

- Most consumer credit agreements which are secured on land are exempt from regulation under the CCA.
- Most *fixed sum debtor–creditor–supplier* agreements where the money is repayable by four or fewer instalments are not regulated.
- A *running account debtor–creditor–supplier* agreement where the debtor must pay back the whole amount is not regulated under the CCA. So, for example, ordinary household bills such as the milkman's bills are exempt as you are required to pay the whole amount back at once. Most credit cards do not fall into this category as the debtor can choose whether to pay the whole amount or whether to spread the payments over some months.
- Small agreements where the amount owed is less than £50 (so the milkman's bill would probably fall under this exception as well).
- Non-commercial agreements, for example, where money is borrowed from family or friends, are not covered by the Act.

4   The protection of the Consumer Credit Act 1974

It is proposed to restrict ourselves to an examination of the way in which the CCA 1974 operates in protecting consumers with regard to:

- the cancellation and termination of agreements
- the protection of goods from seizure by the creditor
- the liability that may be incurred by the supplier and creditor
- the provisions which enable the courts to regulate and control extortionate credit bargains.

4.1   Cancellation of credit agreements

There are complex provisions contained in sections 67–74 of the CCA which give the debtor or hirer under a consumer credit agreement or a consumer hire agreement a limited time to change his/her mind and withdraw from an agreement despite the fact that the agreement has not only been orally concluded but also signed. This *cooling off period* applies to regulated agreements signed at a place *other than the place of business* of the owner or creditor. This provision effectively reflects the fact that if a debtor actually went to visit the creditor, he/she is likely to have wanted to enter into a credit agreement. If on the other hand the creditor, or its representative, visited the debtor, there may have been some pressure brought to bear to persuade the debtor to take on a credit agreement that he/she did not really want.

At the time of signing, the debtor must receive a copy of the agreement; usually but not always he/she receives a second copy within seven days. If the agreement is capable of being cancelled, the second copy must be sent by post and include details of the cancellation rights. If the debtor/hirer wants to cancel the agreement then he/she must serve notice of cancellation within a specified period (usually five days) from receipt of the second copy. (In other words approximately two weeks from the making of the original agreement.)

If the right to cancel the agreement is exercised, the parties are restored to the position that existed before the agreement was signed. Any money received must be returned and any goods acquired by the debtor must be available to be collected.

4.2   Termination of agreements by the debtor

4.2.1   The right to terminate

With regard to regulated hire purchase agreements or conditional sale agreements, a debtor must be entitled to put an end to the agreement. If someone discovers that they have overextended themselves they must be able to withdraw from the agreement. (The creditor is protected by the Act's providing that, unless the contract states otherwise, the hirer cannot terminate the agreement until it has run for at least 18 months.) Written notice of termination of the agreement must be given and the debtor must pay:

- any arrears of payments
- half the total price (with credit being given for any amounts already paid)
- compensation to the creditor for any damage that the goods may have suffered due to the carelessness of the debtor.

4.2.2   The right to pay off the debt early

A debtor under a regulated consumer credit agreement is entitled to pay off the debt early. Once the debt is paid off, the goods, if not already in the debtor's ownership, will pass into his ownership.

For example, imagine that Simon entered into a conditional sale agreement with payments to be made over two years at 23% APR. When visiting his bank manager Simon is told that he can consolidate all his debts with a bank loan at 16% APR. The original company which is owed money over two years at 23% cannot refuse to allow Simon to repay early.

4.3   Control of termination of the agreement by the creditor

Debtors can be particularly vulnerable with a hire purchase agreement or a conditional sale agreement to the situation where a creditor might be able to use a very minor default by the debtor to repossess the goods. If the debtor has paid a large amount of the loan, then the creditor may be using the technical default to 'have his cake and eat it'. The creditor is being paid for goods which it then takes back.

4.3.1   The requirement for a default notice

Regulated agreements protect the consumer against this possible abuse by providing under section 87 that the creditor may not:

- terminate the agreement, or
- demand earlier payment of any sum, or
- recover possession of the goods, or
- treat 'any right conferred on the debtor or hirer as terminated restricted or deferred', or
- enforce any security

until a default notice has been served on the debtor or hirer.

4.3.2   The contents of a default notice

If a default notice is served it must tell the debtor or hirer various things. It must:

- specify the nature of the alleged breach of the agreement
- state what the debtor or hirer must do to put the breach right and by what date
- state what must be paid by way of compensation.

The date specified must not be less than seven days after service of the default notice and the creditor is prohibited from terminating the agreement or recovering possession of the goods until then.

Section 89 of the Act provides that if the debtor/hirer responds to the notice by taking the action required and paying the compensation then the breach of the agreement must be treated as if it never happened.

4.3.3   When is a court order necessary before goods can be repossessed?

Certain goods are protected from being repossessed by a creditor even if a termination notice has been served and is not complied with. The goods are *protected* against repossession unless a court order is first obtained. Goods are protected where the debtor has not terminated the regulated hire purchase or conditional sale agreement, and is in breach of the agreement *but* has paid at least one third of the total price. Even though the ownership of the goods remains in the creditor, the creditor cannot get them back without a court order.

If a creditor were to try to repossess protected goods without a court order, the penalties are heavy:

- the agreement will terminate
- the debtor is released from *all* liability under the agreement *and*
- the debtor is entitled to recover from the creditor any sums paid by him under the agreement.

Some cases illustrate how important it is for creditors to comply with the provisions of the Consumer Credit Act. Although the cases were decided under earlier legislation they remain good authority under the current legislation.

The case of **Capital Finance Co Ltd v Bray (1964)** shows that once the goods have been recovered without a court order there is a breach of the CCA which cannot be rectified by returning the goods. The facts were that a creditor, without having obtained a court order, repossessed a car which fell within the requirements for protected goods. The debtor demanded the return of all his money. The creditor, realising that it had acted hastily, returned the car by leaving it outside the debtor's house. The debtor used the car for a while but failed to pay the instalments under the original agreement. The creditor sued. It was held that return of the car did not reinstate the original agreement, the creditor could not therefore sue based on the original agreement and the debtor was entitled to the return of all the money paid under it.

There are, however, some situations where the creditor may be able to get protected goods back without a court order. Firstly, if goods are returned by the debtor to the creditor this does not bring into play the heavy penalties imposed by the Act.

In **Mercantile Credit Co v Cross (1965)**, a debtor under a hire purchase agreement fell into arrears after paying more than one third of the price. The creditor terminated the agreement and demanded repossession of the motor cycle. The debtor's wife telephoned the creditor and was told to return the motor cycle to the supplier. The debtor did so. It was held that the debtor had voluntarily delivered up the goods and the creditor had merely accepted the voluntary surrender.

Section 90 does provide that the creditor must 'recover' possession. In this case it had not.

Neither is there any problem if the creditor retrieves goods which have been abandoned since section 90 provides that the creditor cannot recover possession from the *debtor*.

> In **Bentinck v Cromwell Engineering Co (1971)** the debtor abandoned protected goods (a car) after it had been severely damaged in a road accident. The creditor repossessed the car without a court order. It was held that as the car had been abandoned, it was no longer in the possession of the debtor and therefore the creditor had not recovered goods from the debtor. The terms of the agreement were therefore still enforceable.

5 Liability of the supplier and the creditor

Where the creditor and the supplier are not the same person (as, for example, in the diagram of a hire purchase agreement on page 239), the CCA imposes on the creditor equal responsibility for any misrepresentation or breach of contract by the supplier.

By section 56, where there is a regulated agreement the supplier is deemed to be acting on behalf of (as the agent for) the creditor. The creditor is therefore responsible for matters which may be amiss in negotiations which are regarded as having been entered into on its behalf.

By section 75, where a debtor has any claim against the supplier regarding either misrepresentation or breach of contract he shall have a similar claim against the creditor. This only applies where it is a *regulated credit agreement* and the cash price of the goods is between £100 and £30,000.

6 Extortionate credit bargains

The Consumer Credit Act gives the courts power to reopen *extortionate credit bargains* so that any injustice can be remedied. An extortionate credit bargain is one which a court finds 'contrary to the ordinary principles of fair dealing'. (There is no £15,000 limit as there is for an agreement to be *regulated* under the Act.) The rate of interest charged will be an important factor which the courts will take into consideration but other more general factors will also be considered. This can be seen clearly by the case of **Ketley v Scott** where the court took into account a number of factors.

In **Ketley v Scott (1981)** a house buyer contracted to buy a flat but because of lack of funds he was unable to complete the purchase on the required date. He therefore obtained a loan from a money lender at 12 per cent over three months. This rate was in fact equal to 48 per cent a year (that is, an APR of 48 per cent). On the money lender's side it is true that he had supplied the loan at very short notice and for little security and despite the fact that the borrower had had his application to the bank rejected. It was held in this particular case that 48 per cent was not excessive, particularly bearing in mind that the borrower was an experienced businessman and so he could not be regarded as particularly vulnerable. The court also took into account the fact that money lenders, unlike building societies, do not usually operate in a comparatively 'safe' part of the market. Money lenders can expect to lend money which they can never get back and that was a valid reason for charging high interest rates.

Summary

You should now:

- understand what is meant by: a conditional sale agreement, a hire purchase agreement and a credit sale
- be able to explain what type of agreements will be regulated under the Consumer Credit Act as consumer credit agreements or consumer hire agreements
- be able to explain what is meant by a cooling off period and when it applies
- explain the purpose of a termination notice
- explain the importance to the creditor of knowing whether the goods are protected goods
- explain the role of the courts in an extortionate credit bargain.

Consider the following situation.

     CASE STUDY

Alison's business over the last few years has involved her in more and more travelling. She therefore decided that she needed a faster car. She saw a car which she liked in the showrooms of Easyride Garage Ltd. She arranged to buy the car for £10,000 and Easyride said that they would 'sort out the finance'. The credit agreement which Alison signed was with Fast Finance Ltd. The agreement provided for 36 monthly payments, whereafter Alison could give written notice to purchase the car for an additional sum of £1.

1 What type of agreement is this?

2 Is the agreement regulated? Would it make any difference if the price of the car had been £20,000? Would it make any difference if Alison had paid cash for half the cost of the vehicle?

3 Who in this arrangement is:
the debtor
the creditor
the supplier?

4 After completion of the transaction who has (a) possession and (b) ownership of the car?

5 If Alison wants to terminate the agreement what must she do?

6 If Fast Finance want to terminate the agreement, can they do so? If they can, what must they do? Does it make any difference if the amount of finance outstanding is £1000?

7 Would your answer be any different if the interest rate was equivalent to 36 per cent APR?

17 How are agents regulated?

Objectives

By the end of this chapter, you should:

- understand what is meant by an agent, a principal and third party
- be able to explain what is meant by express, implied and apparent authority
- be able to assess who might be liable when something goes wrong
- be able to know when an agency agreement might be terminated
- be able to answer the questions in the case study when you have read the whole chapter.

1   What is an agent?

We make use of agents almost every day, both inside and outside work. Examples of agents include:

- a shop assistant
- a solicitor
- a sales representative
- a bank manager
- a travel agent
- an estate agent
- an export agency.

An agent can be defined as a *person authorised or empowered by another (the 'principal') to bring the principal into legal relations with a third party*. This relationship is shown in the diagram below.

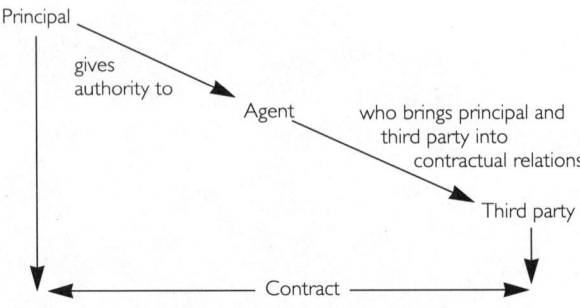

Figure 17.1

An agent may be:

- an employee of his/her principal. For example, the shop assistant (the agent) is an employee of the shop owner (the principal) and the bank manager (the agent) will be an employee of the bank (the principal)
- or act as an intermediary. For example, the travel agent who acts on behalf of a number of travel companies in arranging your holiday may be the agent of the travel company but is not an employee of the travel company.

We generally come into contact with agents in negotiating a contract. As a third party, we might agree the purchase of goods with a shop assistant (agent) on behalf of the shop (principal). As a principal we might authorise an estate agent to sell our house for us to a third party. Finally, we may be agents ourselves, for example as employees in the purchase of goods or services on behalf of our employer.

In a business context, the term is often used to refer to an intermediary acting for a business, for example, in selling goods on commission in an overseas market. However, as we have seen, an agent can be any employee who has the power to enter into legal relations on behalf of a business.

To illustrate some of the key business issues relating to agency, consider the following case study and the questions attached to it.

 CASE STUDY 1

Your manager asks you to buy a PC for the office and tells you to spend no more than £x. You go to a shop and speak to a young sales assistant. After explaining your needs and price range, she shows you a PC which is £50 over your boss's limit. You explain this is too much and she agrees, finally, to reduce the price by £30. You accept, pay using your company credit card, and take it to the office. Later in the day, the shop manager rings up to say the sale is invalid because the assistant was, in fact, a trainee who should have been supervised and had no authority to discount the price. He asks you to pay the remainder. Your boss tells you it's your problem, since you exceeded her limit.

1 What agents, principals and third parties can you identify in this situation?

2 Do you think that the store manager is right to claim the initial sale was invalid?

3 Do you think that your own company can disclaim responsibility for your purchase?

4 Do you think you will have to foot the bill?

Looking at the first question, firstly from your point of view:

- the sales assistant is acting as agent for the shop (her principal) in contracting with you as a third party.

Secondly from the shop's point of view:

● you are the agent for your company (the principal).

A key issue which needs to be clarified before you can answer questions 2, 3 and 4 is, clearly, how far you or the shop assistant can act as agents on behalf of your organisations as principals. We will use this same case study at the end of the chapter to see whether you can then answer these last three questions more fully.

In the following sections, we will need to consider:

● what authority someone can have as an agent
● how far this affects who is liable when something like this goes wrong.

We will also consider when agencies can be terminated.

2   What authority does an agent have?

In many cases, there will be a written contract between an agent and principal defining the scope of the agent's authority. However, this need not be the case. An agent can be appointed orally and the contract may contain few express terms. As an example, a volunteer in a charity shop, although a volunteer and although unpaid, is still acting as an agent for the shop. It is unlikely that, when the volunteer is taken on, a written contract is entered into. Indeed it is more likely that the conversation simply went: 'we'll show you how to work the till and you can work alongside Jenny for the first week'.

Whether or not there is a written agreement, we need to consider three kinds of authority. An agent may have *express authority, implied authority* or *apparent authority.*

2.1   Express authority

Express or actual authority, as the term suggests, covers the formal arrangements there may be between agent and principal. When there are express terms the agent must abide by them.

In some exceptional cases, an agent may be able to vary express terms, in an emergency for example, to protect a principal's property from damage. Providing the agent has been placed in charge of the property, it is genuinely impossible to contact the principal, and the agent is acting in a genuine emergency to protect the property, the agent is considered to have agency of necessity and may be entitled to reimbursement for acting on the principal's behalf. Given the range and speed of modern communications, these circumstances are likely to be rare.

Where there are express terms they are binding on an agent; however, as we shall see, they may not protect a principal from a claim by a third party.

2.2 Implied authority

Even if there is a formal agreement, there will always be circumstances it won't cover. The law recognises, for example, that an agent may carry out activities that are implied in the nature of a job, or are a natural consequence of carrying out express instructions, whether or not those activities have been agreed explicitly. A principal may then become responsible for the agent's actions, even if he or she disagrees with them.

Consider the following example: Mike is employed by Maginet plc. As part of a sales promotion Maginet plc host a publicity launch. Afterwards Mike is asked to take some prospective customers out and entertain them. What the managing director had in mind was a nice dinner. What Mike in fact ran up against the company account included numerous additional and excessive entertainment features.

Maginet, as principal, will be responsible for Mike's actions despite the fact that Maginet would not have approved of the extent of the entertainment.

If there is any ambiguity in these terms, an agent has a duty to clarify them with the principal. If this is not practical for any reason, he or she is justified in acting in good faith on a reasonable interpretation of these instructions, even if it turns out not to be what the principal intended.

In **Hely-Hutchinson v Brayhead Limited (1968)**, the directors of a company allowed the Chairman to act as if he were managing director. He entered into an agreement with Brayhead Limited which his company subsequently attempted to repudiate. The Court of Appeal held that, whilst he had never been expressly appointed as managing director, by allowing him to act in that capacity the company had given him implied actual authority and was bound to honour the agreement.

As we shall see, this case also involves questions of *apparent* authority, which we discuss below. In some areas of business, it may be standard practice for an agent to carry out certain activities or to have certain responsibilities, in which case they may be entitled to act on behalf of a principal without express authorisation.

In **Waugh v Clifford & Sons Limited (1982)**, solicitors were acting for a building firm in a dispute concerning property. The other side suggested a compromise involving an independent valuer. The client did not want to settle on these terms, but his instructions were not passed to the partner dealing with the case, who agreed the compromise. It was held that the builder was bound by it since it was within the usual authority of a solicitor to agree such a compromise and the other side could rely on the solicitor's apparent powers.

2.3   Apparent authority

In both of the above cases, we mentioned the third kind of authority an agent can have: *apparent* authority. To understand this concept, think back to the case study at the beginning of the chapter. When you bought the PC, you assumed the sales assistant had the authority to sell it to you on behalf of the shop. You would think it unfair and impractical to have the responsibility of checking every time you wanted to buy something.

The law recognises that third parties are not always in a position to check the authority of an agent. They have to take a certain amount on trust and proceed on the basis of his or her apparent authority. To illustrate the point, we can consider a situation where, unknown to a third party, a principal has restricted an agent's *express* authority. Although the agent may then exceed this authority, any resulting agreement with a third party may still be binding on the principal. This situation is shown in the following cases:

> In **Mercantile Credit Limited v Garrod (1962)**, G and P were partners in a garage business concerned with repairing cars and letting lock-up garages. They had expressly agreed not to sell cars. Nevertheless, P, without G's knowledge, sold a car to M Limited. It then transpired that P had had no title to the car, so M Limited demanded back the money. When P did not pay, G was held liable as his partner. There was nothing to make M Limited suspect that P and G had restricted their repairs-only authority. Therefore, both of the partners were liable, despite G's express agreement with P.
>
> In **Folkes v King (1923)**, an agent had authority to sell his principal's car for not less than £575. In breach of these instructions, he sold it for only £340. The buyer was able to keep the car because the agent was clearly in possession with authority to sell and the buyer had no reason to suspect the limitation which the principal had imposed.

The case of **Hely-Hutchinson v Brayhead Limited (1968)**, discussed earlier, has been interpreted as one involving apparent authority (also the related case of **Freeman and Lockyer v Buckhurst Park Properties (Mangal) Limited (1964)** where the board of Buckhurst Ltd allowed one of its number to act as though he were managing director. The board were estopped from denying he was managing director and were therefore bound by a contract he had made with the plaintiffs.)

A principal may still be liable even when an agent misuses his position. As an example:

> In **Panorama Developments Limited v Fidelis Fabrics Limited (1971)**, a company secretary used the company name to hire cars for his own use. The company still had to pay the hire company, who acted on the company secretary's apparent authority to hire cars for the company.

To protect its position, a principal needs to make any restrictions on the authority of an agent clear to potential third parties such as occurred in the following case:

> In **Overbrooke Estates Limited v Glencombe Properties Limited (1974)**, the catalogue given to bidders before an auction made it clear that the auctioneer had no authority to make representations about the property. The seller was, therefore, not bound by statements which the auctioneer did make.

More broadly, it is accepted that a third party has a responsibility to check the agent's authority if the appearance of authority is suspicious. This responsibility may also relate to the question of implied authority. As the following case shows, if experience and business practice suggest an agent is acting beyond his or her authority, a third party should query the matter.

> In **Armagas Limited v Mundogas SA (1986)**, an employee negotiated an unusual three-year charter of a ship, purportedly for his employer, claiming he had been given express authority to do so. This was clearly outside his usual powers and the employer had not held out the agent as having power to make it. The agent said that he had express authority, but a prudent third party would have checked this. The principal therefore was not bound.

Although in most cases a principal is likely to want to escape transactions made without his authority, in some cases he may be entitled to ratify them after the event if they are to his advantage.

3   Who is liable if something goes wrong?

Now that we have some rules defining the degree of authority an agent may exercise on behalf of a principal, we can consider who may be liable if any of the parties is unhappy with a transaction. We will consider the respective responsibilities of principals, agents and third parties to one another.

3.1   Is the principal liable?

As we have seen, if an agent is acting with the express, implied or apparent authority of a principal and a third party had no good reason to suspect otherwise, the latter is entitled to think any contractual arrangement binding on the principal. This will be true even if the agent acts fraudulently or negligently.

⚖

> In **Gran Gelato Limited v Richcliff (Group) Limited (1992)**, R's solicitors, acting within their implied authority, negligently gave a false answer to G's question about R's property. The solicitors gave the answer on behalf of their client (R), but without consulting him. Nevertheless, R was liable to G, and the solicitors were not. R's only recourse was to take action against the solicitors.

Looking back to the case study at the beginning of the chapter, you would, in normal circumstances, be entitled to think that the shop assistant had authority to act on the shop's behalf. The shop, as principal in the transaction, would be obliged to honour the arrangement. Similarly, the shop would be entitled, depending on your seniority and the significance of the transaction, to assume that you had authority to act on your company's behalf. The company would, therefore, have to honour the transaction.

A principal still remains liable to a third party, even if an agent has failed to pass on payments for the third party entrusted to him. In such cases, the principal must honour the agreement with the third party and seek redress from the agent. A principal is also responsible to a third party even if an agent fails to disclose the principal's name to that third party. In this case, a third party has the right to sue either the agent or the principal, but not both.

Principals also have a responsibility to honour agreements with agents acting on their behalf. As an example:

⚖

> In **Alpha Trading Limited v Dunshaw-Patten (1981)**, the principals employed an agent to arrange for the sale of a quantity of cement. A contract was concluded, but the principals deliberately reneged on it to take advantage of rising cement prices. The Court of Appeal held that the agent should be paid since there had been no agreement to accept this kind of risk.

The responsibilities of principals to 'commercial agents', defined as independent agents who sell goods on behalf of a business over a long period, have recently been strengthened by the **Commercial Agents (Council Directive) Regulations 1993**. There is now a greater onus on principals to keep agents informed and to act in good faith in honouring agreements with such agents, including prompt payment even when a principal has not received monies due from a third party. In these situations, the courts have sought to maintain a balance between upholding the spirit of an agreement between principal and agent and the agent's freedom in the use of his or her property.

3.2 Is the agent liable?

In some industries, it is accepted that agents may take some personal responsibility for contractual arrangements. If this is widely understood, the courts may make the agent solely responsible.

Particularly in those situations where there is not a clear, written agreement, it may be wise for an agent to make it clear that he or she is acting as an agent in any dealings with a third party – it is less easy then for a principal to try to claim those dealings were undertaken in a purely private capacity.

Agents also need to be sure that they are acting with the continued authority of a principal. Not surprisingly, agents cannot claim exemption from action by a third party if they claim an authority they know they don't possess (for instance, in **Hedley Byrne & Co Ltd v Heller & Partners (1964)**).

Where there is a clear agreement with a principal, an agent has a general responsibility to obey those terms and to use reasonable care and skill in carrying them out. He or she is not generally entitled, unless necessity or trade custom permit, to delegate his/her responsibilities to a sub-agent without the principal's permission. He or she must also disclose any conflict of interest, especially if it benefits him/her or damages the principal.

In **Mahesan v Malaysia Government Officers' Housing Society (1978)**, M was engaged by the Society to find building land. He found a cheap and suitable site, but accepted a bribe from a property speculator to keep silent about it. This enabled the speculator to buy the site cheaply, and then resell it to the Society at a huge profit. The Society was entitled to recover the bribe and the speculator's profit from M.

Finally, under the Commercial Agents (Council Directive) Regulations 1993, a principal may impose a limited restraint of trade on an agent to prevent an agent taking away customers acquired as part of the agency or acting for someone else in contravention of the agreement between them.

3.3 Is the third party liable?

If a third party fails to pay an agent, he can be sued by either the agent or the principal. If he pays the agent who then, for some reason, fails to transfer the agreed remuneration to the principal, the latter can only sue the agent, not the third party.

A third party can be sued by an undisclosed principal unless the contract between the third party and agent specifically excludes an undisclosed principal or where the failure to disclose the existence of the principal is seen as unfair to the third party. As an example, if an employee accepted a job and then revealed she was acting as an agent for someone else, the employer would not be bound to employ the agent's principal.

4 Under what circumstances can an agency be terminated?

In most cases, an agency agreement is terminated voluntarily either by performance, or by expiry of an agreed time limit, providing it meets the minimum standard (1–3 months) of the 1993 EC Regulations. Neither party can terminate the agreement unilaterally before then, unless an extreme event such as death, insanity, bankruptcy or something to cause frustration (such as illegality or illness) occurs to terminate it involuntarily. If no date is given, the courts may apply one they consider reasonable. Normally, an agent would not be entitled to any payment for work undertaken after termination, unless it related to carrying out his/her obligations under the original agreement.

Finally, a principal needs to be careful that a third party is aware of a voluntary termination since, if the latter has no good reason not to assume an agent still has apparent authority, the principal may still be liable for the agent's actions done ostensibly on his behalf.

Summary

You should now be in a position to define:

- an agent
- the kinds of authority he or she might possess
- the essential contractual obligations that exist between an agent, principal and third party.

To test your new skills, re-read the case study at the beginning of this chapter and see if you can now confidently and more fully answer *all* the questions.

Glossary

Agent: A person who has authority to act for another (the principal) and to create between that other and a third party legal relations usually in the form of a contract.

Arbitration: A method of resolving disputes whereby the parties in conflict by agreement submit their arguments to a third party (usually with knowledge of the subject matter) who will decide the issue.

Ascertained goods: Goods selected and identified (after the contract has been made) as the appropriate subject matter of the agreement.

Capacity: The legal ability to enter into a binding contract.

Civil law: The area of law primarily concerned with resolving disputes between individuals.

Condition: An important term in a contract, breach of which entitles the innocent party to repudiate the contract and claim damages.

Conditional sale: A contract for the sale of goods under which ownership does not pass to the buyer until a specified condition (normally the payment of the purchase price by instalment) has been satisfied.

Consideration: An essential requirement in all simple contracts. It is the bargaining aspect of the contract, whereby each party to the contract gives something and receives something in return.

Contributory negligence: A defence or partial defence to negligence which occurs in a situation where the plaintiff has suffered some form of damage through the negligence of the defendant, but has also him/herself contributed to that damage by virtue of his/her own negligence.

Conversion: A tort which is committed when a person deals with the goods of another person in such a way as to show that he calls the ownership of the goods into question. The civil counterpart of theft.

County Court   A court whose purpose is to resolve civil disputes comparatively quickly and cheaply.

257

Court of Appeal: A court split into civil and criminal divisions. The head of the Civil Division is the Master of the Rolls while the head of the Criminal Division is the Lord Chief Justice. The Civil Division hears appeals from the County Courts and the High Court, while the Criminal Division hears appeals from the Crown Courts.

Credit sale: A contract for the sale of goods under which ownership passes to the buyer immediately, the purchase price being payable later.

Criminal law: The area of law primarily concerned with punishing those who are guilty of conduct prohibited by the State.

Crown Court: A court whose main function is to deal with criminal matters; it also hears appeals relating to some civil matters.

Decision: A form of European Community legislation having direct effect and binding in its entirety upon those to whom it is addressed.

Deed: A formal document which is binding on the parties – whether or not it is also a contract.

Defamation: The publication of a statement about a person which tends to lower him/her in the estimation of right-thinking members of society generally (see Libel and Slander).

Defendant: An individual or company against whom a civil action is brought, or who is prosecuted for a criminal offence.

Delegated legislation: The creation of law whereby Parliament delegates to a person or body the power to make law.

Directive: A form of European Community legislation addressed to member states requiring them to pass domestic legislation in order that the directive may be implemented within a specified time.

'Eiusdem generis' rule: A minor rule of statutory interpretation meaning that where specific words are followed by general words, then the general words should be interpreted in the light of the specific words.

Estoppel: Where a person allows another to believe that a certain set of circumstances exists and the other person relying on the information given alters their position to their detriment, the first person is estopped (prevented) from denying that such circumstances exist.

European Community Institutions

i) The Council of Ministers:	The Council is the formal legislative body of the Community, though it only has power to decide whether or not to adopt proposals put forward by the Commission. It consists of one Minister from each of the member states.
ii) The Commission:	The Commission is the executive body of the Community. The 20 members of the Commission are appointed by the national governments, but thereafter act independently in the interests of the Community.
iii) The Parliament:	The members are directly elected by voters in the member states. Originally a purely advisory and consultative body it has, since the Single European Act, acquired increasing legislative powers.
iv) The European Court of Justice	The Court sits in Luxembourg and is the supreme authority on all aspects of European Community law. It ensures that Community law is observed and its decisions are binding on all member states.
European Court of Human Rights	The Court sits in Strasbourg and decides whether states signatory to the European Convention for the Protection of Human Rights and Fundamental Freedoms have breached one of the provisions. It should not be confused with the European Community's Court of Justice.
Exemption clause:	A term in a contract which attempts either to exclude liability altogether, or to restrict such liability to a specific amount (also called Exclusion clause).
Express term:	A term which has been specifically agreed upon by the parties to a contract prior to its formation.
'Expressio unius exclusio alterius' rule:	A minor rule of statutory interpretation meaning that omissions from a statute are intentional and circumstances to the contrary should not be implied.
Frustration:	A doctrine in the law of contract which says that where, due to some external event which is the fault of neither contracting party, performance of the contract becomes either impossible or substantially different from what the parties must have intended when they entered the contract, then the contract is terminated.
Golden rule:	A rule of statutory interpretation in which words are interpreted in such a manner as to avoid ambiguity or absurdity.

High Court: A court dealing with civil matters. It consists of three divisions: Queen's Bench, Chancery, and Family.

Hire purchase: A method of buying on credit under which the buyer initially hires the goods and is later given the option of buying them, normally by paying the last of a specified number of instalments.

House of Lords: The final court of appeal in this country for both civil and criminal matters.

Implied term: A term not expressly mentioned by the parties to a contract, but deemed nevertheless to form part of the contract. Such terms are implied either by the courts, custom or statute.

Injunction: A court order restraining a person from doing something, or, in the case of a mandatory injunction, requiring them to do something.

Joint and several liability A situation in which two or more persons incur liability together as well as separately as individuals. They can be sued together or the whole of the sum can be recovered from only one of them.

Legislation: Law enacted by Parliament in the form of Acts of Parliament (or statutes).

Libel: A defamatory statement in permanent form.

Limitation: Rules which prescribe the time limit within which proceedings are to be brought.

Literal rule: A rule of statutory interpretation in which words are given their common and ordinary meaning.

Litigation: The resolution of disputes in court.

Magistrates' Courts: Courts mainly concerned with criminal matters, but having a limited civil jurisdiction.

Minor: A person under the age of 18.

Mischief rule: A rule of statutory interpretation in which words are interpreted in order to eradicate the problem (mischief) which the statute was passed to eliminate.

Misrepresentation: A false statement of fact made by one party to a contract which induces the other party to enter into the contract.

Necessaries: Anything required by a minor to keep him suitably provided according to his particular standard of living at the relevant time.

Negligence: A tort which is the breach of a duty imposed by law to take reasonable care and which results in damage to the plaintiff by the defendant.

'Noscitur a sociis' rule: A minor rule of statutory interpretation meaning that a word should be interpreted with reference to its context.

'Novus actus' interveniens' In negligence, it is the term applied to an intervening act which breaks the line of causation between the defendant's negligent act and the plaintiff's consequent loss such that the intervening act becomes an independent cause of the harm suffered by the plaintiff.

'Obiter dicta': Statement said 'by the way' during a judgment (usually abbreviated to 'obiter').

Ombudsman: An official, independent of the Government, who has the function of dealing with alleged matters of maladministration by public authorities where such matters are not capable of being resolved through the courts.

Passing off: A tort whereby one party attempts to 'pass off' his goods as someone else's with the result that the other party suffers loss.

'Per incuriam': Through lack of care.

Per se: By itself. A tort is actionable per se where there is no necessity to establish any loss as a result of the tort.

Plaintiff: An individual or company who pursues a legal action requesting a court for some form of remedy.

Principal: A person for whom another person acts as agent.

Private law: Law which regulates individuals and their behaviour towards other individuals.

Private nuisance The unlawful interference with a person's use or enjoyment of land.

Privity of contract: The rule that only a person who is a party to a contract can sue or be sued on the contract.

Public law: Law which regulates the State and its relationship with the individual.

Public nuisance: An act or omission which materially affects the reasonable comfort and convenience of life of a class of Her Majesty's subjects.

'Quantum meruit':   Where, under the terms of a contract, one person performs services for another, he may sue upon a 'quantum meruit' to recover the amount earned by his labours if the other person breaks or repudiates the contract.

'Ratio decidendi':   Reason for deciding – the legal reasoning upon which a judicial decision is based (usually abbreviated to 'ratio').

Recommendations and Opinions: A reflection of the views held by the European Commission and Council on European Community policies.

Rectification: A remedy given by a court so that a document which incorrectly reflects the intentions of the parties to a contract may be corrected in order to reflect the true intentions of the parties.

Regulation: A form of European Community legislation of general application binding in its entirety and directly applicable without the necessity of domestic legislation.

Rescission: A remedy given where it would, on account of mistake, misrepresentation or otherwise, be unreasonable to uphold a contract.

'Res ipsa loquitur'   The thing speaks for itself – it refers to a situation in the tort of negligence where, as a result of it being manifestly obvious that negligence has occurred, instead of the plaintiff having to prove negligence, the responsibility shifts to the defendant who has to disprove negligence.

Romalpa clause: A clause in a contract whereby the ownership of goods is to remain with the seller until such goods have been paid for.

Slander: A defamatory statement in the form of spoken words or gestures.

Small claims: An expression used for cases referred automatically to County Court arbitration when the claim is small.

Specific goods:	Goods identified and agreed upon at the time a contract of sale is made.
Specific performance:	An order of the court ordering a defendant to perform his obligations under a contract.
Tort:	A civil wrong which occurs where a person is in breach of a duty imposed upon him/her by law.
Trespass:	A tort in which there is direct interference with either the person, land or goods of another without lawful justification.
Tribunal:	A term usually applied to a type of dispute resolving mechanism outside the court structure.
'Uberrima fides' (or 'uberrimae fidei'):	'Of the utmost good faith' – a term applied to certain types of contract, e.g. insurance contracts, in which it is absolutely essential for a party in receipt of material facts to make a full disclosure.
Unascertained goods:	Goods comprising the subject matter of a contract of sale which have yet to be identified and appropriated to the contract.
Vicarious liability:	A situation where A is liable to C for the tortious acts of B. The most common application is where an employer can be vicariously liable to a third party for the torts of his/her employee, where such torts are committed during the course of the latter's employment.
Void contract:	A void contract is a nullity and no rights can be acquired under it.
Voidable contract:	A contract which may be treated as ineffective by one of the parties to it, subject to certain conditions.
'Volenti non fit injuria':	A defence available to a defendant in an action for negligence. It is usually abbreviated to 'volenti' and means 'no harm is done to one who consents'.
Warranty:	A less important term in a contract, breach of which entitles the innocent party only to sue for damages.
Writ:	A form of written command. A writ of summons notifies the defendant of a claim against him/her and orders him/her to submit to the jurisdiction of the court to answer the claim.

Index

264